Documentation Project Committee:
Herbert Prokle, Georg Wildmann, Karl Weber, Hans Sonnleitner

Genocide of the Ethnic Germans in Yugoslavia 1944–1948
European English-Language Edition

Documentation Project Committee

Genocide
of the Ethnic Germans
in Yugoslavia
1944–1948

München 2003

Published by:	Board of Directors of Donauschwäbische Kulturstiftung – Stiftung des bürgerlichen Rechts –, München, Germany

Donauschwäbisches Archiv, München

Series III:	Contribution to the Danube Swabian Heritage and Home Country Research ISSN 017–5165–96
Publisher:	Verlag der Donauschwäbischen Kulturstiftung, München 2003 D-81929 München, Schädlerweg 2, Germany Tel./Fax 0 89/93 77 93 ISBN 3–926276–47–9
Branch Offices:	D-71065 Sindelfingen, Goldmühlestr. 30, Germany D-76571 Gaggenau, Max-Hildebrandt-Str. 9, Germany
Title:	Genocide of the Ethnic Germans in Yugoslavia 1944–1948 European English-Language Edition
Published:	2003
Circulation:	2500 Copies
Editorial Project Comitee:	Herbert Prokle, Georg Wildmann, Karl Weber, Hans Sonnleitner
Graphics:	Magdalena Kopp-Krumes MA, München
Typesetter:	Fotosatz Völkl, Türkenfeld
Printed by:	Jos. C. Huber GmbH & Co. KG, Garching-Hochbrück

Casualties of Ethnic German Civilians in Yugoslavia
(numbers rounded off)

Up to World War II the total ethnic German population in Yugoslavia amounted to

> **540,000**

After the dismemberment of Yugoslavia in 1941, 95,000 were drafted by the German, Hungarian or Croatian armies and 245,000 civilians were evacuated to Germany before Yugoslavia was restored – under Communist rule. Between October 1944 and April 1945 the remaining

> **200,000**

fell under Tito's control and became victims of the genocide perpetrated by his regime.

Already between July 1941 and October 1944

> **1,500**

civilians had been **killed bestially** during partisan raids on ethnic German settlements.

From October 1944 to June 1945

> **9,500**

men and women were **cruelly murdered**, most of them during the *bloody autumn 1944*.

Of the 8,000 women and 4,000 men **deported to the Soviet Union** by the end of 1944

> **2,000**

succumbed to the martyrdom they had to suffer for years.

With the exception of about 8,000 persons all the remaining 170,000 ethnic German civilians (from babies to old age) were concentrated in camps.

> **51,000**

of these **children, women and old age perished miserably** within three and a half years, mostly from **starvation and intentionally uncontrolled epidemics**.

Hence, the **total number** of **ethnic German civilians** who became **mortal victims** of the **premeditated genocide 1944–1948** amount to

> **64,000**

More than **40,000** of these victims are **registered by name** in the documentation series *Leidensweg der Deutschen im kommunistischen Jugoslawien.*

Source: *Verbrechen an den Deutschen in Jugoslawien 1944–1948*

Table of Contents

Foreword

By Alfred M. de Zayas

"The right not to be expelled from one's homeland is a fundamental right ... I sub-mit that if in the years following the Second World War the States had reflected more on the implications of the enforced flight and expulsion of the Germans, to-day's demographic catastrophes, particularly those referred to as 'ethnic cleansing', would, perhaps, not have occurred to the same extent ... There is no doubt that during the Nazi occupation the peoples of Central and Eastern Europe suffered enormous injustices that cannot be forgotten. Accordingly they had a legitimate claim for reparation. However, legitimate claims ought not to be enforced through collective punishment on the basis of general discrimination and without a deter-mination of personal guilt."[1]

These words of the first United Nations High Commissioner for Human Rights, José Ayala Lasso (Ecuador), were spoken at the Paulskirche in Frankfurt am Main on May 28th, 1995 on the occasion of the solemn ceremony to remember 50 years since the expulsion of 15 million Germans from Eastern and Central Europe, including the Danube Swabians of Yugoslavia.

There is no question that in international law mass expulsions are doubly illegal – giving rise to State responsibility and to personal criminal liability. The expulsions by Germany's national socialist government of one million Poles from the Warthe-gau 1939/40 and of the 105,000 Frenchmen from Alsace 1940 were listed in the Nürnberg indictment as "war crimes" and "crimes against humanity". The Nürn-berg judgement held several Nazi leaders guilty of having committed these crimes.

It is an anomaly that in spite of this clear condemnation of mass expulsions, the Allies themselves carried out even greater expulsions in the last few months of the Second World War and in the years that followed. Article XIII of the Potsdam Pro-tocol attempts to throw a mantle of legality over the expulsions carried out by Czechoslovakia, Hungary and Poland. Nothing is said about the eliminations from

---

[1] The complete text in German was published in Bonn, 1995, in: Dieter Blumenwitz, ed., *Dokumentation der Gedenkstunde in der Paulskirche zu Frankfurt am Main am 28. Mai 1995; 50 Jahre Flucht, Deportation, Vertreibung*, p. 4. Excerpts from the English original are quoted in A. de Zayas *The Right to One's Homeland, Ethnic Cleansing, and the Inter-national Criminal Tribunal for the Former Yugoslavia*, Criminal Law Forum, Vol. 6 (1995), p. 257–314 at 291–92.

other countries like Yugoslavia and Romania. However, the victorious Allies at Potsdam were not above international law and thus could not legalize criminal acts by common agreement. There is no doubt that the mass expulsion of Germans from their homelands in East Prussia, Pomerania, Silesia, East Brandenburg, Sudetenland, Hungary, Romania and Yugoslavia constituted "war crimes", to the extent that they occurred during wartime, and "crimes against humanity" whether committed during war or in peacetime.

Moreover, the slave labor imposed on persons of German ethnic origin as "reparations in kind", which was agreed by Churchill, Roosevelt and Stalin at the Yalta Conference[2], also constituted a particularly heinous crime, which led to hundreds of thousands of deaths during the deportation to slave labor, during the years of hard work with little food, and as sequel of this inhuman and degrading treatment.

American and British historians have not given the flight and expulsion of 15 million Germans, in the process of which more than two million perished, the attention that this enormously important and tragic phenomenon deserves. Nor has the American and British press fulfilled its responsibility to inform the general public about these events. On the contrary, the issue has been largely ignored and subject to taboos, even to this day. Only the occurrence of the ethnic cleansing in the former Yugoslavia during the last decade of the 20th century allowed obvious parallels to be drawn, and some discussion on the subject of the Germans as victims has finally ensued. Much more is necessary.

Whereas some studies about the expulsion of the Germans by Poland and the former Czechoslovakia have been published, there is relatively little information available concerning the fate of the Germans from the former Yugoslavia. That is why the publication of this book must be welcomed, and its dissemination among the press and in the schools should follow. Testimonies of survivors of this "ethnic cleansing" of Germans should be recorded in video and on paper for future generations. Survivors of this awful crime against humanity should also speak to students in high schools and universities.

Let us remember the words of the noted British publisher and human rights activist, Victor Gollancz, one of the first courageous voices to recognize the moral implications and thus condemn the mass expulsion and spoliation of the Germans:

"If the conscience of men ever again becomes sensitive, these expulsions will be remembered to the undying shame of all who committed or connived at them … The Germans were expelled, not just with an absence of over-nice consideration, but with the very maximum of brutality."[3]

---

[2] A. de Zayas, *A Terrible Revenge. The ethnic cleansing of the East European Germans 1944–1950,* St. Martin's Press, New York 1994, p. 81.

[3] Victor Gollancz, *Our Threatened Values,* London 1946, p. 96.

But in order that the conscience of mankind become sensitive, it is necessary to have full information, open discussion without taboos – i. e. freedom of expression. Let us hope that this book will help us understand that all victims of "ethnic cleansing" are deserving of our attention and of our compassion.

Alfred de Zayas, J. D. (Harvard), Ph. D. (Göttingen), Senior Fellow, International Human Rights Law Institute, Chicago Member, International P.E.N. Club.
Author of *Nemesis at Potsdam*, 1998, Picton Press, Rockport, Maine,
A Terrible Revenge, 1994, St. Martin's Press, New York,
The Wehrmacht War Crimes Bureau, 2000, Picton Press, Rockport, Maine.

Prologue

During the last ten years of the 20th century the whole world followed, with horror and detest, the terrible events in the multiethnic nation Yugoslavia. These events were not merely wars between enemy armies, they were indescribable, cruel annihilation actions against entire ethnic groups. Children, women, old and invalid people were brutally murdered because they belonged to certain ethnic or religious groups. Human beings were robbed of their possessions, disfranchised and expelled from their native soil. Whole regions were "ethnically cleansed". Public and world opinion rightfully demanded that this cruel genocide be stopped and the perpetrators be punished. An international Yugoslavia-tribunal was established in Den Haag for this very purpose and one hopes that it will demonstrate to the world that war crimes, crimes against humanity and genocide will no longer be tolerated.

However, hardly anybody knows that 50 years earlier, in this very nation, a gruesome genocide, preplanned and directed by its highest leadership, took place. At that time ethnic German citizens of Yugoslavia were the victims, but the civilized world closed its eyes. World War II was just coming to an end and nobody wanted to come to the aid of humans whose mother-tongue was German. The bloodthirsty Communists, led by Tito, could commit their atrocities without interference and none were held accountable.

The fate of some 15 million ethnic Germans who, during the final phase of World War II and immediately thereafter, were inhumanly and illegally removed from their native soil is hardly known in the public consciousness of Europe. German-language historical records largely skip over this topic. However, without adequately recognizing history's largest expulsion of humans, history writing remains a one-sided endeavor. An honest and everlasting reconciliation of the European people requires that all sides distance themselves from lies and injustices. This generates mutual respect and trust which is an indispensable precondition for a solid foundation of the communal House of Europe.

All the injustices committed by the national-socialistic regime in Germany of some 50 years ago were prosecuted in court as soon as they were discovered and, whenever possible, subjected to rehabilitation. This is correct and necessary since a casual acceptance of committed injustices would destroy the human esteem as well as sense of value and could lead to the danger of repetition. However, this is true not only for Germany but for all countries as well. Criminal political systems and individuals could be encouraged if they know that crimes against humanity and genocide will not be punished and will eventually be forgotten.

The most recent history of Yugoslavia's ethnic people would probably have taken a different course if the serious crimes of Tito's criminal Communist regime, particularly the genocide of the ethnic Germans during 1944–1948, were immediately disclosed and prosecuted. But the criminals of that time were never held accountable, their crimes were concealed or even glorified. Thus it is hardly surprising that their children and grandchildren feel encouraged to follow such examples.

After 1944, about 500,000 ethnic German citizens of Yugoslavia have disappeared from their native land. Since Tito assumed power, and during the reign of his successors up to the deposition of Milošević, Yugoslavian historical writings with reference to their former ethnic German citizens contained only lies, concealment of crimes and disavowal of the genocide. During more than 50 years the systematic falsification of history was also practised by the Yugoslavian writers – partly because of the political pressure they were subjected to, partly due to ideologic communist or nationalistic delusion. Unfortunately this is also true for very prominent and capable literary men whose works were even translated into other languages. Being embeded in good literature the historic untruth assumed a strong semblance of seriousness, convincing even those readers (specially younger ones without own personal experience), who would not necessarily believe the politicians. Only now, after they have overcome dictatorship, local people are gradually beginning to ask that the truth be told. The purpose of this book is to help them in this endeavor. It is a terrible, cruel, truth; not a pleasant but a necessary reading.

The ethnic Germans whose ancestors were residing since 1686 in the area of the middle Danube region, then part of Hungary which in turn was part of the Habsburg Empire and since 1918 attached to Yugoslavia, are of the opinion that world conscience cannot remain silent about the crimes and atrocities committed against them. But without knowledge, conscience cannot be raised. In order for world consciousness to learn about their fate and bring it to its conscience, the fact of the genocide and committed atrocities have to be recollected: orgies of murder, confiscation of properties, disfranchisement, shipment to concentration camps, planned annihilation by starvation, epidemics, and ethnic re-education of children.

For that purpose, this books attempts to fight against the suppression, concealment and forgetfulness. The authors are also convinced that knowledge of the history of the 15 million ethnic Germans expelled from their native lands and the refugees constitute an integral part of the German and Austrian history and has to become a permanent part of the historic and cultural consciousness of both nations.

Over many generations the Danube Swabians, as the majority of the ethnic Germans in Yugoslavia were called, lived peacefully among other nationalities in their native homelands which were incorporated in the newly formed Yugoslavia after World War I. For the reader who is not familiar with this area and to better understand these events, we briefly explain the development of this new nation up to World War II, the first disintegration, the following civil war and the attainment of power by the Communists. The ethnic Germans in Yugoslavia could not evade these historic developments and when the Communists prevailed, their fate was sealed.

In the title and throughout the book the authors have used the term "genocide" for the crimes committed against the ethnic Germans in Yugoslavia. In chapter 13 they present the objective proof that the legal facts of genocide within the definition of the UNO Convention of December 9th, 1948 are clearly established. In order for the reader to arrive at his/her own conclusion, the Appendix of this book contains the complete text of the relevant UNO documents including the Convention of November 1968 which deals with Non-Applicability of Statutory Limitations to War Crimes and Crimes Against Humanity.

Individuals as well as all associations of ethnic Germans from Yugoslavia do not consider the prosecution of the crimes committed against them subject to time limitation since Article I of the Convention specifically states that no Statutory Limitations apply to such crimes. Nor do they consider the robbery of their property as a settled matter. By publishing this book they want to draw world attention and the attention of the pertinent nations to the fact that the moral and legal rehabilitation and an adequate restitution for the ethnic Germans in Yugoslavia is still an open file. A settlement of this matter will contribute to the peaceful cohabitation in a new Europe.

This book is based on the four-volume documentation *Leidensweg der Deutschen im kommunistischen Jugoslawien* (The suffering of the ethnic Germans in the Communist Yugoslavia), compiled 1990–1995 and the companion pocket book *Verbrechen an den Deutschen in Jugoslawien 1944–1948* (Crimes committed against the ethnic Germans in Yugoslavia 1944–1948) which was published in several editions since May 1998. It is, however, a distinct edition. Due to space limitation, this English-language book dispenses with detailed source references; interested readers can obtain these from the aforementioned documentation series which have been compiled in a scientific and responsible manner.

The project committee *"Documentation"*, which is responsible for the content of this publication as well as for the entire documentation series has been authorized by the Donauschwäbische Kulturstiftung München, and the Federal Danube Swabian Associations of Germany and Austria to document the genocide events. But it also undertook this task out of its own initiative since most of its members are eyewitnesses and personally experienced these terrible events, surviving thanks to merciful higher guidance.

Last but not least, this book was created out of respect for the immeasurable suffering of the victims. The solidarity of remembrance, a dominant feature of a new humanity, mandates that the suffering of the innocently killed shall not be forgotten. This book also wants to prevent the exclusion from memory the suffering of the ethnic German victims. It wants to give those dead victims a voice.

Acknowledgements

Many have contributed to this book but the following authors should be especially recognized. As adolescents they experienced first hand the power grab of the Tito-Partisans. They lost their parental home, all belongings and suffered in the labor and liquidation camps. Family members and close relatives were murdered. Their sense of responsibility for a competent and truthful record and judgement of the events induced them to make themselves available for this project.

Herbert Prokle (Project Manager of the present book), born 1933 at Modosch/Banat, studied mechanical engineering at the Technische Universität München (Dipl.-Ing.). Senior and chief executive positions at BBC/ABB Konzern, particularly in Mexico. Retired in 1992. Chairman of the HOG and Publisher of *Modoscher Heimatblätter,* Contributor to newspapers and journals. Co-founder and member of the Advisory Board of the Donauschwäbische Kulturstiftung. Deputy-Chairman of the Landsmannschaft der Donauschwaben in Germany (Federal Association of Danube Swabians in Germany)

Georg Wildmann, born 1929 at Filipowa/Batschka, studied theology and philosophy (Dr. Theol. and Lic. Phil.). Professor at the Theologische Hochschule Linz and Colleges. Editor of the *Filipowaer Heimatbriefe,* Member of Board of Directors of Donauschwäbische Kulturstiftung. Publications: *Personalismus, Solidarismus und Gesellschaft* (Wien 1961); Author of the eight volume illustrated series: *Filipowa – Bild einer Donauschwäbischen Gemeinde,* as well as the graphic series of Sebastian Leicht: *Weg der Donauschwaben;* Co-author of the documentation series: *Leidensweg der Deutschen im kommunistischen Jugoslawien* and the three-volume *Donauschwäbische Geschichte* (Universitas, München). Numerous contributions to books and journals. Bundesverdienstkreuz 1. Kl.

Karl Weber, born 1933 at Bulkes/Batschka. Mechanical engineer at the BASF Chemical Corporation. Member of Advisory Board of the Donauschwäbische Kulturstiftung. Author of volume IV *Menschenverluste – Namen und Zahlen,* and Co-author of volume II of the documentary series *Leidensweg der Deutschen im kommunistischen Jugoslawien.* Responsible for all population and casualties statistics in these publications.

Hans Sonnleitner, born 1931 at Karlsdorf/Banat. Studied economic sciences at the Verwaltungs- und Wirtschaftsakademie München (Dipl. Econ.). Retired senior manager and Division Director at the Siemens Corporation. Chairman of the Donauschwäbische Kulturstiftung, München. Co-author of the documentary series *Leidensweg der Deutschen im kommunistischen Jugoslawien.* Author and contributor of numerous articles to journals and publications and the books *Karlsdorf im Verlauf Donauschwäbischer Geschichte, Aktion Intelligenzija in Karlsdorf; Donauschwäbische Todesnot unter dem Tito-Stern; Etymologie des Familiennamens Sonnleitner.*

Ernst Ott (Translator of the book *Genocide of the Ethnic Germans in Yugoslavia 1944–1948),* born 1928 at Lugasul de jos, Transylvania. Education: Languages, International Trade, Publishing. Senior Executive positions; Retired President of International Operations, Jockey Intl., USA; Chairman, Advisory Board, Apparel Management School, University of Missouri; guest lecturer at US Universities and Colleges; President, German American National Congress; Editor-in-Chief, German American Journal; numerous articles and translations; Co-author of the book *Heimat North America:* Bundesverdienstkreuz 1. Kl.

Chapter 1: The Ethnic Germans in Yugoslavia – Historical Summary

This book deals with a subject which has largely been kept secret by the Yugoslav Communist regime and by government decrees, systematically falsified for school teachings and publications: the historic truth of the genocide of the ethnic Germans of Yugoslav nationality in Yugoslavia during World War II and particularly thereafter and their flight and expulsion from their ancestral homes. The events detailed here took place particularly between the fall 1944 and spring 1948.

It is, therefore, not surprising that after 50 years the likelihood that this crime will be forgotten is great and the false Yugoslav history version could prevail.

At the beginning of World War II, about 540,000 people whose mother-tongue was German lived within the national boundaries of the then Yugoslav kingdom. About 510,000 belonged to the ethnic group of Danube Swabians, which comprise the ethnic Germans of the West Banat, Batschka, Belgrade and Serbia, Syrmia, Baranja Triangle, Slawonia, Croatia and Bosnia. Additional groups were the Germans (formerly Austrians) of Slovenia, mainly the German Untersteirer, German Oberkrainer and the Gottscheer.

1.1 The Danube Swabians

The Danube Swabians are descendants of the Southwest Germans and Austrians who, between 1689 and 1787, were settled in the Pannonian Basin by the Habsburg emperors after the liberation of Hungary from Turk rule (which at that time belonged to the Habsburg empire).

1.1.1 Origin, Settlement and Colonial Achievements

The defeat of the Turk armies at the battle of *Kahlenberg* (1683) at the end of the siege of Vienna led to the gradual retreat of the Ottoman Empire and the liberation of the Danube region. After 160 years of Turk domination, the victories of the Imperial Armies, under the military leadership of Karl of Lorraine, Ludwig of Baden and Prince Eugene of Savoy, laid the foundation for the reconstruction of the region.

Vienna proved to be not only a bastion against the expansion of the Turk military might, but also a launching pad for the political, cultural and economic reconstruction of the Hungarian region. Already in 1689 the Habsburg decree called for the resettlement of the depopulated Hungarian Kingdom.

In the years 1722/23 the Hungarian representatives to the national assembly (Landtag) at Preßburg demanded that "people of all walks of life be recruited and exempted from all public taxation for a period of six years".

The Monarch Karl VI was requested to issue appropriate decrees in the entire Roman Empire and neighbouring countries. The colonization was carried out in a peaceful manner and with the consent of the landowners. Among the settlers from several countries, those of Germanic origin were an important and preferred group.

During the 18th century over 150,000 immigrants arrived from various German and Austrian areas and settled in the then historic Hungarian boundaries. Since many of the settlers and their descendants were of Swabian origin, historians later (1922) referred to them collectively as Danube Swabians *("Donauschwaben")*.

The immigration which took place throughout the 18th century reached three peak periods: 1723 to 1726, 1764 to 1771 and 1784 to 1787. They were called the Swabian treks *(Schwabenzüge)*. Instead of the "Promised Land", touted by the recruiters, they encountered, particularly during the earlier phases of the colonization, harsh living conditions in the swampy lowlands and mines of the mountain regions causing hardships, epidemics, diseases and many casualties over several generations.

Fittingly, this led them to coin the phrase "The first encountered death, the second distress and only the third bread" ("Den Ersten der Tod, den Zweiten die Not, erst den Dritten das Brot").

It was due to a well programmed settlement policy which led to the creation of many new, attractive villages, substantial increases in agricultural, commercial and industrial production and growth of national prosperity. Thus, the Pannonian lowlands developed, with considerable contributions by the settlers of the 18th century and their descendants, into the "breadbasket of the Danube Monarchy".

The Austrian settlement program must not be interpreted as a tendency of Germanization, as some today's adversaries argue. It was the principles of practicality, trade and national interests which called for the recruitment of colonists, merchants, artisans and skilled laborers from the German and Austrian territories.

Most of the immigrants in the Banat mining district were miners, foundry workers, charcoal burners and forest workers who, shortly after the retreat of the Turks, were recruited to reactivate the abandoned copper, silver and iron mines. It was their efforts, which, in the 19th century, established the basis for the largest mining and industrial region of Southeast Europe.

The Danube Swabian poet Stefan Augsburger-Roney aptly characterized his countrymen's achievements with the words: "Conquered not by the sword, but by the plow, children of peace, heroes of labor" ("Nicht mit dem Schwert, mit dem Pflugschar erobert, Kinder des Friedens, Helden der Arbeit").

The 19th century was highlighted by positive economic growth of the rural communities. However, adverse circumstances prevented the Danube Swabians from developing their individualistic intellectual strata, since the strengthening Magyar (Hungarian) society attracted and assimilated the intellectual forces emerging from the rural peasantry (Ingomar Senz, 287–319).

1.1.2 The Danube Swabians in Yugoslavia 1918–1941

After the dismantling of Austria-Hungary in 1918, the community of the Danube Swabians (numbering 1.5 Million at that time) was dissected and – disregarding President Wilson's proclamation of self-determination rights of the people – distributed among the three successor nations Hungary, Romania and Yugoslavia (Josef V. Senz, 182 ff.).

As an ethnic entity and "a people in three fatherlands" it was difficult for them to find their common identity. They had to make do and go their own way in their respective new nations. According to their individual interests they formed their own different cultural, political and economic organizations.

The majority of the Danube Swabians, their mother tongue being German, became involuntary Yugoslav national citizens and lived in the Westbanat, Batschka and aranja, which was collectively termed Vojvodina. This province never before belonged to a South-Slavic nation. Its population was multiethnic and none of its segments had an absolute majority. The composition of the Westbanat, for example was: 39 percent Serbs, 33 percent Germans, 13 percent Romanians, 9.5 percent Hungarians and 5.5 percent other minorities. In relation to Yugoslavia as a nation, the Germans, Romanians and Hungarians were a relatively small minority. Such comparisons, however, are misleading since, in their former home territory they represented considerable ethnic groups.

Restrictive Minority Politics

In the 1919 newly created Kingdom of Serbs, Croats and Slovenes (renamed Yugoslavia in 1929) the Danube Swabian national minorities accounted for approximately half a million citizens. As a condition to be internationally recognized as a nation, at the Paris peace agreements, Yugoslavia had to grant contractual minority protection guarantees which provided for their individual ethnic development. However, these constitutional provisions were never carried out and an effective control system did not exist. Thus, the Serb authorities largely ignored the minority guarantees (Wildmann, 2001, esp. 57 f.) Nevertheless, during the first two years the German minority was, temporarily, able to improve its school system, establish the basis for a German-language press and, in 1920, establish the Swabian-German Cultural Association *(Schwäbisch-Deutscher Kulturbund)*, in 1922 the German Party *(Partei der Deutschen)* and the very successful German cooperative society *Agraria*. These initial concessions, however, disappeared after a few years.

The restrictive school policy of Belgrade – it was only in 1940 that Belgrade permitted the first German-language full grade high school (Vollgymnasium) – the prohibition of German societies and other restrictive measures considerably impaired the ethnic-political situation of the German community (Josef Senz, *Schulwesen*, 82–87; 92–100).

New restrictive property legislation made the purchase of real estate within 50 kilometre of the national border subject to governmental approval. The purpose was to stop the acquisition of real property by foreigners. However, this legislation was quickly used to also make it impossible for Germans of Yugoslav citizenship to acquire property. This measure was devised to further limit the economic base of the ethnic Germans (Janko, Weg und Ende der deutschen Volksgruppe in Jugoslawien, 50 f.). The situation of the Germans in Yugoslavia began to improve only in the thirties after Germany began to strengthen its political posture.

Transformation of the Ethnic German Group (Volksgruppe)

About the middle of 1939 the old national-conservative cultural respectively national-liberal society leadership *(Kulturbundführung)*, after intense internal struggle, was replaced by representatives of the national-radical Renewal Movement *(Erneuerungsbewegung)* which was supported by the German government. Its leadership consisted of a handful of young intellectuals.

Dr. Sepp Janko, its leader was elected in 1939 upon strong pressure brought about by the German government Office for Germans Living Abroad *(Auslandsdeutsche)*. For him the principal idea of "Nationalsozialismus" was the total unity of the ethnic group, rooted in the same blood. He was convinced that the blood relationship with the German Nationals *(Reichsdeutsche)* necessarily united them all. The destiny of Germany would also become the destiny of the Danube Swabians (Wildmann, 1993, 132 f.).

Similar developments took place in Hungary as well, where in 1938 the *Volksbund der Deutschen in Ungarn* ("Alliance of the Ethnic Germans in Hungary") was established.

An opposition against the Renewal Movement was started by a Catholic Action *(katholische Aktion)* under the leadership of the priest Pfarrer Adam Brenz. From 1935 to 1944 he conducted an intense ideological battle against the anti-Christian excesses and abuse in his weekly periodical *Die Donau* (The Danube) (Lehmann, *Die katholischen Donauschwaben*, 242 ff., 421 ff.).

The ethnic German group leaders *(Volksgruppenführer)* began adopting organizational and image models, patterned after those of Germany. Thus, after the "April War" of 1941 which led to the first partition of Yugoslavia, organizations such as *Deutsche Mannschaft* (Body of German Men), *Deutsche Jugend* (German Youth), *Deutsche Frauenschaft* (German Women's Group) became established. In the independent Croatia, *Arbeitsdienst* (Work Team Service) and *Winterhilfswerk* (Winter Aid Society) were founded.

The group leaders had idealistic conceptions of Germany's "Nationalsozialismus". They had great hopes that such joint common cultural and socially strengthened groups with the interchange of the larger Germanic cultural community could give them a real chance to ensure a continuation of their own identity in this multiethnic and multi-cultural Southeastern Europe. Until well into the course of the war they held those idealistic notions of the Nationalsozialismus and the merits of the fight against Bolshevism of which the German propaganda projected a dramatic image.

There was another opposition group to the Nationalsozialismus which was rooted in political, ideological and religious doctrines. It included mainly the Catholics and Protestans of the middle and western Batschka and had the belief that one could also be a good German if he had role models other than the National Socialistic ones. The majority of the Danube Swabians were, in general, non-political. The renewed strength of Germany after 1933 increased her esteem in middle-eastern Europe. It kindled the hope of the Danube Swabians that Germany's influence would bring an end to the discrimination of the German speaking people in Yugoslavia and give them a cultural autonomy (VDJ, 21 f.).

1.1.3 A Military Coup and its Consequences: The Disintegration of Royal Yugoslavia in 1941 – Establishment of Communist Yugoslavia in 1944/45

Both, the Yugoslav government of Prime Minister Dragisa Cvetkovic and the German government, were interested in preventing an expansion of the war in the Balkan. (World War II began September 1939.) Cvetkovic wanted to protect Yugoslavia from territorial claims by Italy and Hungary. Hitler was preparing his attack on Russia and did not care to tie up his military forces in the Balkans. He also wanted to ensure a peaceful Yugoslavia. Given those circumstances, Cvetkovic's government accepted the invitation to join the Axis Powers (Germany, Italy and Japan), particularly since his neighbouring countries Hungary, Romania and Bulgaria had already done so and the conditions were favorable for Yugoslavia (no commitment on the part of Yugoslavia to participate in the Axis war or to permit transit of foreign military forces) (Wüscht, *Jugoslawien und das Dritte Reich,* 153–158).

The pact was signed on March 25th, 1941. However, two days later, a military coup in Belgrade, led by General Dusan Simovic toppled the Cvetkovic government and thus prevented the ratifications of the pact. Anti-German slogans and an agreement with Russia indicated a change of Yugoslavia's political direction. The participants of the coup were mainly members of the Serbian general staff. Documents of their secret negotiations with the Allies fell into German hands during her war with France (Wüscht, *Jugoslawien und das Dritte Reich,* 159–180).

The reasons for Hitler's quick decision to attack Yugoslavia were his concern of the creation of a southern front by the Allies and his desire to protect his flanks during the planned attack on Russia. The simultaneous attack on Greece was to support the Italian army which became bogged down there. The Yugoslav war began on April 6th, 1941 and ended on April 18th, 1941 with the unconditional surrender of the entire Yugoslav army.

Contrary to some defamatory reports, the conduct of the ethnic Germans was that of loyalty to their home country Yugoslavia. 80 to 90 percent of those subject to draft followed the call, compared to only 60 to 70 percent of the Slavic population. Accusations that members of the ethnic German group acted as a "Fifth Column" against their home country are without merit (VDJ, 44).

The New Constitutional Position of the Danube Swabians

As a result of the partitioning of Yugoslavia following the April war, the ethnic Germans became subjects of the independent nations Croatia (Syrmia and Slavonia), Hungary (Batschka and Baranya) and the German-occupied Serbia (West Banat). The Germans of Lower-Styria became citizens of Germany (Austria), since their homeland was annexed by Germany. Because the homeland of the Gottscheer was given to Italy, they were resettled to Lower Styria.

The partitioning of Yugoslavia created complex international and constitutional situations. In addition, the infighting among the Tschetnics, Communist partisans and Croatian Ustaschas was leading to civil war-like conditions. The German and Italian occupation forces and Hungarian government were further power factors in the former kingdom. On July 8th, 1941 Germany and Italy declared that Yugoslavia had ceased to be a legal international formation due to its unconditional surrender, even though the exiled king and his government-in-exile, which had fled to London, claimed the continuation of the country's existence.

Hungary, Romania, Bulgaria and the newly created Independent State Croatia (USK) which had joined the Axis powers adopted the same position. The legal consequences were that the inhabitants of the annexed areas, including the Danube Swabians, became national citizens of these countries, subject to their laws and compulsory military service. It was beyond their political understanding that they could, therefore, be considered traitors to a (no more existing) kingdom of Yugoslavia or the terroristic partisans' "liberation" movement.

Legal Position and Military Objectives of the Tschetnics

The National-Serbian Tschetnics led by the Chief of the General Staff Dragoljub-Draža Mihajlović did not recognize the unconditional surrender. For them the kingdom did not cease to exist as a legal entity. Accordingly, the government-in-exile appointed Mihajlović Secretary of Defense and Commander-in-Chief of the Yugoslav Army in the home territory. He considered himself the Commander of the surviving armed forces, continuing the fight. In reality the Tschetnics carried on a gang-like war.

His objectives were:
a) the liberation of the country, re-establishing Yugoslavia's former govern-mental, legal and social structure with a strong Great-Serbian, centralistic domination,
b) fight against communism which, in his declaration of allegiance to the Western Powers, he considered an internal Yugoslav matter and
c) an "ethnic cleansing" of Yugoslavia, in which only Serb, Croats and Slovenes, but no minorities were permitted. This resolution was adopted at the end of 1942 at Sahoviči (Montenegro).

The Partisans and their Strategy for Seizing Power

In 1939 the illegal Communist Party of Yugoslavia (KPJ) numbered only about 2000 members. A tightly organized underground group of several hundred persons was already active since the end of the twenties. They had an influential following among students and intellectuals and were able to infiltrate the government appa-ratus. In 1937 the Croat Josip Broz became Secretary General of the Central Com-mittee of the KPJ.

When Germany attacked the Soviet Union on June 22nd, 1941 the Komintern (In-ternational Communist Committee) called upon all Communist parties of Europe to rise up. As a national section of the Komintern the KPJ also did its duty in the service of the "world revolution". On the same day the central committee of the KPJ issued a proclamation calling for the Proletariat of Yugoslavia to come to the defense of the Soviet Union, "the beloved socialistic Fatherland". On July 4th Tito, as Josip Broz now called himself, issued the call for the KPJ to rise up against the occupational forces. The same month German officers and soldiers were ambushed and killed, the rail line Belgrade-Agram sabotaged and Communists were liberated from prisons, including Alexander Ranković, who later became Tito's Minister of the Interior and chief of the notorious secret police OZNA.

The assigned tasks of the KPJ were:
a) tying up as many enemy divisions as possible on the secondary Balkan front and
b) protecting the Balkan from a British landing. For the latter purpose Tito even was willing to collaborate with the Germans. Therefore, the initial objective of the par-tisans was not the "liberation of the people", but grasping the historical opportu-nity to enforce Communism in Yugoslavia according to Moscow's plans.

The Status of the Tschetnics and Partisans According to the International Convention on the Conduct of War

As far as the German military was concerned and according to the International Convention on the Conduct of War (International Law), neither the National-Serbian Tschetnics nor the ethnically mixed partisans had the status of "combatants" (soldiers). They were considered "guerrillas" or gangs. According to the Convention only combatants are authorized to carry out acts of war (VDJ, 40).

The ambush and murder of German soldiers which started on July 7th, 1941 led, on August 11th to a new appeal to the Serbian people by the German military in Serbian newspaper to cooperate with the occupying forces. The same appeal was made in public posters. The disregard of these appeals by the partisans led to the notorious order #888/41 of the German Army Command (OKW) of September 16th, 1941 which ordered the execution of 100 hostages for each murdered German soldier and 50 hostages for each wounded soldier. The express purpose was of deterrent nature. This action was purposefully provoked by the partisans as admitted by Serbian historians. The German retribution, however, far exceeded the principle of "adequate numbers", as provided by the Convention (VDJ, 41; Wüscht, *Jugoslawien und das Dritte Reich*, 193–200).

The strategy of the partisans, however, was to provoke the occupation forces to retaliatory actions against the civilian population including the threatened summary executions of hostages. It induced many to seek refuge with the partisans in the forests (VDJ, 38).

During the course of the civil war the creation of a Communist Yugoslavia became an increasingly greater objective of the communist party's central committee. For tactical reasons, however, it was necessary to expand the war and not make it appear to be a fight of the unpopular and, by the government-in-exile, unrecognized Communist party, but a national "Revolutionary War" of the Yugoslav people, for the liberation from the fascist occupiers and their collaborators. Hence the slogan "Death to Fascism-Freedom to the People". This became the "signature" of the Tito-movement. This popular-front image was the concept for the realization of a Communistic Yugoslavia in order not to scare away non-Communists but rather to induce them to join and fight with them.

Autonomous Administration of the Danube Swabians in the West Banat 1941–1944

With the authorization of the German government, the group leadership under Dr. Sepp Janko moved to the West Banat, which belonged to German-occupied Serbia and was permitted to establish an official autonomous self-administration of the ethnic German group. The Banat model was supposed to show that a peaceful coexistence of different ethnic nationalities in the same living space was entirely possible. It was also supposed to prove the Pannonian lowlands could, when properly managed, deliver extraordinary economic results (Janko, *Weg und Ende*, 89–205; VDJ, 45–49).

Tito-Partisans planning the annihilation of the Danube Swabians as an Ethnic Group

After the German attack on the Soviet Union, the Tito-partisans also began their terroristic attacks in the Banat. This action in itself made it clear that the Tito-movement considered the Danube Swabians collectively as allies of the German enemy. Dr. Janko reported that during the fighting which led to the retreat of the partisans from their temporarily established "Uzice Republic", the "Resolution of the Executive Committee" of the "Anti-Fascist Front" was seized. It prescribed the manner in which the ethnic German group was to be destroyed. After the "punishment of the culprits", all others were to be dispersed among all areas of the country and integrated into the Slavic population. According to Dr. Janko, after this resolution became known, the leadership in the Banat came to the conclusion that there was no other alternative for the ethnic Germans in Yugoslavia than to put their trust into Germany's support and protection. At any rate, the ordinary person had to feel that his fate was that of all Germans. The conviction that only Germany could protect them, was the major reason for strongly defending themselves against the actions of the partisans (Janko, *Weg und Ende*, 231 f., 237; LW I, 942).

Aside from the obvious genocidal intentions, the partisans also jeopardized public safety and order, which an occupying force, according to the International Law on the Conduct of War, was obligated to uphold regardless whether such occupation of a country was legal or not. According to this international law, partisans can be executed.

As the terror actions of the partisans increased, the group leadership decided to organize a home guard regiment, named Prinz Eugen, consisting of Banat citizens, for the sole purpose of the defense of the Banat. This was entirely legal according to the Haag Convention on the Conduct of War (HCCW). In April 1942, however, Hitler ordered the formation of the "SS Volunteer Mountain Division Prinz Eugen" instead of the home guard regiment. The service became compulsory for all ethnic Germans since there were only very few volunteers. The Division had a German-national leadership, German-national officers, and, against the original intent of the ethnic German leadership, was deployed against the Communist Tito-partisans outside of the Banat.

Sepp Janko, leader of the ethnic German group was concerned about this turn of events and argued with the SS headquarters that such deployment of Banat Germans was against the laws of the HCCW. However, he had to yield to the SS pressure. Based on this fact, the Danube Swabians had to reject the later accusations of treason (Janko, *Weg und Ende*, 206–237; VDJ, 47–49).

This Waffen-SS division (SS = acronym for "Schutzstaffel"), was a German military organization parallel to but independent of the main army called "Wehrmacht", however, did not cooperate with the Ustascha units (Croatian military units) which tried to exterminate the orthodox Serbs in Croatia and Bosnia.

The Danube Swabians of the Batschka and Baranja – Hungary, 1941–1944 (LW I, 378–407; VDJ 49–54)

After the incorporation of the Batschka and the Baranja into Hungary, the Schwäbisch-Deutscher Kulturbund (Swabian-German Cultural Alliance) became affiliated with the Volksbund der Deutschen in Ungarn (Alliance of the Germans in Hungary). The latter was established on November 26th, 1938. Its founder Dr. Franz Basch now also became the leader of the Germans in the Batschka and Baranja. His program included, in addition to the legal recognition of the ethnic group, the establishment of schools and church services in the German mother tongue.

At the Vienna meeting, on August 30th, 1940, the German and Hungarian governments, without the participation of the ethnic Germans, agreed upon the following status of the ethnic German group in Hungary:

a) Member of the group is a person who professes to be of German heritage and is accepted by the leadership of the ethnic alliance.
b) Members of the alliance have the right to organize and form societies.
c) All ethnic German children should have the opportunity to receive a grade school and higher education in their mother tongue. The necessary training of teachers will be supported by Hungary.

The Vienna agreement, however, did not grant the alliance a legal status. Nevertheless, it succeeded to establish 300 local chapters with about 50,000 members. After the second Vienna agreement, following the incorporation of North Transylvania and Sathmar into Hungary, the membership increased to 97,000 and the incorporation of the Batschka and Baranja, as a result of Yugoslavia's partition, added another 100,000.

The leadership of the German army and lawyers of the German State Department took the position that according to the Haag Convention, the German army could not legally recruit soldiers in the allied nations Hungary, Romania and Slovakia and let them fight outside their own borders. Thus, the ethnic Germans in the Banat should not have been deployed outside their home territory.

The SS leadership, however, and its leader Heinrich Himmler insisted on the overriding concept of *Volksrecht* (Right of the People) and the *blood brotherhood*. "Same ethnicity same people", as it was called at that time, meant the same destiny and the same obligation of military service, regardless of nationality. Therefore, Himmler considered his actions in the Banat justified.

After the start of Germany's war against the Soviet Union, the Waffen-SS needed additional soldiers to make up for its losses. Himmler saw in the ethnic Southeast Germans a welcome human resource and decreed in summer 1942 that, while there was no legal requirement, there was a moral requirement based on ethnicity for the ethnic Germans living outside of Germany, to fulfill military service in the German armed forces. The governments of Hungary, Croatia and Romania were put under pressure to enter into an agreement allowing Germany to draft their able-bodied ethnic Germans into the German Army, preferably into the Waffen-SS.

To stay within international law, the SS leadership declared the recruitment to be of a voluntary nature. Furthermore, the drafted ethnics serving in German military forces automatically received the German citizenship. This made them German soldiers, in accordance with the HCCW Convention.

The agreements which served as the legal basis for the drafting of able-bodied Germans were made without participation of the respective ethnic German leadership. However, the task to direct the draftees to the induction centers was given to the ethnic organizations, thus absolving the respective governments from taking legal actions against those not complying with the draft notices.

In the third agreement regarding the Waffen-SS action, the Hungarian government transferred the military service jurisdiction over its ethnic Germans to Germany and required them to serve their military service in Germany's armed forces. Simultaneously it reversed its earlier cancellation of the Hungarian citizenship of the Hungarian-Germans, serving in the German armed forces. Therefore, the Hungarian Germans drafted in 1944 into the Waffen-SS were neither volunteers nor formal German citizens (VDJ, 52 f.; LW I, 401–404).

During World War II, about 93,000 Danube Swabians of the former Yugoslavia served as soldiers in various national armies. One in four, 26,000, did not return. There are no records of any war crime trials of ethnic Germans of Yugoslavia, serving in the Waffen-SS.

Danube Swabians in the independent Croatia 1941–1945

The Croatian Germans, referred to here collectively as definition for all Danube Swabians living at that time in the various regions of the independent nation Croatia (USK), which included Syrmia, Slavonia, Croatia and Bosnia, did not consider themselves any longer citizens of the partitioned Yugoslavia, whose government-in-exile was in London, but citizens of the newly created nation Croatia and subject to its jurisdiction (VDJ, 34–36).

The Croatian Germans led by Branimir Altgayer, were given legal status of ethnic citizens and enjoyed considerable cultural autonomy. As members of a recognized ethnic group, they enjoyed equal rights in education. The central issue of cultural autonomy was schooling in its mother tongue to a degree not imaginable in the former kingdom of Yugoslavia (Oberkersch, 441–447).

The Tito-partisans were operating mainly in Krajina, Bosnia, Syrmia and Slavonia, areas, which since the April war of 1941 belonged to the now independent nation Croatia. The Croatian Ustascha-regime was allied with Germany and persecuted the Serbs living within its territory. This caused many of them to join the Tito-partisans who fought a cruel and bitter war against the Croats and to some extent against the Muslims as well. For the National Fascist Ustascha it was an ethnic-motivated civil war. For the Tito-partisans it was primarily a war leading to the Communist take over. Thus, the partisans considered the Danube Swabians of Croatia also their enemies.

In view of the growing hatred and cruel actions of the Tito-partisans against everything German, the leadership of the ethnic Germans considered their own fate as inadvertently and unavoidably intertwined with that of Germany. This led the leadership and majority of the Danube Swabians to conclude that their survival as an ethnic entity was only guaranteed by a peace favorable to Germany (VDJ, 54 f.).

Resettlement of the Germans in Bosnia and West Slavonia

The widely scattered Danube Swabian settlements in Bosnia and West Slavonia became a major problem for the ethnic German leadership. With the beginning of the partisan activities in summer 1941, it already became evident, particularly in Bosnia, that the German settlements could not be sufficiently protected. The Bosnian Germans suffered considerable casualties inflicted by the raids of the partisans. The local home guard was simply too weak to protect the scattered settlements. In late fall 1941 and in cooperation with the Croatian government, all endangered German settlements were evacuated. The 18,360 residents were shipped to various camps inside Germany and Austria.

In 1943, the situation in Slavonia became increasingly critical due to the frequent partisan raids on the scattered German settlements, particularly in West Slavonia. It was therefore decided to resettle the German inhabitants of 50 communities. They were moved to the area between Essegg, Vinkovci and Vukovar. In total 20,206 persons had to leave their homes (VDJ, 56; Oberkersch, 387–397).

The Partisans: Raids, Murders and Lootings in Syrmia and Slavonia

Some of the partisans used the following strategy. They operated only at night, while at daytime pretended to be peaceful citizens pursuing their normal activities. These "night partisans" were particularly successful in West and East Slavonia as well as in Syrmia.

However, when Croatian or German forces were further away, regular partisan units settled down in the conquered villages and coordinated their activities with the night partisans. "Settling the score" with non-Communists, particularly government-loyal Croats and Germans were daily occurrences (VDJ, 56–62).

Flight and Evacuation, Fall 1944

When Soviet forces approached towards the end of September 1944, the order of the German military to evacuate the Danube Swabians in the Banat and Batschka came too late (VDJ, 67; Janko, *Weg und Ende*, 249–288). Hence only relatively few from the West Banat, in some of the Batschka villages only one percent, in others up to 90 percent, fled by the time the Red Army and the partisans were getting ready to cross the Theiss river (Wüscht, *Beitrag*, 130 ff.; VDJ, 67–72).

Major reasons for this tragic evacuation delay were the tactical and political dilemma of Germany's leadership. The evacuation of the Danube Swabians was tantamount to admitting that large areas of Hungary and Croatia were considered lost, risking that the Hungarians would immediately capitulate and the Croats lose their willingness to continue the fight. On the other hand, if one did not evacuate the ethnic Germans, one risked the loss of *German blood* which again was contrary to the philosophy of Germany's Nationalism. It is known that Colonel General (equivalent to a US four-star general) Alexander Löhr pleaded for a timely evacuation. A few days after Romania's capitulation (August 23rd, 1944) in a meeting with ethnic German leaders at Belgrade he said: "If you want to save German blood in this region, we have to do it immediately" (VDJ, 66).

Beginning October 1944, the German military began a systematic evacuation of the Danube Swabians in Croatia, mostly by rail and horse-drawn wagons. The evacuees loaded onto open railroad cars tried to protect themselves from rain and cold with wooden boards and tarps. The horse-drawn wagons were traveling for weeks. The search for fodder for the horses and lodging for the nights were daily struggles. Some of them had to travel over 1,000 kilometre (621.4 miles) to reach their allocated destinations.

By fall 1944 almost 225,000 Danube Swabians fled or were evacuated. Several thousands returned to Yugoslavia under great difficulties and were immediately forced into internment camps. Between October 1944 and May 1945 well over 200,000 civilians, whose mother tongue was German, fell into the hands of the partisans.

The escapees and surviving Danube Swabian prisoners who could not go back totalled about 300,000. Thus, Yugoslavia achieved a first "ethnic cleansing" of more than half of its 540,000 ethnic German citizens.

1.2 The Germans of Lower Styria (Untersteiermark)

The German Untersteirer are the former inhabitants of the Untersteiermark (Lower Styria) which – since 1147, for over 770 years – belonged to the Styria duchy. In 1910 the population was 74,000.

For hundreds of years they were dominant in cultural life, trade, industry and mining. At the peace treaty of Saint-Germain, the Lower Styria was separated from the Styria which belonged to Austria and was made part of the newly created Slovenia which in turn was incorporated into the Kingdom of Serbs, Croats and Slovenians (renamed Yugoslavia in 1929). After the partitioning of Yugoslavia (1941) the Untersteiermark was joined with the old Steiermark and both were attached to Germany.

"By Hitler's orders", the entire historic Steiermark was to be "germanized". All South Slavs who had immigrated into the Untersteiermark after 1918, about 10,000, and about 20,000 Slovenians, who openly opposed the germanization, were expelled. The former were moved to what was left of Serbia and the latter to the German *Reich*.

In their place the Gottscheer and the resettled ethnic Germans from Bukovina and South Tyrol were transferred to the southeast of the historic Steiermark, which now belonged to Germany.

It is not surprising that these measures disappointed not only the Slovenes who had put their trust into the Germans, but also incited the hatred of the Slovenian Nationalists which led to the partisan uprising. The "Slovenian Liberation Movement" was created April 27th, 1941. Initially, it consisted mainly of Communists and radical Nationalists who soon were joined by desperate citizens. The partisans' actions were brutal. Resorting to executions and torching farms, they forced the farmers to feed and support them. German counter-measures were equally brutal, but could no longer contain the fire they had ignited.

Understandably, the Deutsch-Untersteirer were initially enthusiastic about their incorporation into the German *Reich*. However, their disappointment came rather quickly as they found out that they had no voice whatsoever in the administration of the territory. Many warned against the expulsions, executions of hostages and forced political re-education; but they were told that the nature of the war required such measures and were given glorious postwar promises.

Since their fate was intertwined with that of Germany, they had no choice but to support the German administration.

Even as the course of the war turned more menacing and eventually hopeless, with few exceptions, people were not permitted to leave. About 4,300 ethnic German-Slovenian civilians perished as a result of the partisan war, mostly by executions, torture and starvation in the camps at the end of the war: Thus about 1,000 Gottschee civilians, and about 3,300 Deutsch-Untersteirer became victims of the genocide. Approximately 90 percent of the surviving Deutsch-Untersteirer found a new home in Austria. Since 1948 they are organized in a *Hilfsverein* (an aid society) with its headquarters in Graz.

1.3 The Gottscheers

The *Gottscheers* are inhabitants of the German-speaking language enclave *Gottschee,* situated in the former Habsburg crown land Krain. It was established in 1330, about 660 years ago, by German settlers from Carinthia and East Tyrol, due to an initiative of the Carinthian counts of Ortenburg. In 1918, the naturally developed language enclave numbered 18,000 inhabitants, living in 25 communities and 172 villages. At the peace treaty of St. Germain (September 10th, 1919), it became part of Slovenia and the newly created Kingdom of the Serbs, Croats and Slovenians.

After the collapse and partitioning of Yugoslavia in 1941, Gottschee became Italian territory and the Gottscheer (about 11,200) were moved to the Southeast Untersteiermark (Lower Styria).

Like the Germans in Slovenia, they too initially were forbidden to leave when the Russians approached. The order to evacuate was issued only beginning May 1945, which for most of them was too late. While the exact number of those who perished during the flight or in camps is not known, estimates of the casualties including those of soldiers, run around 1,000. A large number of Gottscheer found a new home in Austria; however, other significant groups emigrated to the USA.

Sources to 1.1

Arbeitskreis Dokumentation, *Leidensweg der Deutschen im kommunistischen Jugoslawien,* Vol. I–IV, Donauschwäbische Kulturstiftung München, München/Sindelfingen 1991–1995. Abbr.: LW I etc.

Arbeitskreis Dokumentation, *Verbrechen an den Deutschen in Jugoslawien 1944–1948. Die Stationen eines Völkermords*, Donauschwäbische Kulturstiftung München, 3. Aufl., München 2000. Abbr.: VDJ.

Beer, Josef, *Donauschwäbische Zeitgeschichte aus erster Hand*, Donauschwäbische Kulturstiftung München, München 1987.

Djilas, Milovan, *Krieg der Partisanen.* Memoiren 1941–1945, Molden/Wien 1978. Jugoslawisch: *Revolucionarni Rat*, 1977.

Janko, Sepp, *Reden und Aufsätze*, Betschkerek 1944.

Janko, Sepp, *Weg und Ende der deutschen Volksgruppe in Jugoslawien*, Graz/Stuttgart 1982.

Lehmann, Michael (Hrsg.), *Die katholischen Donauschwaben in den Nachfolgestaaten 1918–1945*, Pannonia-Verlag, Freilassing 1972.

Oberkersch, Valentin, *Die Deutschen in Syrmien, Slawonien, Kroatien und Bosnien. Geschichte einer deutschen Volksgruppe in Südosteuropa*, München 1989.

Scherer, Anton, *Die Deutschen in der Untersteiermark, in Ober-Krain und in der Gottschee*, in: E. Hochberger/A. Scherer/F. Spiegel-Schmidt, *Die Deutschen zwischen Karpaten und Krain*, München 1994.

Schieder, Theodor u. a., *Dokumentation der Vertreibung der Deutschen aus Ost-Mitteleuropa*, Vol. V: *Das Schicksal der Deutschen in Jugoslawien*. Herausgegeben vom Bundesministerium für Flüchtlinge und Kriegsbeschädigte, Bonn 1961. Abbr.: Dok V. Unveränderter Nachdruck: Deutscher Taschenbuchverlag (dtv reprint 3274), München 1984 und Weltbild-Verlag, Augsburg 1994.

Senz, Josef V., *Geschichte der Donauschwaben. Von den Anfängen bis zur Gegenwart*, Donauschwäbische Kulturstiftung München, München 1989.

Senz, Josef V., *Das Schulwesen der Deutschen im Königreich Jugoslawien*, Verlag Südostdeutsches Kulturwerk, München 1961.

Senz, Ingomar (Hrsg.), *Donauschwäbische Geschichte*, Vol. II: *Wirtschaftliche Autarkie und politische Entfremdung 1806–1918*, Universitas, München 1997.

Völkl, Ekkehard, *Der Westbanat 1941–1944. Die deutsche, die ungarische und andere Volksgruppen*, München 1991.

Wildmann, Georg, *Die Donauschwaben und der Nationalsozialismus*, in: Franz Roth (Hrsg.), *Beiträge zum Geschichtsbild der Donauschwaben* (Donauschwäbische Beiträge 97), Salzburg 1993.

Wildmann, Georg, *Die politische und rechtliche Lage der deutschen Volksgruppe im König-reich Jugoslawien 1918–1941*, in: Felix-Ermacora-Institut (Hrsg.), *Europa und die Zukunft der deutschen Minderheiten* (Bd. 1 der Schriftenreihe *Geschichte, Gegenwart und Zukunft der altösterreichischen deutschen Minderheiten in den Ländern der ehemaligen Donau-monarchie*), Wien 2001, 52–73.

Wüscht, Johann, *Beitrag zur Geschichte der Deutschen in Jugoslawien für den Zeitraum 1934–1944*, Kehl am Rhein 1966.

Wüscht, Johann, *Die Ereignisse in Syrmien 1941–1944*, Selbstverlag, Kehl am Rhein 1975.

Wüscht, Johann, *Die magyarische Okkupation der Batschka 1941–1944*. Dokumentarische Stellungnahme zur jugoslawischen Darstellung, Selbstverlag, Kehl am Rhein 1975.

Wüscht, Johann, *Jugoslawien und das Dritte Reich*. Eine Dokumentierte Geschichte der deutsch-jugoslawischen Beziehungen 1933 bis 1945, Stuttgart 1969.

Wüscht, Johann, *Ursachen und Hintergründe des Schicksals der Deutschen in Jugoslawien*. Selbstverlag, Kehl am Rhein 1966.

Sources to 1.2

VDJ, 26–29, 68 f.; LW I, 826 f.; Scherer 130 f.; Wüscht, *Slowenen und Deutsche*, 39–59; Karner, Stefan, *Die deutschsprachige Volksgruppe in Slowenien. Aspekte ihrer Entwicklung 1939–1997*, Hermagoras, Klagenfurt/Ljubljana/Wien 1998, 11–168; , Dušan Nečak, *Die "Deutschen" in Slowenien* (1918–1955), Znanstveni Institut Filosofske fakultate Ljubljana 1998. Mit einer deutschen Kurzfassung.

Sources to 1.3

VDJ, 29 f.; 63 f.; 68 f.; Erker, Ernest in LW I, 869–873; Scherer, 134–154; Dok. V., 31–37; Karner, Stefan, *Die deutschsprachige Volksgruppe in Slowenien. Aspekte ihrer Entwicklung 1939–1997*, Hermagoras, Klagenfurt/Ljubljana/Wien 1998, 93–105.

Yugoslavia 1918-1941
Residence Areas of Ethnic Germans (hatching)

Formed after World War I as a successor nation of the Austro-Hungarian Empire, Yugoslavia also incorporated many territories, where the ethnic Germans represented a high portion of the established population.

Central Europe Before World War I

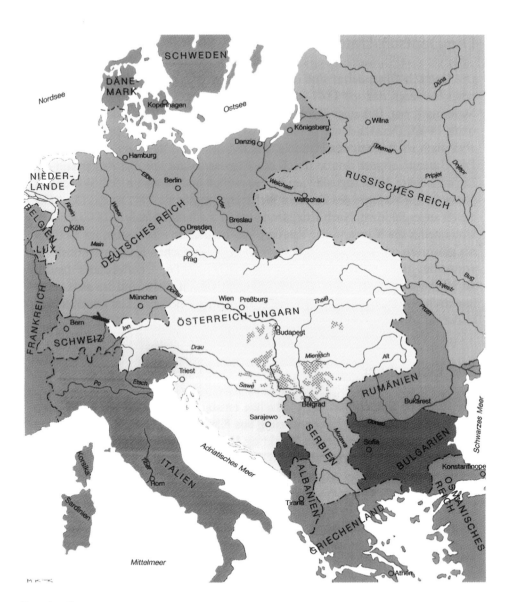

Danube Swabian settlements on both banks of the central Danube River - from the Raab River in the Northwest to the Iron Gate in the Southeast within the Dual Monarchy Austria-Hungary (shaded-in).

Central Europe After World War I

Danube Swabian settlements within the successor nations of Austria-Hungary:
Hungary, Yugoslavia, Romania (shaded-in).

The Partitioning of Yugoslavia After the April War 1941

Independent country **Croatia**

Territory under the jurisdiction of the German military command in **Serbia**

Planned country **Montenegro** (occupied by Italy)

Kosovo attached to **Albania** (occupied by Italy)

Territory annexed by **Hungary**

Territory annexed by **Germany**

Territory annexed by **Italy**

Territory annexed by **Bulgaria**

International boundries
before the partitioning of Yugoslavia

International boundries
after the partitioning of Yugoslavia

Chapter 2: The Tito-Regime – Executor of the Genocide

The above mentioned 200,000 Danube Swabian civilians, the German-Unter-steirer, the Gottscheer and the ethnic German prisoners, who fell into the hands of the partisans, were victims of a cruel genocide committed from 1944 to 1948. Before entering into details of these atrocities which give evidence of genocide, a historical analysis of the reasons is made, that led Tito's partisan movement and subsequent Communist government to the genocide of the ethnic Germans of Yugoslavian citizenship of the former Yugoslav Kingdom.

A careful examination of the events and review of the Tito-partisans own statements lead to varying reasons which induced the annihilation of the ethnic Germans in Yugoslavia. The causes are of ethnic, national, ideological, economical, power-oriented and personal nature.

Hate of everything German

A primary reason is the hate of everything German which has its main origin in the course of World War II. Beginning April 1941 and following orders of the Komintern, under the command of party leader Josip Broz, also called Tito, the Yugoslav Communists began their fight against the German and Italian occupation and shortly thereafter also against the Serbian Tschetniks who were loyal to the monarchy as well as against the Croatian Ustaschas – all in support of the Soviet Union, the "Socialist Motherland".

In 1942 the Tito-partisans infiltrated the autonomous West Banat, administered by the ethnic German group. The "Volksgruppe's" leadership wanted to organize a battalion, called "Prinz Eugen", consisting of Banat ethnic Germans for protection, a form of home guard, considered legal by international conventions, and turned to the German occupation forces for weapons.

Himmler, head of the SS, however, had other plans. In order to circumvent the *Hague Convention on Conduct of Warfare* he declared the recruitment as "volunteer actions". The originally intended Banat home guard battalion "Prinz Eugen" became the "SS Volunteer Mountain Division Prinz Eugen". Against the wishes of the ethnic German leadership the division was used in the war against the partisans outside of the Banat. For the Tito-partisans, this was reason enough to identify the Danube Swabians with their main enemy: Hitler's Germany (Janko, 217 ff.).

The Power of the Communists

During its battle, the Communist Tito-movement changed direction. It saw its chance to grasp the power in Yugoslavia, provided Germany would lose the war. For tactical reasons the Tito-movement no longer preached the "Communist Revolution" as its objective, but the "Liberation of the People" and developed a popular-front movement to entice as many non-Communists as possible to join its fight.

This patriotic approach was used in the interest of the Communist's power grab and to mobilize many patriots who loved their own country – while Tito had greater Yugoslavian aspirations. He succeeded to maintain this national patriotism, if not by conviction, then by force.

After Tito's death the individual Serbian, Croation, Slovenian, Macedonian, Bosnian, Kosovo-Albanian Nationalisms suddenly resurfaced. We all have witnessed the horrible consequences during and after the unraveling of Yugoslavia since 1990.

The Aftermath of Jajce

During its second meeting, November 21–29th, 1943 at Jajce in Bosnia, the "Anti-Fascist Council for the Liberation of Yugoslavia" (AVNOJ), an interim ruling commission of the Partisan Movement, declared the national equal rights of the South Slav peoples of the Serbs, Croatians, Slovenes, Macedonians and Montenegroans, as well as their right to form states within the Yugoslav Federation. Tito was elevated to the rank of Marshal of Yugoslavia. Recognition of the government in exile, operating out of London, was withdrawn and King Peter II was prohibited to return to Yugoslavia. The outline of the partisans' policy regarding the Germans was also drafted. The ethnic Germans were not recognized as a national minority. Instead, the *Proclamation of Jajce,* that dealt with the ethnic Germans, was forged and served as guideline for the subsequent measures to be taken against the ethnic Germans of Yugoslavia.

This decree was dated November 21st, 1943 and signed by Moša Pijade who, together with Eduard Kardelj, drafted all proclamations of Jajce. The disposal was probably a kind of leaflet and, apparently, not included in the currently available published collection of the AVNOJ proclamations (Karner, 125 f.).

It reads as follows: 1. All ethnic German persons living in Yugoslavia will automatically lose the Yugoslav citizenship as well as all civic and nationality rights. 2. The entire movable and non-movable property of all ethnic German persons is considered confiscated and becomes state property. 3. Ethnic German persons are prohibited from claiming any rights, nor exercise the same or seek legal or personal protection from courts or institutions (Werther, 46).

The proclamation of Jajce is obviously the basis of the decisions which the AVNOJ adopted during its fourth meeting on November 21st, 1944 at Belgrade which dealt with the "transfer of enemy property to State property" and – as the interpretation of June 8th, 1945 shows – preordained the ethnic Germans' loss of citizenship rights. Article I reads: "On the day this proclamation comes into force, the following become property of the State: 1. all property of the German *Reich* and her nationals located on Yugoslav territory. 2. all property of ethnic Germans, except those who fought with the National Liberation Army and the partisan units or those who are nationals of neutral countries and did not engage in hostile acts during the occupation. 3. all property of war criminals and their helpers, regardless of their nationality, and all property of any person who, by the judgement of a civil or military court, was sentenced to loss of property and confiscation by the State." Article 12 declares the effectivness of the proclamation to be the date of its publication, which was February 6th, 1945 (Dok. V, 180 E–183 E).

A June 8th, 1945 interpretation of the proclamation stipulates that those ethnic Germans living in mixed marriage with one of the Yugoslav nationalities or recognized minority shall not lose their citizenship rights and their property shall not be confiscated (Dok. V, 183 E f.).

The intent to eliminate the ethnic German population from the People's Republic of Yugoslavia and to adopt the position of "collective punishment" is confirmed in a declaration of the "Supreme People's Liberation Committee of Vojvodina", which reads: "The Hungarian population, as an indigenous population, shall enjoy all civic rights; only the criminals and servants of the Horthy occupation regime shall be punished. The ethnic German population which, collectively, stood in the service of German fascism … deserves no place in our country. However, those ethnic Germans who fought in the ranks of the partisans and the Yugoslav liberation army or supported in other ways the people's liberation battle, shall enjoy all civic rights" (Schweissguth, 88).

Indicative for the "Spirit of Jajce" is the *Draft of the Declaration of the Basic Rights of the Peoples and Citizens of the Federative Democratic Yugoslavia* which was elaborated by Mose Pijade on April 17th, 1944 with reference to the *Declarations of Jajce*. Paragraph 11 reads: "Every citizen of Yugoslavia who during the war acted as a traitor of the people and fatherland or served in the armed forces of the enemy, fought with him against the liberty of his people, shall be excluded from all civic rights, also from acceptance in public service, grant of pension or of any support. In addition, he will be prosecuted in court for treason, service for the support of the occupiers or espionage for the benefit of the enemy and is subject to the death penalty" (LW III, 62–68; VDJ, 83 f.).

The "spirit of Jajce" removed all killing restraints for the partisan leaders and gave the murders a semblance of legality. The results were tens of thousands of victims: Croatian Ustachas, Domobrans, German soldiers, whole sections of the division Prinz Eugen and about 8,000 Danube Swabian mainly male non-military victims during the fall 1944 massacres in the Banat, Batschka and Syrmia.

The genocide of the ethnic German population, branded as fascists, proved to be an important factor in stabilizing the Communists' power since it was an effective intimidating factor against the national-conservative forces and loyal monarchists. At the same time the annihilation of the Germans suited the Communist concept in removing a segment of the population which, in a Communist society, would have been the greatest source of resistance.

Danube Swabian Property – Reward for the Tito-Partisans

There was, as admitted by the partisans, another motive for the annihilation of the ethnic Germans: the confiscated property was to serve as a reward for the fighters of the "liberation battle". In the relatively barren revolutionary regions of the country, there was a dearth of fertile agricultural soil. A large percentage of the land, if not most of it, which was redistributed by the Agrarian Reform, belonged to the Germans. Thousands of active partisan fighters and their families from these barren areas, particularly from Krjina and Lika, were rewarded with the homes of the escaped or interned Germans in the Vojvodina. They had to learn how to cultivate the fertile land of the evacuated villages within the Communist's communal property doctrine (Djilas, 540).

Confiscation of German Property – A Step towards a Government-planned Economy

The extensive Agrarian Reform of August 23rd, 1945 confirmed again the collective confiscation, regardless of individual culpability and the transfer of the entire tillable land belonging to "persons of German ethnicity" to the land trust of the Agrarian Reform. These former German properties were to be granted preferably to Yugoslav partisans and soldiers. This clearly illustrates that the annihilation of the Germans was contemplated simultaneously as a step towards a government-managed economy. The confiscated real property of the Danube Swabians, double the size of Luxembourg, appeared to be particularly suitable to carry out the ideology of the government.

Effects of the planned German expulsion from East/Central Europe

Causes only become reality if certain circumstances prevail. The Serb Djilas, in his book *Revolutionary War* writes: "Our warriors, as well as the people, became so weary of 'our Germans', that in our Central Committee we repeatedly touched on the subject of expelling the ethnic German population. However, we might have thought differently, had not the Russians, Poles and Czech already decided the expulsion of the Germans from their territories and started doing so. We arrived at our position, without discussion or negotiations, a matter that was understandable and justified because of the 'German crime' (Djilas, 540).

The intent of the Yugoslav government to effectively "cleanse" the country of her ethnic Germans is also evident in Yugoslavia's approach to the Western Allies in a Aide-memoire on January 19th, 1946 asking to agree to a collective transfer to Germany of the 110,000 ethnic Germans that survived the first persecution year. It repeated this request on May 16th, 1946; however, it did not receive any reply (Dok. V, 113 E).

At a January 1947 London meeting of the Deputy Foreign Ministers in preparation of a peace treaty with Germany the Yugoslav delegate Dr. Mladen Ivecović again raised this request, however, it was not considered (Dok. V, 468).

In spring 1946 the US government intervened at the Yugoslav government on behalf of American citizens of Yugoslav heritage and protested repeatedly against their internment in forced labor camps.

On October 18th, 1946 the US ambassador at Belgrade delivered a note of protest to the Yugoslav government in which the actions of the Yugoslav government were declared a violation of the human rights of American citizens of ethnic German heritage, who were interned without any judicial process (Dok. V, 435; LW III, 116 f.).

Ethnic Germans declared "Enemies of the People", expropriated and disfranchised of all Civic Rights

Under different political conditions, the partisans could have possibly refrained from the annihilation of the Germans. However, on November 21st, 1944 the AVNOJ issued an ex-judicial decree declaring the Germans "Enemies of the People" and stripped them of all civic rights. All their personal properties were confiscated by the government without any compensation (Geršković, 133 ff.; Dok. V, 104 E).

Exempt were only those married to other nationals or active fighters belonging to or supporters of Tito's communist "Peoples' Liberation Movement". To give this action a semblance of legal justification the decree had to be made by an ex-judicial process. This meant that they did not lose their citizenship, but were deprived of civic rights.

Thus, the ethnic Germans could, without providing any reason, be expelled from their homes, coerced into forced labor, put into labor camps or camps for children or extermination camps for sick persons.

Among the criteria for genocide the UNO Convention of December 9th, 1948 specifies: "Genocide means – c) Deliberately inflicting on the group conditions of life calculated to bring about its physical destruction in whole or in part".

The AVNOJ decrees provided exactly these conditions and are the basis and justification for the planned and government-sanctioned genocide of the Danube Swabians.

Great-Serbian Nationalism, a Partial Reason for Elimination

The question, as to what extent the elimination of the Germans in Yugoslavia was also due to the desire of the Serbs for territorial expansion, is actually the most controversial debate among Danube Swabian and Serb authors.

Historically the Serbs were only a minority in the Banat, Batschka and Syrmia (now called Vojvodina). These areas, which for about 1,000 years belonged to Hungary, were given to Serbia after World War I at the 1920 peace treaty of Trianon desragarding the long-established population's desire. The strongest ethnic groups which suddenly came under Serbian domination were the Germans and Magyars (Hungarians). In spite of immediate Serb colonization efforts, in 1941 the Serbs still did not represent more then 37 percent of Vojvodina's total population, in the Batschka only 23 percent!

Objective of the Chauvinists: Nationalization of the "Serbian People's Soil"
(Jojkić, 7)

The objectives of the Great Serbian nationalism to squeeze the ethnic Germans and – to a lesser extent – the Hungarians out of the Vojvodina were demonstrated in three *ways*: by Statements of Serbian politicians, in specific nationality politics and political writings of representatives of the Great Serbian policies.

The Serbian politician Nikola Pašić (1847–1926) who was primarily responsible for the realization of the *Kingdom of Serbs, Croats and Slowens* in 1918 (in 1929 renamed Yugoslavia), wanted to expell the ethnic Germans immediately. Vladimir Matijević who, in 1916, was commissioned by the Serbian government to develop a plan for the expropriation of large landowners, also states his opinion that the German farmers should be completely expropriated and expelled. According to Matijević, the army should, immediately after occupying the Vojvodina, set on fire some of the villages to cause the inhabitants to flee and to bombard those that refused to leave. "The military will execute a part of the inhabitants, the other part will then flee until everything has been cleansed." These statements are contained in the memoirs of the well-known sculptor Ivan Meštrović who died in the USA in 1962.

During the 1920s Serbian members of parliament considered to resettle the Danube Swabians to Macedonia. Thus the Wojvodina, annexed after World War I, would be "cleansed" of them. Furthermore the Danube Swabians co-mingled with the Macedonian population would simultaneously teach the latter to operate more efficiently.

With the beginning of 1918 the Yugoslav governments pushed through a series of anti-German measures. *In matters of "National Policy"*: they prevented to give constitutional rank to the obligations contained in the minority protection agreements. Thus these could be easily ignored and not legally claimed by those affected.

National Agricultural Policy: Within the framework of the Agrarian Reform of 1919, 40,000 hectare (400 square kilometre) of real estate was taken away from the Danube Swabians. However, not a single member of this ethnic group, of which 40 percent owned no real estate, received any part of the confiscated land. Everything was given to Serbs (volunteer war veterans, wounded and landless).

School Policy: Abolition of German-language classes at high schools and secondary schools. German-language classes at elementary schools only if at least 30 German children were registered. (Other ethnics were not allowed to attend these.)

Property Policy: Controls and restrictions in the real estate business. According to the finance decree 1937/38 the transfer of real estate to non-Slavs within a 50 kilometre wide belt of the national borders was prohibited. Even purchase and inheritance contracts between ethnic Germans were often disallowed. The purpose was to effect a gradual transfer of real property to Slav nationals.

Taxation Policy: An "exploitation strategy" was enacted which had the result that the northern regions (where mostly Germans, Hungarians, but also Croats lived) had to pay double or even triple the tax rate of the southern areas.

Administration: Non-hiring of ethnic Germans as administrative officials and non-admission of German as an official language (contrary to the minority protection agreements).

Cultural Policy: Repeated prohibition of the "Schwäbisch-Deutscher Kultur-bund" and the "Deutsche Partei".

The Great Serbian Nationalization objectives also were evident in the literary-ideological area. In 1931 a book was published at Neusatz/Novi Sad by the Serbian Nationalist Vladan Jojkić, titled *Nationalization of the Bačka and Banat,* which caused a stir. It described the "ethnic nationalization" of the Batschka and Banat, a vital problem of national politics. Jojkić recommends as the most successful method for the "de-population of non-Slavs" their "outsettlement beyond the national borders". The topic of reduction of the ethnic German percentage in the Vojvodina was also taken up by Toše Iskruljev in his book published in 1936. He called for a forced resettlement of the poor part of the minorities to South-Serbia.

All these measures collectively established a system of planned "Nationalization" of what was called "Serbian people's soil" in the Vojvodina. These facts prove an anti-German ground swell since the founding of the multiethnic nation Yugoslavia, fostered by Serbian nationalism (particularly against the largest non-Slav minority, the ethnic Germans), as well as envy (the Germans were also the wealthiest). Of course, this intolerance does not pertain to the entire Serbian people and it is not the purpose to create the impression of a collective guilt. However, one has to point out that hatred of the ethnic Germans did not emerge all of a sudden with World War II, but has always been stoked by this fanatic Great-Serbian group.

After the April War of 1941 which led to the demise of the Yugoslav kingdom, the anti-German ground swell in the Serbian political thinking began to increase and accelerated within the Chauvinist circles the pre-existing wish to eliminate the ethnic Germans. The main cause may be attributed to the mental-emotional mechanisms, referred to as "projections". Even though it was their own doing, the Serbs blamed Germany for the demise of the Serbian kingdom and transferred this enemy image to the ethnic German fellow citizens in their own country.

The Intent to eliminate all non-Slavs after the War

During World War II, nationalistic Serbian circles also expressed their intent to expel minorities. In 1942, the monarchy-loyalist, but nationalistic Tschetniks, at their Congress at Sahoviči (Montenegro) adopted a resolution that stipulated: "Within the territory of the future nation there can only be Serbs, Croats and Slovenians. No minorities are tolerated" (Wüscht, 11).

The Secretary of War of the Government-in-exile and leader of the Tschetniks, General Draža Mihajlović, intended to expel all Germans, Magyars and Romanians after the hoped for victory of his Tschetniks. By the way, after the renewed recent break-up of Yugoslavia the resurrected Tschetniks retained their radical nationalistic Great-Serbian course. 50 years later, during the wars in Bosnia and Kosovo, their paramilitary units committed bloody massacres.

Even General Milan Nedić, the Prime Minister of German-occupied Serbia and installed by the Germans in 1941, did not want to have any national minorities in a future postwar Serbia (Wüscht, 12). In 1944, the Communist party of Yugoslavia, however, became the executor of the elimination plans.

The conclusion of those who cite Great-Serbian Nationalism as a major reason for the expulsion and annihilation of Yugoslavia's ethnic Germans is the following: The three leading Serbian, respectively Serb-dominated groups, the Tschetniks, partisans and Nedić-followers, who were fighting each other during World War II, towards the end of 1942 all agreed on the elimination of the Germans from a future Yugoslavia. At the very least, the intent was to make them disappear as an ethnic group by integrating them forcibly into the Slavic ethnic sections.

Disputes of today's national-conservative Serbs

Lately, national-conservative Serbian authors have strongly objected against the theory that Great-Serbian Nationalism was the virus which infected the movement of the Tito-partisans and thus injected them with the idea of the expulsion of the Germans. They claim that the Great-Serbian Nationalism had no decisive influence on the *Politbureau* (the political leadership) of the partisan movement which at that time consisted of Tito, Kardelj, Ranković and Djilas. They offer the following reasons:

1. The AVNOJ (Serbian acronym for Anti-Fascist Council of Yugoslav People's Liberation) of the partisans was dominated by Communists. The decisive motivation for the decision of the AVNOJ to expel and annihilate the Germans was that the Germans did not join the "People's Liberation struggle" of the partisans and that they defended themselves against the guerilla attacks on their villages.

2. Alexander Ranković, although being a Serb, but a radical Communist, and since 1944 chief of the OZNA (Yugoslav secret police), controlled the leadership policies and issued the instructions to the OZNA chiefs of the country's regions, as well as to the other members of the political leadership. He was considered the "executor of the political suppression and annihilation of all real or suspected enemies of the regime" (Libal, 136). Therefore, the policy of political terror was communist motivated.

3. Edward Kardelj was a Slovene, leading party ideologist and second in command after Tito. He pursued the transformation of the society according to the communist doctrine. He considered the Germans potential opponents and enemies and he needed their property values to carry out the agrarian reform according to the communist pattern.

4. Josip Broz Tito was a Croat, had a Croatian father and Slovenian mother. The actions of the genocide were subject to his approval and tolerance. He was hardly influenced by nationalistic-Serbian considerations since he had a schismatic re-

lationship with the Serbs. He toned down the Great-Serbian ambitions and limited the sovereignty of the Serbian part of the nation by establishing the two autonomous provinces Wojiwodina and Kosovo.

5. According to the national-conservative Serb Zoran Žiletić, not enough consideration is given to the sufferings of the anti-Communist, Serbian intelligentsia, middle class, commercial and industrial citizenry and all other "South-Slavs" in the AVNOJ of Yugoslavia (Grimm et al., 232).

6. Zoran Žiletić and the Danube Swabian Hans Sonnleitner believe that the Atheism of Communism is the predominant cause of the inhuman, gruesome and bestial actions of the Tito-partisans against the defenseless ethnic German population. The ungodliness of the Communist zealots diminished, even eliminated all moral restraints Žiletić in the prologue to Nenad Stefanović's book *Ein Volk an der Donau – Gespräche und Kommentare* (A people at the Danube – Discussions and Commentaries), published 1996 in Belgrad, writes: "The dictators in 1944–1948 also expelled our God" (Stefanović, 18).

Final Comment by Herbert Prokle, another Danube Swabian eye witness: Even if Great-Serbian Nationalism did not provide the impulse for the crime, it certainly facilitated it. The execution of the indescribably fiendish genocide between 1944 and 1948 on such a national scale required a large number of participants, not all of whom were Communists. Furthermore, there was a large segment of the Serbian population that, while not wanting to "dirty their hands", were quite in agreement with the annihilation of the Germans. The pathologically extreme Nationalism of a part of the Serbs may very well be responsible for it.

Sources

Arbeitskreis Dokumentation, *Leidensweg der Deutschen im kommunistischen Jugoslawien,* Vol. II and III. Abbr.: LW II, LW III.

Arbeitskreis Dokumentation, *Verbrechen an den Deutschen in Jugoslawien 1944–1948,* 3rd edition, München 2000. Abbr.: VDJ.

Djilas, Milovan, *Krieg der Partisanen.* Memoiren 1941–1945, Molden/Wien 1978 (Serb Title: Revolucionarni Rat, 1977 = Revolutional War).

Geršković, Leon, *Historija narodne vlasti* (History of People's Power), Belgrad 1957.

Grimm, Gerhard/Zach, Krista (Hrsg.), *Die Deutschen in Ost-, Mittel- und Südosteuropa: Geschichte, Wirtschaft, Recht, Sprache,* Vol. 2, München 1996, 232.

Janko, Sepp, *Weg und Ende der deutschen Volksgruppe in Jugoslawien,* Graz/Stuttgart 1982.

Jojkić, Vladan, *Nacionalizacija Bačke i Banata. Etnopolitička studija,* Novisad 1931 (The Nationalisation of Batschka and Banat. Ethnopolitical Studies).

Karner, Stefan, *Die deutschsprachige Volksgruppe in Slowenien. Aspekte ihrer Entwicklung 1939–1997,* Klagenfurt/Ljubljana/Wien 1998.

Libal, Wolfgang, *Die Serben – Blüte, Wahn und Katastrophe*, München/Wien 1996.

Schieder, Theodor u. a., *Dokumentation der Vertreibung der Deutschen aus Ost-Mitteleuropa*, Vol. V: *Das Schicksal der Deutschen in Jugoslawien.* Herausgegeben vom Bundesministerium für Flüchtlinge und Kriegsbeschädigte, Bonn 1961. Abbr.: Dok V.

Schweißguth, Edmund, *Die Entwicklung des Bundesverfassungsrechts der Föderativen Volksrepublik Jugoslawien.* Studien des Instituts für Ostrecht, Vol. 9, München 1961.

Stefanović, Nenad, *Jedan svet na Dunavu – razgovori i komentari*, Beograd 1996 (German Edition: *Ein Volk an der Donau.* Das Schicksal der Deutschen in Jugoslawien unter dem kommunistischen Tito-Regime, München 1999).

Werther, Oswald, *Die Untersteiermark von 1918–1945*, in: Ernest Erker u. a., *Der Weg in die neue Heimat. Die Volksdeutschen in der Steiermark*, Graz/Stuttgart 1988, 46.

Wüscht, Johann, *Ursachen und Hintergründe des Schicksals der Deutschen in Jugoslawien*, Selbstverlag, Kehl am Rhein 1966.

Žiletić, Zoran, in: Grimm, Gerhard/Zach, Krista (Hrsg.), *Die Deutschen in Ost-, Mittel- und Südosteuropa: Geschichte, Wirtschaft, Recht, Sprache*, Vol. 2, München 1996, 232.

Chapter 3: The Carnage

The Tito-partisans appeared behind the advancing Red Army. By October 6th, 1944 the Soviets occupied the Western Banat (Yugoslavian Part) and by October 23rd, 1944 the whole Batschka.

During their occupation of the Banat and Batschka the Russian soldiers rarely wantonly killed Germans, however, they did commit numerous rapes of German girls and women and destruction of property. The first action of the partisans was usually to establish local "People's Liberation Committees". Then began the arbitrary detention, brutal mistreatment, rapes, executions and murders, particularly of Germans, but also of Magyars (ethnic Hungarians), loyalist Serbs and other Slavs. Especially during the first two months of the partisans military administration there was a period of widespread arbitrariness and despotism. During this period a great number of murders of Germans were committed, therefore it was called "the bloody autumn 1944" of the Vojvodina.

In the Banat and Syrmia during the *bloody autumn 1944* at least 5,000 and in the Batschka 2,000 Danube Swabians were murdered. The analogous losses in Slovenia (Untersteiermark, Oberkrain, Gottschee) are not included in these figures. Between 1941 and October 1944, about 1,100 lost their lives during partisan raids on German communities. These are very conservative figures. Names and localities are documented on page 1019, volume IV of the German-language book *Leidensweg der Deutschen im kommunistischen Jugoslawien,* published 1994 (The ethnic Germans tragedy and sufferings in the Communist Yugoslavia).

Source References: The identification of the most important localities where the murders and massacres committed on the ethnic Germans of Yugoslavia as well as various murderous acts occurred, are based on statements of the surviving victims themselves. They were recorded and published 1990–1995 in four volumes *Leidensweg der Deutschen im kommunistischen Jugoslawien.* The major part of these first-person reports are located at the *Deutsches Zentralarchiv Bayreuth* (German Central Archives at Bayreuth, formerly Koblenz). So far, access for the Danube Swabians and most foreign researchers to the Yugoslav military archives at Belgrade has been denied. Also, according to a statement by the director of the Yugoslav archives, Miodrag Zečević in the Belgrade paper *Borba* of July 24th, 1987, large scale destruction of archive material took place in the immediate postwar period.

A major difficulty has been the determination of individual responsibility. The reports do not always specify which of the various groups or authorities encouraged, authorized or carried out the tortures and murders and whether they were based on individual/decentralized decisions or on orders from higher up.

3.1 The Seven Executors

The first-person reports from Banat, Batschka and Syrmia indicated that there were seven authorities or groups acting as the direct executors of the killings. Events in Slovenia were more complicated, since additional factors were involved.

3.1.1 Spontaneous Groups

Occupying partisans and citizens in some ethnically mixed communities spontaneously formed groups that engaged in murderous activities. One of the worst incidents took place in the Banat village Deutsch-Zerne. After it was seized, a spontaneously formed group of Serbs, Russian soldiers and gypsies engaged in pillage and mass rapes of German girls and women which caused at least 55 (documented) victims to commit suicide.

Another example is the tragedy at Palanka in the Batschka where local gypsies joined an invading group of partisans. This group executed a number of prominent Germans, Magyars and Serbs. Some of the latter were killed just because they pleaded on behalf of the Germans. In Obrowatz, the partisans and local Serbs tortured and murdered 33 Germans, six Magyars and two Serbs after Russian troops moved on. At Towarisch, 36 of the 48 Germans, that had stayed behind, were also killed.

3.1.2 Private Persons

Personal revenge was also a motive for the murder of individual Germans. A tragic example is what happened at Homolitz. When males between 14 and 70 years were led away for execution, the Serbs decided to spare the locksmith Kudjer since he was deemed to be useful. His young son, also in the group, pleaded: "Father, don't leave me." The partisans were ready to release the son too because of his young age, but as eyewitnesses testified, a young Serb of the same age objected since the two boys had a previous quarrel. So the boy had to die as a revenge for a quarrel among children.

3.1.3 The Local People's Liberation Committees

Some local People's Liberation Committees (NOO = Narodno Oslobodilacki Odbor) took a liberal interpretation of the Declaration of Jajce as an opportunity to liquidate influential Germans without formal court action by branding them "enemies of the people", "fascists" or "supporters of the occupation".

At India, Syrmia, on November 11th, 1944 nine men were shot. The following day an additional 64 persons, among them children, were killed with a hand grenade or beaten to death with hatchets. The names of the torturers and murderers are registered in the India chronicle.

At Sombor, Batschka, November 5th, 1944, 52 men from Kolut were taken to the OZNA jail. None of them came out alive.

3.1.4 Revenge Groups and "People's Courts"

Serbian revenge groups in the part of the Batschka, which was occupied by Hungary during the war, took revenge on the Magyars for executions committed by the Hungarian military during a 1942 raid. The Serbs from Schajkasch and Tschurug are reported to have personally asked Tito for permission to take revenge on the Hungarians, which was granted (reported by the Hungarian historian Enikö A. Sajti). The ethnic Germans, who had nothing to do with the Hungarian military actions, were nevertheless included in the orgiastic murders.

The "People's Court" for the areas of Batschka, Banat and Baranja instructed the partisans to collect several thousand men, mainly Hungarians and Germans, but also Serbian intellectuals and trucked 2,500 of them at night to the forest near the Danube where they were shot and dumped into mass graves. This massacre is also documented by Hungarian sources. Beginning 1945 the Communist leaders stopped the actions against ethnic Hungarians due to political reasons: Hungary had to be considered a "socialistic brother country", the barbarous extermination of the ethnic Germans, however, continued until 1948.

3.1.5 The Military Courts of the Partisans

Immediately after conquering an area, the partisans declared martial law and court-martialed important German personalities. A most striking example was the case of Dr. Philipp Popp, Bishop of the German Protestant Church of Yugoslavia. On the pretext that he was a collaborator, he was sentenced to death and shot on June 29th, 1945.

It was likely that the military courts and prisons of the partisan's army served the power-grab strategy of the partisan regime. They were used according to their policy to achieve their "political cleansing". In the Batschka, former German soldiers and members of the Schwäbisch-Deutscher Kulturbund (Swabian German Cultural Society) were picked up and shipped to the military prison at Sombor.

3.1.6 The OZNA

The Germans in cities and county seats were particularly targeted for murder by the OZNA (acronym for Office for the Protection of the People), the secret police of the partisan movement. It was established in 1944 by the Communist Party of Yugoslavia (KPJ). The head of the national OZNA was Alexander Ranković. He was simultaneously Secretary of the KPJ. All heads of the Federal States ("Republics") were important functionaries and simultaneously members of the regional KP (political arm of the communist party). The regional OZNA organisations selected their victims rather arbitrarily and according to their own criteria. They arrested well-known ethnic German citizens, members of the "Deutsche Mannschaft" and alleged saboteurs. Particularly notorious was the OZNA central prison at Sombor (Batschka). Generally speaking, the OZNA was the main instrument of the Communists power-grab strategy and served to carry out the "political cleansing" in the conquered territories.

3.1.7 The "Action Intelligentsia"

Beginning about the middle of October 1944, mobile execution commandos in the Banat and Batschka began entering the communities and arresting leading, respected and well-off Germans – sometimes against the objections of local Slavic citizens. The victims were later cruelly tortured and murdered. Targeted were also "leading heads" of the communities, occasionally also Slavic followers of the previous monarchy, former leaders of the bourgeois-Serbian parties, industrialists, well-off trades people, rich farmers, professionals, clergy and intellectuals. All persons that were categorized as "capitalists", "class enemies" and potential " counter-revolutionaries". Most were males. The selection of these persons indicates their liquidation was carried out according to the Stalinistic pattern. Evidently, the purpose of these actions was to eliminate the leadership, intimidate the people and make them obedient.

3.1.8 The Question of Responsibility

From the day of seizure of power in autumn 1944 until April 15th, 1945 the "liberated" territories were under the reign of the partisans' military administration. Commander of the military administration in the Banat was Jovan Beljanski ("Lala"). Commander in the Batschka was major – general Ivan Rukavina. It is known that Rukavina was directly subordinated to Tito. So it may be taken as a fact that Tito was not only very well aware of what was going on, but authorized or even ordered the partisans' military administration to allow the aforementioned groups like local committees, "People's Courts", OZNA, individuals and of course the partisans' own military courts to wantonly persecute alleged "enemies of the people", "Fascists" and "supporters of the occupiers". Since all ethnic Germans collectively had been declared fascists, enemies of the people etc., there was no lack of pretext to persecute them. The Action Intelligentsia was obviously planned, organized and directed by the fanatic Stalinist Communists Moscha Pijade and Alexander Ranković. But also here, Tito is the main responsible authority since nothing could be done without the "Highest Authority's" approval.

54

Other fully responsible top leaders were Edward Kardelj and Ivan Ribar. Toma Granfil was political commissar. Secretary of the Communist party for the province of Vojvodina was Jovan Veselinov Žarko. The OZNA chief Vid Dodik was commander of all concentration camps in Vojvodina.

3.2 Some Selected Reports

The following are *just a few examples* out of many similar gruesome events that took place during the *bloody autumn* of 1944.

3.2.1 Banat

The murders and massacres in the Banat were partly carried out in the respective localities and partly concentrated in regional camps of the district capitals.

The Sovjet army conquered the western Banat (belonging to Serbia) beginning of October 1944 and ceded the power to the Communist Tito-regime. In almost all places immediate sporadic revenge actions occurred. A few days later general persecutions started against the ethnic German population which obviously were predetermined as they all followed the same pattern. About 4,000 victims are registered by name, however, many more ethnic Germans of the Banat were murdered with unimaginable cruelty during this *bloody autumn 1944*. Since many families and kinships were completely exterminated from 1944 to 1948, there was nobody left who knew and could have registered all victims of that family circles.

About 90 percent of the *bloody autumn* victims were men and an obvious aim of the partisans was to liquidate the Danube Swabian males of the Banat. Since all those liable for military service were in combat at the front-lines, the partisans mainly seized very young and relatively old men. Youngsters of 14 years upwords and seniors up to over 70 years were murdered.

The first killing phase generally took place in their respective home places during first half of October 1944. Most of the victims were intellectuals, leading and respected persons as well as well-off farmers and tradesmen ("Action Intelligentsia"). Starting by the middle of October 1944, the second killing phase continued through December 1944 and to a lesser extent until spring of 1945. Now all ethnic German men (and some women) within the specified age limits were arrested and taken to regional liquidation camps, regardless of their economic situation or education. Many of them were tortured for days and then murdered. The most notorious regional liquidation camps were the "Milk Hall" in Kikinda for the northern region of the Banat; the "Old Mill" in Betschkerek for the central area of the Banat; and the "Stojković-Telep" in Werschetz for the southern Banat. To a smaller extent but nevertheless with bestial cruelty the local camps in Deutsch-Zerne, Pantschowa and Kubin also were used to liquidate ethnic Germans from other villages.

In the course of 1945 all ethnic Germans were expropiated and interned in camps (see chapter 5). During this process the regional liquidation camps where gradually integrated in the system of local and central civilian labour camps (see chapter 6). In order to demonstrate the special status of these regional liquidation camps during the *bloody autumn* 1944 the specific reports on them are comprised in a coherent subchapter, separated from some selected reports on the massacres perpetrated in individual villages during the *bloody autumn 1944*.

3.2.1.1 Reports from Individual Localities

Deutsch-Zerne (Nemačka Crnja)

Most inhumane atrocities were committed against Danube Swabians in Deutsch-Zerne. After the retreat of the German armed forces, a spontaneously organized group of Serbs, Russian soldiers and gypsies turned into a psychotic victory and hate orgy, resulting initially in mass rapes of German females and looting. At least 55 persons (documented by names) committed suicide out of despair and sense of shame. This is a local report on some events: "On October 5th, 1944 at 2 pm, the first Russian troops appear. Already at 3 pm the first German men, including Father Franz Brunet, are beaten to death or shot. At the same time, a large number of German men are already locked up in the Serbian town hall. On October 6th, Peter Schweininger with his horse-drawn wagon has to report to the town hall and is beaten to death. A drunken soldier starts shooting wildly in the cellar, killing five and wounding four people." Margarethe Themare further relates, how she is taken to the town hall together with two more women. Eleven women are already there. The first corpse is brought out and thrown onto the wagon. A young Serb and a gypsy order them to sing. They have to sing until all dead are on the wagon, then they have to run behind the wagon, clapping their hands. At the knacker's yard a gang of gypsies with shovels is already waiting. The women take the wagon back.

"On October 24th, 1944 around 4 pm a first group of men and women, all from Deutsch-Zerne, tied in pairs by wire to a rope are led to the knacker's yard. Young Serbs and gypsies with clubs escort the column and commit excesses at will. Those collapsing during the march are clubbed and dragged along. The "column of death" is flanked by Serbian men and boys with cow bells. Church bells are ringing too. On this day three groups are being murdered. Head executioner of all three groups is the female partisan leader Ljubica from the Batschka, who lives in the Catholic rectory. All the victims have to undress; those unable to do so are undressed by the gypsies. In groups of five to six they have to stand before the grave and are killed with machine guns. The next group of victims always has to push down the bodies of the previously shot who did not fall into the hole. The bodies of the first group were not covered with earth to leave space for the next ones.

Meanwhile several hundred Serbs have congregated as spectators. There are some victims in the pit who are not yet dead and their death struggles evoke laughter from the spectators. At dusk the second group is not quite finished yet and the third is disposed of by moonlight. Towards 9 pm having completed the murder orgy, the partisans return singing to the village."

Charleville, Soltur, St. Hubert (three sister communities, now called *Banatsko Veliko Selo*)
These three sister communities with a total of 3,300 inhabitants were founded by French settlers, who assimilated with the Danube Swabians. So 3,050 inhabitants' mother tongue was German.

On October 6th, 1944 the Russian troops entered without resistance. Indescribable scenes of rape by Soviet soldiers and partisans and looting, in which civilian Serbs and gypsies from the surrounding villages participated, took place.

On October 11th, 1944 Adam Weissmann, a well-known farmer, was tortured to death. The next day, five additional men and two 15 year old youths were arrested and locked in the town hall. After a drinking bout, the partisans began a gruesome torture process: The victims were burned behind their ears with red-hot phosphorous rods and their soles beaten with bullwhips. Their screams were heard in all the surroundig houses. On October 17th they were taken to Kikinda and to never appear again.

During the night of October 31st, 1944 the partisans surrounded the three villages, gathered all the men they could capture and took them to the "Milk Hall" at Kikinda. There were about 70 men from Charleville, 93 from St. Hubert and 76 from Soltur. Until the end of November 1944 all of them were killed. The Catholic priest Anton Adam was among them. 194 victims are documented by name.

Kubin (Kovin)
The partisan rule in Kubin, a community of 8,000 inhabitants (2,300 ethnic Germans), was particularly cruel. The partisans moved in on October 2nd, 1944. According to Johann Fischer, the first arrests and tortures of leading personalities, including the mayor Sava Gulubić, started already the next day. During the persecutions from middle of October onwards, one German girl was hung with wire slings in a doorframe and split in half with a butcher hatchet. Fischer also states that he was an eyewitness when Hilde Knecht, leader of a women's society, had her breasts cut open and pieces of flesh cut from her abdomen. Several people were tarred, bound together in a group and set aflame. Such burnings were also carried out on barges which then floated down the Danube as flaming torches. The 54 year old Jakob Fitschek was sawed apart alive. 108 murdered victims of Kubin are documented by name in volume IV of the documentation series *Leidensweg*.

Ernsthausen (Banatsko Despotovac)
During the months of October/November 1944 all men in the village that could be tracked down (old men as well as teenage youths) were herded into the Betschkerek regional liquidation camp. Ladislaus Schag was one of them. In the very first

days, 24 succumbed to the terrible tortures and lack of nourishment. The camp was also kwon as "death mill" and the dead were taken away by the cart load.

Later on in December, some of those about to die were shipped out of the camp into surrounding villages (in the camp they concentrated able-bodied people to be deported to the Soviet Union). One week before Christmas, L. Schag being one of them, together with 38 victims, was taken to his home village Ernsthausen. They were completely exhausted, the skin covered with sores and dirt from all the beatings. They were too weak to step down from the wagon and village dwellers had to assist them. One of these unfortunate fell down and could not get up. A partisan shoved his rifle into his stomach and the man made one more attempt, fell back and died. After the few weeks at the Betschkerek death camp, Ladislaus Schag was so disfigured that his own daughter did not recognize him. She found him among the rags and wrapped in the inner lining of his coat, shriveled to a skeleton, but still alive. The local partisan commander, for whom she worked, allowed her to take him home; all others, including the two Modosch villagers Ernst Wabersinke and Mathias Fuderer, were thrown into the Schlitter inn.

The partisans began getting drunk. During the night they brought the prisoners out to the bowling alley, one at a time. They had to bend over and received axe blows to their back. The mortally struck bodies convulsed while the partisans erupted in sadistic laughter. The apparently lifeless bodies were then hacked into pieces to be buried in the neighbourhood manure piles. This, however, was not possible since everything was frozen. The next morning some old men from the neighbourhood were chased out to load the dismembered pieces onto a horse-drawn wagon and take them to the cementary. It took three wagons, dripping with blood, to complete the transport, watched by the horrified inhabitants.

A young partisan from a Hungarian neighbourhood village was standing guard that night and watched the whole hideous crime. He was still in shock when he re-ported the occurrence to Elisabeth Schag the next day. The inn was still covered with splattered blood, human pieces, hair and bloody axes. Although the partisans had threatened to kill them, if they talked to anybody, some of the old men also informed their wives before they died.

Next day the local commander reported to the Betschkerek Liquidation Camp that all 39 prisoners had died of typhoid. It was a general practice of the partisans to register all victims of their sadistic murder orgies as natural causes.

Homolitz (Omoljica)

Homolitz in the county of Pantschowa had about 5,200 residents, over half of ethnic Germans. On October 3rd, 1944 Serbs and gypsies took over the admi-nistration of the town. Overnight local Serbs became partisans; however, it was the mobs that were the rulers. Russians and partisans raped women and girls. One girl, only 14 years old, was raped at gunpoint in front of her parents by five Russian sol-diers. On October 27th, an execution squad of the Sremska brigade appeared and surrounded the village. The partisans of the brigade, led by locals, went from house to house and arrested all male German youths and men between 14 and 70 they could find. They took them to an inn and wrote down their names and occupations. 15 to 20 craftsmen were sorted out for later use and the rest taken to a tile shed at the Danube reed. There they had to strip and stand in front of a previously dug pit. Machine gun bursts ended the lives of 173 youths and men. Up to the end of the year 1944, 49 additional men and women of Homolitz were murdered.

Pantschowa (Pančevo)
The city of Pantschowa had about 22,000 inhabitants, about 8,000 ethnic Germans. Before the general internment 222, recorded by name, were murdered. Immediately after the occupation by the Russians and partisans and the resulting rapes and pillage, all men were arrested. Some were held in a camp at the "Fischplatz"; men of the intellectual level and women in the Stockhaus jail. A partisan court martial dispensed the sentences. Each morning women and wealthy intellectuals, after night-long torture, were led out and shot. Then, a few days later, all the other prisoners were killed as well.

Zichydorf (Veliko Plandište)
Zichydorf in the Werschetz district had a population of about 3,300, almost 2,000 were ethnic Germans. 149 of them became victims of the Action Intelligentsia. Most of the men jailed in the village hall during October did not survive their tortures.

On November 2nd, 1944 about 200 partisans disembarked from a freight train and arrested all males age 14–70, in total 350 persons. They were taken to the "Stojković-Telep" at Werschetz which had acquired the sad reputation as being the liquidation camp for the Danube Swabians of the South Banat. There about 160 males from Zichydorf were murdered, according to the Zichydorf home town book.

3.2.1.2 Regional Liquidation Camps in the Banat

In these camps ethnic Germans were sadistically tortured and brutally murdered during the *bloody autumn 1944*. The inhuman crimes committed there are beyond the imagination of any normal being.

Since only very few of the inmates survived and these had no possibility at all to take notes, the exact number of victims cannot be determined and it is even difficult to give realistic estimates. Certainly the number of dead is not comparable to those perished 1945 to 1948 in the later liquidation camps for children, old and disabled ethnic Germans (see chapter 7). On the other hand these regional liquidation camps represent the first and most brutal station of the genocide committed against the ethnic Germans in Yugoslavia and therefore require a coherent presentation.

Considering the atrocious sufferings of all victims, no comparisions should be made. Even so, the camp at Betschkerek was named the worst one. It also was the one, where sporadic tortures and murders went on for a considerable time after the orgiastic killings of the bloody autumn and its conversion to a "normal" labour camp took quite some time. Furthermore, being the capital of the Banat, Betschkerek was also the headquarter of the supreme camp command. For all these reasons the regional liquidation camp at Betschkerek is selected as main example and described in more detail. The presentation of the other camps with similar function will be kept short.

Regional Liquidation Camp "Milk Hall" at Groß-Kikinda
On October 7th, 1944, one day after the occupation of the town Groß-Kikinda (30,000 inhabitants, 6,000 ethnic Germans), a prison was set up for German men. Already on this first day 28 men were murdered. The following day more victims from Kikinda were interned in the "milk hall" and the partisans also started to confine there the ethnic Germans from the following villages: Banater Topola, Botschar, Bikatsch, Charleville, Heufeld, Mastort, Mokrin, Nakodorf, Ruskodorf, St. Hubert, Sanad and Soltur.

A documentation issued by Dr. Peter Binzberger contains a register by name of 668 victims (618 men and 50 women) murdered in Kikinda. With the exception of Mokrin all the mentioned villages are included, but there is no doubt, that the real number was considerably higher. Evaluating all eyewitness reports, an estimate of 800 to 1,000 murdered is realistic.

According to unanimous eyewitness reports the imprisoned were subject to continuous inhuman, sadistic tortures. Whenever the partisans felt like, they wantonly pulled out some Germans; the victims were beaten to death or butchered with knives like pigs. Among the first ones were most of the intellectuals, including Father Michael Rotten of Kikinda. November 5th, 1944 became a real bloody Sunday: The partisans murdered around 100 men "just for fun", among them Father Anton Adam from Charleville. Notoriously the weekends from Friday to Sunday were the most horrible days for the defenceless prisoners. The partisans' way of celebrating the weekend was to get drunk and torture and kill Germans. Weekdays the gaps left by the dead were filled up with new "human material".

Rose Mullarczyk from Heufeld writes about a Friday butchering in the "milk hall": "On November 3rd, 1944 I was eyewitness of the slaughter of a larger group of men. Individual people were already previously liquidated. This group of 22 men, among them two I knew from our neighbouring village, were fiendishly murdered. First, the men were disrobed, had to lie down, their hands tied behind their back. Then they were subjected to a terrible lashing with whips. Then, strips of flesh were cut from their bodies. Some had their noses, tongues, ears or genitals cut off. Their eyes were cut out and in between the beatings continued. I could witness all these terrible atrocities since I was, at that time, together with another female prisoner in a room on the ground floor. The victims screamed, convulsing in pain. This went on for about an hour, then the screams became weaker and eventually ceased. Even the next day, when we walked across the yard, one could find tongues, eyes, ears, and other human body parts scattered all over and the entire yard was covered with blood."

Siniša Jakonić, a Serb born 1961 in Kikinda and still living there published a book in December 2002. The main purpose of his book is to settle accounts with the collapsed National-Communist regime. A secondary aspect in this context is the gruesome liquidation of the ethnic Germans to which he dedicates one chapter titled "The Blood of our Germans".

For about two and a half years (1985–87) Jakonić was an officer of the Yugoslavian State Police SDB and had access to pertinent documents. In addition, Serb eyewitnesses (their names indicated in the book) informed him of the occurrences in 1944 to 1948. Among many details about the murders, Jakonić also relates how a group of about 80 German girls between 14 and 19 years were systematically exploited for the partisans' and their guests' sexual "amusement".

According to Jakonić one of the camp commanders was Nikola Popović, a 22 years old partisan officer from Krajina (ethnic Serbian part of Bosnia). He also enumerates the following murderers: Arkadija Trifunac, Neša Demić, Klakavi Sremac, the gypsy " Šantavi Cigan", Brile and Dronja.

The author further confirms, that most of the victims were thrown into mass graves close to the "Railway Cementary" and just slightly covered.

With regard to the graves the following deposition of the ethnic Hungarian Szabó Karoly (born 1933 in the Banat, still living in Kikinda) formally taken down by Dr. Peter Binzberger is very significant: "In summer 1963 the company for which I worked at that time as a dredger operator sent me to the 'milk hall' area. The hall was being demolished and the whole terrain had to be flattened for industrial settlements. During this work I found several human skeletons lying in group graves behind the 'milk hall' just slightly under the surface. We were ordered to cover these group graves with some more ground. I was certain that these mortal remains belonged to the Danube Swabians who were killed in the 'milk hall' in 1944–1947.

In 1979 or 1980 a cold-storage depot ("Hladnjača") was built on that area. As dredger operator I had to dig up the soil for the foundations and found ten to fifteen skeletons. These were cart away, but nobody told us where to. Not far away, beyond the former football court ŽAK (Željeznički Atletski Klub), where the ground was more sloping, the graves were just covered with sand. For me there is no doubt that these horrible findings were the mortal remains of the Danube Swabians murdered in the 'milk hall' in 1944 and the following years. Many people knew about those massacres and the mass graves, but it was strictly forbidden to talk about them."

After the fall of the dictatorship in Yugoslavia there is no longer a personal risk and it is very important that Serbs and other non German ethnics reveal their knowledge of this terrible historic truth.

Regional Liquidation Camp "Stojković-Telep" at Werschetz (Vršac)

After heavy fighting Werschetz (29,000 inhabitants, 12,000 ethnic Germans) was occupied by the Soviet army on October 2nd, 1944. Already on October 3rd, the partisans arrested several hundred ethnic German men, about 200 were immediately murdered. In the course of the month 700 local Germans were killed. On October 17th the mayor Geza Frisch together with five prominent citizens were chased through the town in front of a horse-drawn cart and killed at the knacker's yard. On October 23rd, 35 well-to-do citizens were taken to the jail, continuously tortured for two days, then shipped away by trucks and murdered.

Among the Werschetz camps there was also the "Camp No. 233", the most inhumane torture place for German prisoners of war known in history. Out of several camps for Danube Swabian civilians, the "Stojković-Telep", close to the railway station was the worst one. The guarding partisans had full authority to torture and kill the inmates whenever they felt like. Also sadists from outside the camp were free to enter and harass the Germans. The partisans' wives came and enjoyed torturing sick and wounded people. Many men died of the continuous misstreatment and were put in mass graves directly aside the camp. The ones who endured for some time, were taken off by trucks, generally at night, and murdered outside.

From October to December 1944 several thousand civilians, predominantly German men, but also others, like Serbian monarchists and Croat anti-communists were taken to the regional liquidation camp "Stojković-Telep". By December 1944 the number of surviving inmates was about 300, that means the "work" of the murderers was done. However, the place was still far from being a "normal" labour camp. A Werschetz' woman reports: "… one and a half years after the end of the war executions without any legal verdict still take place … the Zoffmann family was taken out of the camp and shot in the mouth without any cause."

The Danube Swabians murdered in Werschetz during the "bloody autumn 1944" were mainly citizens of the following locations: Alt-Letz, Georgshausen, Groß-Gaj, Groß-Sredischte, Heideschütz, Kudritz, Setschanfeld, Werschetz, Zichydorf. A total of 1,038 victims are known by name, of which 647 are from the city of Werschetz. However, as already stated, complete lists of all murdered people do not exist. Based on many individual reports a figure of 1,500 to 1,800 ethnic German civilians may be considered a realistic estimate.

The report of Dr. Josef Wüst from Georgshausen may be taken as example of what happened in the mentioned villages: "Day by day the partisans became bolder, they took whatever they liked. Soon they started violence. The teacher Karl Petri was beaten to death by a former pupil. Some other men were taken to the village hall and tortured until they perished. Also the women and girls were not spared; the partisans repeatedly brought Russian soldiers to the village to whom they had to submit. But this was only the beginning.

On November 1st, 1944 a first group of 20 men were apprehended, tied together and transported to Werschetz. After unbelievable torturing all were finally murdered. On November 3rd the remaining men of our village, including boys of 16 years and older, were taken to the 'Stojković-Telep' camp. Except for three young boys none of them left the Werschetz camp alive."

Regional Liquidation Camp "Old Mill" at Groß-Betschkerek
(Veliki Bečkerek, Zrenjanin)
On October 2nd, 1944 the Red Army occupied, without meeting any restistance, Groß-Betschkerek, the main city of the Western Banat which, since 1918 belongs to Serbia (Yugoslavia). At that time it had more than 30,000 inhabitants, of these 7,500 were ethnic Germans. The partisans arrived with the Russian troops. They set up two camps for ethnic Germans. According to all eyewitnesses, the camp "Old Mill" served, since the beginning of October, to systematically liquidate the Danube Swabian men of the central region of the Banat.

Already on October 5th, 1944 the first ethnic German citizens of the city were taken to the "Old Mill" camp. On October 10th a large scale massacre of German men took place. The partisans surrounded the German section of the city, moved from house to house and took all male ethnic Germans whom they found, including youths from 14 years upwards, to a side street of the market place. There all had to strip down to the waist and kneel; then they were cut down with machine guns. According to Hans Diwald 250 men were victims of this massacre.

For further systematic executions, the German men from surrounding communities were also brought to Betschkerek. The headquarters of the camps at Betschkerek ordered the local powers to dispatch the required fresh supply as needed for the continuing murders. Thus, starting October 12th, 1944 the first groups of males from the Middle Banat communities Modosch, Perles, Rudolfsgnad, Sartscha and Stefansfeld were requested and sent. Apparently it was up to the local powers whom they selected and whether they complied with the number called for. For example, Lazarfeld was requested to send 60 men. The commander, a local Serb, had the courage to dispatch only half the number and that was accepted. Of these 30 men, 14 were killed within a few days. Modosch sent, in addition to the men, several young women, among them Anna Rischar (married Gajdics), Hedwig Lambrecht (Kaiser), Carolina Pleli (Becker), Magdalena Samson (Seifert), Lydia Junger (Lickfeld) and Irene Vasilitch (only her mother was German). So, among a total of about 30 females in the "old mill", eight to ten were from Modosch. The local OZNA chief Jovo Zec and the physician Dr. Slepčev (the latter seething with hatred) had great influence in Modosch and may, therefore, be considered as mainly responsible for the German victims shipped from this village to the "Old Mill". We have to give credit to the young women for furnishing us with several personal experience reports; most of the men were murdered, thus unable to report.

The camp: along the street a two-story building, downstairs the rooms of the camp commander, the political commissar, the commander of the guards and partisan guard unit. Above, the rooms for the interned women and the "Slobodnjaci" (camp inmates for internal camp duties). At the right angle, a long building with three large halls, completely locked, where the men were cooped up. Under the staircase section were the notorious "bunkers" (torture chambers). These were built-in concrete cells, three to four on each side; in the middle a gutter so the blood of the victims could flow off. Across the halls were a machine shop and the offices and across the camp gate the latrines. The total forming a completely enclosed rectangle. The camp had a steady flow of 2,000-inmate occupancy. The vacancies caused by the liquidation process were continuously refilled with new groups of men from the "supplying" communities.

Anna Rischar describes her arrival at the camp end of October 1944: "It was evening when we arrived at the large gate. In front of the stone walls stood heavily armed partisans who received us. The guards who brought us were not allowed into the camp. As we went inside we were blinded by strong floodlights and the guards shouted and screamed at us like wild animals. It was the entrance to hell. A 'Kommandir' asked all men that went to secondary schools to raise their hand. Some did – a derisive laughter followed. They had to take off their shoes, lie down on their backs and lift up their legs. Then their soles where whipped." Generally all new arrivals were received with beatings. Then they were robbed of all their belongings, left only with minimal clothing. Then everybody was registered by name and hometown and allocated to a room.

The camp commander hailed from Melenci. According to Walter Neuner he was a 19 years old secondary school student by the name of Živko. The chief of the guards was a Serb from the village Višnićevo. The guards were mainly gypsies and young local 17–20 year old Serbs. These so-called "Kommandirs" conducted a cruel reign of terror and were lords over life and death. Milorad was considered the worst sadist, but his comrade Brko was almost as bad. According to Adam Feketitsch they both came from Tschenta in the Banat. The 16 years old Kurutschki was feared for his brutal whippings. The gypsy Milan, also called Zigo, also liked to use the metal-studded whip.

Until they were murdered, the men served the partisans as laborers in the city, for bridge building and the supply bases of the Russians. The day usually started with "morning gymnastics", already at 2 or 2:30 am: The men had to roll around in the wet and muddy autumn soil. The partisans trampled on them with their heavy, nailed shoes. Then they had to get their "breakfast", in small groups. The partisans counted up to three and everyone had to finish his cup of a quarter liter no-fat, watery and almost saltless soup. He who lagged behind received a beating. After "breakfast" work assignments were given out. All left for work at 7 am. At the

64

camp exit everybody received 100 gram of bread which had to last till the evening. They usually returned at about 6 pm and whoever was late, missed his soup.

In the evening, when they returned exhausted from work, they had to worry whether or not they would survive the night. The "interrogations", beatings and torture, often with fatal consequences, took place mostly during the nights. Whoever was selected during the evening reviews or dragged from his bunk in the middle of the night and taken to the "bunker", was considered lost. He was usually cruelly tortured or beaten to death in the "bunker" or courtyard by the mostly drunken guards. The screams of the victims, magnified by the echo of the "bunker" cell walls, heightened the fright and desperation of the men, huddled in the crowded halls.

Hedy Lambrecht had to watch how her father was almost beaten to death: "It was the beginning of November 1944. At 4 am everybody who could stand up, had to stand in formation to be assigned his work duty. Many of our poor men were so weakened by their terrible mistreatments that they could hardly stand up, but gladly went to work to get away from the hell, at least during the day. We girls and some women had to bring the 'breakfast'. While the men were trying to drink the warm water with some hard peas as fast as possible, the partisans indiscriminately lashed them with their whips.

My father, Christof Lambrecht, was in the first row, about four paces from where I stood. Zigo watched us and noted that a Modosch compatriot whispered something to me even though it was strictly prohibited to talk to each other. Zigo knew my father and also knew that I was his daughter. He thought we had also talked to each other and dragged my father out. He also grabbed my arm and led us into the camp hall. I was prepared for the worst. My father was asked what he whispered to me. He truthfully answered that he did not talk to me, but Kurutschki pulled out his gun and ordered my father to open his mouth. He knocked the two lower teeth into his mouth and screamed 'gutaj … gutaj' (swallow). I shall never forget the shouts of this torturer. My father swallowed his two teeth, was then knocked down and whipped. Zigo stood on one side, Kurutschki on the other and they took turns lashing my father till he lost consciousness. I could no longer watch and closed my eyes. Suddenly someone grabbed me from behind and said 'bezi' (run). I ran to our room and was convinced I would never see my father again. After the torture he was left lying there for a while. Later two men were ordered to carry him to their room. It was probably God's will that these two were his best friends from Modosch (Landgraf Philipp and Hackbeil Hans). They and other 40 men were detailed to work at the oil factory and also to live there for a while. Somehow they were able to drag my father along, which was his salvation. However, he suffered severe internal injuries and never recovered again. He died in 1954."

Lydia Junger, who was also an eyewitness to this brutal mistreatment, adds the following events, which Hedy, in her anxiety about her father, did not register: "… Mr. Kesselring from Modosch was beaten to death, my father's kidneys were severely injured, also Hedy Lambrecht's father's kidneys." This means that more camp inmates were beaten at the same time, at least the three named Modosch people, one of them fatally.

Anna Rischar describes how, one night, the guards, after cruel mistreatment of several men in the bunker, gang-raped a young women from Stefansfeld till she lost consciousness. The partisans locked ten to twelve women into the bunker, while they were brutally mistreating some men in the hallway. The women could not see anything, however they did hear everything. Suddenly the cell door was thrown open and the women ordered to run to their rooms. Anna Rischar: "We ran through the blood, some slipped. Panicked we ran across the yard, past the kitchen and up the stairs. Nobody paid attention to anybody else until we laid down on our bunks and noted that our quiet woman was missing. She was the victim of that evening.

She was somewhat different from us. She was young, attractive, but had a frightened look in her eyes. She hardly spoke and one had to ask her questions. She was the wife of a wealthy farmer from Stefansfeld. The commander of the guards worked as a farm hand at their farm and she sensed what fate was awaiting her. He had her brought into the camp and planned her torture. He probably savored her fright all along. This night he carried out his satanic plan.

At first one could still hear the voice of a woman among the wild shouting of the guards coming from the courtyard. The turmoil kept on for a long time. Each of us was thinking of oneself and hoped they did not desire any additional victims. Nobody dared to go to the window. After a while heavy steps came up the stairs. The door was thrust open and something like a bag thrown into the room. There was no wailing nor groaning, the woman was unconscious. Two older Hungarian women (their husbands were executed as collaborators) looked after her and put her down on the bunk. Then, being exhausted, we all fell asleep. The next days the poor woman was lying on the bench. She no more came for the meals. Fright and insanity was in her eyes. One night, upon our return from work, she was gone. Nobody knew what happened to her and nobody dared to ask."

By the middle of November 1944, Anna Rischar and Hedy Lambrecht were assigned to work at the camp office, because they knew how to type. When the Serbian secretary found they could write better letters than he could, their positions were "secured". Anna Rischar: "From now, Georg Schneider from Betschkerek who had a legal education, Karl Leidecker, former operations manager of a factory, Hedy Lambrecht and I did all the office work." They continued in the camp's office until spring 1946, so they were better informed than the "ordinary" camp inmates.

The secret police OZNA attempted to extract "confessions" from some ethnic Germans, probably to justify their brutal procedures. Adam Feketitsch reports about his own case. During the night of October 4th, 1944 he and two other ethnic Germans from Betschkerek were bull-whipped for hours by the partisans. They rubbed salt into his open wounds and when he fainted, they poured cold water over him so they could continue their torture. Anton Hufnagel, one of his companions, was murdered in the process. He and the second victim were handed over to the

OZNA. For three weeks they were interrogated and beaten during the nights. Since the OZNA could not prove that they had committed any punishable acts, they were returned to the "old mill". There they were beaten again for six days. Brko and Milorad knocked out his teeth with the revolver. Then he was returned to the usual camp life. His wounds, which he treated with urine, took many weeks to heal.

The systematic executions of major groups of ethnic German men took place mainly at weekends. It didn't matter whether anybody was guilty of anything or not. Everybody had to line up and a certain number, apparently pre-determined, were taken out. Better-dressed and physically stronger as well as unable-to-work men were chosen. In a separate room the victims had to undress down to shirt and trousers and then in the courtyard four each were tied together with wire, always being savagely beaten. Then they were taken to the former military rifle range and shot to death. According to Hans Diwald, the second mass execution of 200 men took place on October 20th, 1944. 30 were murdered on October 23rd, and 152 more on October 28th. Walter Neuner also states that within five weeks a total of 600 camp inmates were shot to death.

According to Dr. Wilhelm Neuner (also confirmed by other eyewitnesses), one of the most hideous crimes was the butchering of the sick which took place on November 17th, 1944. A new commander, appointed for a limited time, at the evening review asked the sick to report for their transport to the hospital. About 60 persons reported to the so-called sick room. At night the hapless were driven, in groups of ten, into the camp courtyard and beaten to death with shovels by the partisans. One of the victims was Christian Kaufmann, a cousin of Anna Rischar.

The weekly mass executions and daily torture and murders lasted till the end of November 1944. The continuous supply of the desired number of victims from many communities indicates a central organisation of the procedure. Michael Kristof comments: "Talking later to people who were in other, similar camps, I could determine that such liquidations took place there at about the same time and in the same manner which indicates a central direction of the procedure against the ethnic Germans." Even ethnic German refugees from Romania who definitely could not be accused of any crime against the Serbs, were tortured and murdered in Betschkerek. This is one more proof for the country-wide intent to systematically liquidate the ethnic Germans.

Starting December 1944, the torture and mass-murders werde notably reduced. This was evidently due to Russian intervention who presumably already knew that the able-bodied internees were destined to be shipped to the Soviet Union and therefore should not be killed. Nevertheless, the inmates were still subjected to the sadistic guards. Anna Rischar comments: "The tortures were no longer systematic, but more sporadic. Beatings continued almost like before. The 'hearse' continued its morning routes with the victims of the night. However, these were mainly people who died of disease, since they were totally emaciated and still starving; infections could not be cured and their resistance was drained ... Now we received a new camp register into which we had to enter all those that were still alive. The names of the arrivals during October and November, so far as they were still legible, also had to be transferred into the book. The dead, regardless whether they were shot or tortured to death or died of starvation or illness had only the entry 'deceased' and the date." Professor Michael Kristof also refers to this camp register: "I was only one week in the office, during the middle of February 1945. During that time I perused the register. My own number was 3214. Looking through the register I could see that people I knew well and of whom I was aware that they were murdered, were only listed as 'deceased'."

Betschkerek had a second camp "oil factory" which was set up in November 1944. It contained a large part of the local ethnic Germans, including many women. It was more of a work camp, as in many other communities. Initially there was no interchange between the two camps, until Christmas 1944. Anna Rischar: "At Christmas Eve, an order was received from the central camp administration (in the center of Betschkerek) to designate December 25th a day of rest. Even though it was highly unlikely that the Communists considered Christmas a holiday, we were naïve and lauded the partisan administration. After the 5:00 o'clock morning review and the soup we were even allowed to return to our rooms.

Suddenly a buggy came through the large gate. Four Russian officers with stern faces descended and ordered all inmates, without exception, to stand in formation. Hedy and I and each of the two men who worked in the office went with a Russian officer and wrote down the names of the 'selected'. Every able-bodied man and all German girls in the camp, including myself and Hedy, were put on the list. At the end we had to type all the lists. The camp commander was ordered that everyone on the list, without exception, had to be ready to march on December 29th. Now the inmates from the second Betschkerek camp (the existence of which we did not know) were also brought in; also the German women and girls from the surrounding Banat communities. Hedy and I had to continuously write new lists."

On the day of departure to the railroad station (an endless column) one of the Russian officers made sure that the two office girls came along. They did not trust the partisans. At the freight station the two girls succeeded to escape with the help of the guard Zigo. Initially he hid them in a hospital and than he brought them back to the camp. Anna Rischar: "Now the camp inmates were much reduced, but new shipments came from the communities and we had much work in the office."

Dietmar Prokle from Modosch, not yet 16, was taken to Betschkerek with the last few remaining "men" (adolescents and aged ones). He recalls: "In January 1945 I was sent to the camp "old mill". For a long time we had to stand in the courtyard, then were individually taken to the small room next to the entrance where, as a greeting, we received a beating, were registered and assigned to a room. The next day a man approached me and asked about his wife and daughter. I did not recognize him. He was our neighbour Stefan Landgraf. The mistreatment during the time of October 1944 to January 1945 made him unrecognizable. Two weeks later he was dead.

68

During the nights nobody was allowed to go to the latrine. Instead, each room had a large bucket, and when it was full, two men who had night bucket detail carried it downstairs. Since just everybody suffered from diarrhea, somebody occasionally missed; if the partisan saw it, he forced the bucket detail to lick it up.

On weekends the partisans were almost always drunk. When they came in we all had to stand at attention. Then the 'boxer' passed by us and everyone who looked at him got punched in the face and fell onto his bunk. One dropped onto the floor and the 'boxer' jumped onto his stomach until he was dead. We named this partisan 'boxer' because of his punching, but he called himself 'bog batina', god of beatings.

A partisan, I think he was Czech, wanted to treat us youths in a better way. He even took us to a separate room and lectured us on German communists (Rosa Luxemburg and Karl Liebknecht). He told us that soon there would be a communist Germany and we could hope for a better future. Obviously, he departed from the prescribed line whereby all Germans from the baby to the old aged were 'enemies of the people'. At any rate, he was removed after one week.

One day all of us youths had to work at the sugar factory. The administrator of the factory cursed our guards because they brought 'children' and ordered them to take us to the back, at the fence and shoot us there. The guards refused, telling him that they had their orders to bring us in the morning and take us back to the camp in the evening. The administrator insisted that we be shot. A loud quarrel ensued which caught the attention of a Russian officer. That was our salvation. He ordered that we not be shot and even told his soldiers to help us with our work – they were simultaneously our protection.

At the end of February 1945 I was lucky to be assigned to work at an agricultural estate (Luisa Puszta) together with some companions. At the 'old mill' I would not have survived. I'll be gratefull to the Hungarian workers at the Puszta for the rest of my life. Even though they themselves did not have much, each Hungarian family gave us something to eat. However, we still were under the jurisdiction of the Betschkerek camp. Spring 1946 a supervising unit arrived and we were individually inspected. The Beschkerek partisans beat each and every one of us. This showed that their attitude had not changed. Nevertheless, we were allowed to stay at the Puszta from where we were soon able to escape to Romania."

By the middle of 1945 the camp was transferred within Betschkerek. Anna Rischar reports: "Initially we were moved to the old sugar factory. For some reason the administration was not satisfied with the location and in late summer 1945 we were moved again to the other side of the city, to the silos. The soup now had more of a nutritional value although we still were subjected to mistreatments and whims of the commander and the guards. But one can say that Betschkerek now was no longer a liquidation camp, but more of a work camp."

By November 1945 Hedy Lambrecht and Anna Rischar were detailed to work in the headquarters of the camp administrations, housed in a large administration building at the main square of Betschkerek. Anna: "The Supreme Commander was a young partisan with fanatical blue/gray eyes, a dark face and razor-sharp voice. He was frightful. All camps in the Banat were under his administration and our task was to record all still living inmates. After we finished one camp list, the lists of the dead were added. When we recognized acquaintances we coughed softly; we did not dear to speak loudly since next door was the dining room of all partisans. Rudolfsgnad was the worst death camp that winter."

There is no doubt, that during 1944/45 the camp "old mill" at Groß-Betschkerek, today called Zrenjanin, was the main regional center of the Tito-annihilation drive for the ethnic German men in the Banat. It is very difficult to state reliable numbers of victims since on the ethnic German side no registration was possible. Should the mentioned partisan's camp lists ever be accessible (provided they still exist) our documentation will have to be amended accordingly. A careful, conservative evaluation of all individual reports available today leeds to an estimation of 1,000 to 2,000 murdered ethnic Germans in Betschkerek.

3.2.2 Batschka

The Batschka was occupied by the Red Army during the second half of October 1944, i. e. about two to three weeks later than the Banat. Since the Batschka had been incorporated into Hungary after the Yugoslav kingdom had colapsed in 1941, many of the local ethnic Hungarians were also victims of the emerging Serbian revenge groups during the first days and weeks of the communist partisan rule. This was, however, soon stopped by the authorities as Hungary became an ally within the communist bloc. On the other hand, the ethnic Germans of the Batschka, who had nothing to do with any oppressive measure of the Hungarian troops, were nevertheless persecuted and liquidated as brutally as in the Banat. This is another proof for the premeditated, countrywide organized elimination of the ethnic Germans in Yugoslavia.

The mass executions and other murders (by stabbing, beating etc.) of ethnic Germans in the Batschka during the *bloody autumn 1944* in the individual communities were, as a rule, carried out in a single day or night. The mobile "special commandos" selected male youths from age 16 and adults up to 60 for executions. This happened for instance in Bajmok, Bezdan, Filipowa, Hodschag, Kischker, Kolut, Obrowatz, Weprowatz and Werbass. Exceptions were the districts of Palanka, Sombor and Kula.

Sombor (Zombor)
The former regional capital of the Batschka had 32,300 inhabitants, thereof 2,500 ethnic Germans. Russians and partisans moved in on October 21st, 1944. The OZNA confiscated the Kronics-Palais and converted it into its central prison. The district administration building Županija became the prison of the partisans military administration. Both buildings also served as the partisans' military court. The

barrack camp at Bezdan Street became a labor camp for the Danube Swabians from the districts Sombor, Apatin and Hadschag.

Just a few days after the partisans occupied the city, they started to arrest ethnic Germans and Hungarians. Specially all those who were taken to the Kronics-Palais disappeared for ever. First they were sadically tortured and then beaten or shot to death. Josef Gassmann, a cinema owner from Apatin, was killed in his cell. Another inmate from Batsch-Sentiwan had to carry him out and only recognized him by his clothes; the head was completely mutilated from the mistreatment. Helene Rajal, who was arrested on November 20th, 1944 at Apatin and taken to the Kronics-Palais, had to take the food to the prisoners who were locked in a garage. She describes the conditions of that place: "About 150 men, in chains, were in this garage for seven weeks. The chains were so tight that the men had sores on their hands. During the seven weeks the chains were not removed once, not even for eating or performing bodily functions. Their clothing was scant and infested with lice. During the cold December days, they had to lie down on the concrete floor of the unheated garage. It was only at Christmas 1944 that a new judge arrived from Novi Sad and ordered the chains be removed."

Notorious was the Kronics-Palais, but in the Županija people were also heavily tortured. The interrogations combined with continuous mistreatments rarely referred to the own, personal conduct of the victims; generally they were asked about other persons (most of whom they did not even know) and the partisans obviously expected them to denounce these people: The Communists needed arguments against local Serbs and Hungarians whom they wanted to get rid of (revenge and "Action Intelligentsia"). So they could liquidate Serb and Hungarian "traitors", "fascists", "enemies of the people" etc. under the pretence of legality.

The ethnic Germans were anyway outlaws and the partisans did not really care to prove any personal defaults in order to justify their executions. The OZNA's "judicial proceedings" against some ethnic Germans were just a farce. Martin Reinspecht informs of the arbitrary liquidations, without trial nor sentence, in the Kronics-Palais: "In February and March 1945 a militiaman of the Kronics-Palais, the OZNA's central prison, came almost daily to see me and have his glass of wine. He became talkative and repeatedly he described how he had liquidated one or several prisoners the night before. His narrations usually sounded like that: 'Yesterday the Poručnik (1st lieutenant) told me, Milan today room no .... I answered: razumem (I understand). As soon as it gets dark, I go to the poor inmate and tell him: druže (comrade) get ready, you're going home. He is happy. However, I don't take him to the street, but to the yard. I let him go in advance, towards a wall, discretely release the safety catch of my machinka (machine gun) and after the crack the good guy still moves his leggs convulsively, then he becomes quiet.'" Martin Reinspecht, an ethnic German himself and fearing to be arrested any moment, adds: "I looked to the weapon which this brutal murderer always kept ready at hand and I imagined that perhaps tomorrow the safety catch would be released behind my back. I was close to fainting, but I ought not to give evidence of my feelings and had to clink glasses with the monster."

Among some larger groups of ethnic Germans, who were tortured in the Kronics-Palais before being redeemed by death, were those from Apatin (13,400 inhabitants, of which 11,700 were Germans) and from Kolut, a multiethnic village in the Sombor district. The Kolut group consisted of 52 Germans and eight other nationals. None of them survived.

Batsch-Brestowatz (Bački Brestovac)

A bestial crime was committed in the multiethnic community Batsch-Brestowatz (8,500 inhabitants, 4,450 Germans). Magdalena Thorer née Ament, after her escape from the camp, described how the partisans summoned her to the deathbed of a Brestowatz Serb and forced her to forgive the dying man, who was not able to die since he considered himself a murderer. He confessed that he had participated in the murder of her brother Stefan Ament and eleven other Brestowatz Germans. He narrated how these men had to bury each other up to the neck in a field outside the community. Then their heads were bashed in or hacked off.

Palanka (Bački Palanka)

The district of Palanka experienced the first partisan actions against the ethnic Germans in the Batschka since it was situated at the front line and for quite a time German troops were keeping up on the other side of the river Danube. The city of Palanka had a population of about 13,200, thereof about 6,800 ethnic Germans. The district of Palanka had a total population of 42,700, the ethnic Germans being the majority with 24,700. There lived additionally 12,450 Serbs, 2,450 Croats, 2,150 Slovaks and 1,400 Hungarians.

The first partisans appeared in the city on October 20th, 1944 and a few days later also partisans from Syrmia moved in. These and the gypsies were particularly rough. According to Dr. Wilhelm Neuner, president of the local court, the partisans committed terrible massacres already during the very first days of the occupation. First they arrested a group of distinguished and well-to-do German men (including some Hungarians), tortured and beat them to death. Some days later in October 1944 they dragged 70 German youths between 15 and 19 years old out of their houses, handcuffed and took them to a near forest. The boys were forced to excavate their own mass grave, then all of them were murdered.

On October 26th, 1944 around 100 German men were arrested, tortured all night and on October 27th taken to the same forest and killed. On November 17th, 1944 all men between 16 and 62 years from all communities of the Palanka district were taken to the city, tortured and some of them killed. The next day the whole group – 1,200 persons – were chased to the regional concentration camp at Neusatz (Novi Sad). This march of 40 kilometre became mortal for many of them. They were continuously mistreated and he who could not follow was killed on the spot.

Klein-Ker, Kischker (Bačko Dobro Polje)

On November 9th, 1944 the partisans arrested 98 men and women from the two main streets (Haupt- und Spitalgasse). They followed a name list established in the town hall. Men and women were separated by gender and crowded into separate small rooms that gave them hardly space to breathe. The partisans continuously threatened to execute them, pushing the poor victims even closer together. After midnight the execution squad arrived. The trembling men and women were taken out one by one and hauled into the interrogation room. The "interrogation" was mainly an unbelievable sadistic torture, the screaming of the victims could be heard far away. The question they asked everybody was whether he or she was a member of the Kulturbund (German Cultural Society). The interrogator then decided whether the person was assigned to "group I or II".

A woman who survived relates: "When brought into the room, the interrogator shouted at me, asking whether I was a member of the Kulturbund and where my husband was. I answered that we had to be in the Kulturbund, otherwise our son could not have attended the German high school and that my husband was also here. Shouting again he decided 'group II', but my husband was put in group I." Out of the 98 persons, 78 were put in group I (56 women and 22 men), among them a 77 year old woman and mothers that were torn from their babies. One mother left behind six children, five of them were less than ten years of age. Group I was murdered the same night. The reporting woman adds: "My grandparents had a son, two daughters, two daughter-in-laws, one son-in-law and two grand daughters among the murdered." The 20 persons of group II were held prisoners for some days in the city hall, then they were chased to Werbass.

On November 14th, and November 20th, 1944 the same procedure was repeated. Again the partisans followed a list from the town hall, now, however, they arrested people of the whole village. They also seized some persons who accidentally came to the city hall. On 14th the victims were twelve women and 34 men and on 20th, nine women and five men. They were all murdered.

Werbass (Vrbas)

The twin city of Werbass (Old-, New-W.) was the most important school center for the ethnic Germans in the Vojvodina. Of a total of 13,900 inhabitants about 8,000 were Germans. The Sovjet troops occupied the city by middle of October 1944. There was only a very weak resistance by Hungarian troops, who quickly withdrew.

Following the Russian troops, the partisans' "People's Liberation Army" moved in. A local committee was formed by native Serbs and some Hungarian and German communists. An ethnic German tailor, called Hengel (or Henkel) became mayor.

Karl Mengel, an ethnic German eyewitness reports: "The executions began towards the end of October. Initially 20 respected citizens and one woman, they are all recorded by name, were herded together, tortured and shot at the cemetery. The same fate happened to three young soldiers who had returned home. Repeatedly Germans were taken from their homes and disappeared without a trace.

Interventions by known Serbs were fruitless. The leader of the partisans was a certain Anton Heller, 28 years old. He was conscripted by the Germans into a so-called work unit, serving on Germany's eastern front and deserted to the Russians. With the advancing Russians he returned to his hometown Neu-Werbass and assumed a leading role among the partisans. Under his command 22 workers from the sugar factory, Germans as well as ethnic Hungarians, were arrested and put to death."

The liquidations culminated on November 9th–11th, 1944. Karoline Zepp née Michel, another Danube Swabian eyewitness, reports: "During the night of November 9th 570 men and youths were removed from their homes and incarcerated in the city hall. The partisans were guided by local Serbs (one of them Pero Djakula and a gypsy called Lalo). In the central cemetery at the separation line between the catholic and the protestant part, about 150 metre away from the protestant mortuary, five mass graves were dug out by order of the partisans. Shortly afterwards the 570 prisoners had disappeared from the city hall. On November 14th, 1944 three of the five mass graves were covered. The relatives of the disappeared asked mayor Henkel about the fate of their family members: 'What do you think is in the holes at the cemetery, perhaps frogs?' was his answer."

Karl Mengel relates that he was first informed of these mass murders by a Serbian acquaintance. The informant knew of about 150 Germans and the same number of Hungarians who were rounded up and beaten. At midnight they were shackled to a long wire and chased nude to the central cemetery. In groups of two they had to stand before the pit and were killed by neck shots. Among the murdered was Jakob Lotz, the former director of the Alt-Werbass high school. These reports were later confirmed to Karl Mengel by Karl Schimony, who was one of the victims, but was only wounded and able to crawl out of the pit, as well as by the Serb shoemaker Novo, performing guard duty during that night.

Hodschag (Odžaci)

November 23rd, 1944 became the "black day" for the district city of Hodschag (5,900 inhabitants, thereof 4,750 Germans). On that day a partisan commando – they supposedly belonged to the Krajinska brigade – arrived at the place. Anton Mathes reports on the crimes of this troop:

"On November 23rd they started a large scale raid; 181 men and two women were herded into the house of photographer Johann Raab. Meanwhile, 40 young people dug a large mass grave in a field along the road to Karawukowa. At that time the city council consisted of three Serbs: Dobranov, Urbas and Pavkov. They knew what was going to happen and succeeded to free some of the prisoners. Thus innkeeper Franz Kraus, merchant Ladislaus Kollmann and Hans Petko were saved. The three Serbs genuinely tried to prevent the mass murder, however, without success. Towards midnight the prisoners had to undress and line up in rows of four and were marched to the mass grave. There they were brutally murdered and the corpses thrown into the pit which was then closed. Hans Mayer was the only one who managed to escape during the night. For many days the mass grave was guarded and nobody allowed to go near."

Filipowa (Bački Gračac)
The murder of men and youths of Filipowa (an entirely ethnic German community of 3,500 inhabitants) in the Hodschag district during the night of November 25th, 1944 was probably the peak – at least as far as the number of victims was concerned – and almost the end of the "bloody autumn" in the Batschka. These were the sequences of events, as researched by Dr. Georg Wildmann:

"The evening of November 24th a squad of partisans belonging to the Krajinska brigade arrived at the village. On the 25th they surrounded the village. After the morning mass the 'Kleinrichter' (village drummer) went through the village and announced: All males between 16 and 60 have to report immediately to the village hall. Anybody not doing so and caught by the partisans will be executed on the spot. Towards nine o'clock more than 300 men and youths congregated at the village hall. Towards ten o'clock they were ordered into the fenced churchyard and to form into files of four. A table was brought and some Serbian clerks sat down. Two partisan officers were in command, one Serb and one Hungarian. Then the men and youths were motioned to the table, their names recorded and divided into two groups. Early afternoon the larger group of 212 had to form lines of four. Partisans stood between them. A leader, on horseback, assumed command as the condemned moved out of the village, watched by horrified women and children behind drawn curtains. The church clock struck 3 pm. The ones left behind, about 100, were chased into the church and locked up for the night. If a villager showed himself as the condemned left the village he was shot at immediately. At one of these shots fired by the commander, his horse rose up and he wounded himself and fell from the horse. He was said to have died the next day.

Some distance outside the village, at the 'Roth-Sallasch' (farm of Josef Roth), the procession stopped. First the men were encouraged to squeal on each other. He who would tell which ones of the co-prisoners were members of the Swabian Cultural Society (Schwäbisch-Deutscher Kulturbund) would be freed. Nobody squealed. That's when the tortures started. The partisans' execution commando had been reinforced by 50 men from the Batschka: Serbs, Slovaks, Bunjewatz and Hungarians. One of these auxiliaries, a Bunjewatz recognized Ludwig Vogl, the Filipowa pharmacist and requested that he be released, since he knew he was not guilty. Arguments started and a major part of the Vojvodina men joined the Bunjewatz in refusing to participate in the torture and execution of the Filipowa men. A messenger on horseback was dispatched to notify the higher ups of the situation. He returned the same night with the order that the protesters should be immediately withdrawn."

75

From Roth-Sallasch the men were chased onto the 'hay-meadow' that contained pits which were used to protect the anti-aircraft guns of the former German airfield in the Hodschag area. The men had to undress in front of these pits and then were beaten to death, butchered with knives or shot and thrown into the pits. No one survived. Among the victims of this massacre were 35 youths age 16 to 19 years. Officially all 212 murdered were termed 'fascists' and 'war criminals'.

In spite of the imposed silence on the participating partisans, the familiy members of the victims later were able to learn of these tragic events that transpired. Various camp inmates (after the total internment of the ethnic Germans) who were bought as workers by Vojvodine Slavs obtained details from their masters. An - eyewitness from Piwnitz told Sister Lea Helfert of the Order 'Arme Schwestern' (Poor Sisters): "I was drafted into the Home Guard and had to participate in the 'cleansing action' on November 25th, 1944. I was not with the armed guards, but with the ones who had to hold together the ropes so nobody could run away. What I tell you now I'll never be able to forget in all my life. Most of the men prayed and made the sign of the cross before they were killed. When both father and son were together, the father made the sign of the cross on his son's forehead before they were murdered." Another eyewitness report was given to Father Friedrich Gillich by Bunjewatzen citizens who, unarmed, also had to participate. They stated that the screams and praying only ceased after the last victims expired and that this hideous night gave them endless nightmares.

3.2.3 Syrmia

Fortunately most Danube Swabians of Syrmia were evacuated before the partisans took over. However, the fate of the ones that stayed at home was tragic.

India (Indjija)
In the multiethnic community India (8,100 inhabitants, thereof 5,900 Germans), it was the local "People's Liberation Committee" which cruelly persecuted the ethnic Germans that stayed behind.

On October 22nd, 1944 the partisans occupied India without any resistance. On October 28th, 1944 in the evening a first group of ethnic German men were imprisoned in the former Hungarian school. The executers were mainly local Serbs of India, among them Braco Vujanić and Jovo Kovačević.

On November 2nd, 1944 Elisabetha Wertatschnik née Sturtz was taken to the city hall. She was terribly tortured and finally beaten to death. During the torture four men played the harmonica as loud as possible to outdo her screeming. When she was dead, her husband had to carry her down to the yard. Her dead body was covered with blood, the flesh was torn to shreds, both eyes were punched out. In this crime participated various local Serbs, their names are registered in LW I.

On November 6th, 1944 all German men, who had not yet been arrested, were also taken to the Hungarian school. On November 11th, 1944 nine well-known men were summond to the school yard, tied with wire and chased to Alt-Pasua eight kilometre away. On the way they were beaten with clubs and guns. There they had to dig their graves and then were executed by a machine gun salvo. Gypsies with hatchets in their hands checked whether all were dead and split their heads. Some Croatians from the area were also murdered.

On November 12th the rest of the prisoners were taken from the Hungarian school, two each tied together and each one was also tied around the waist with a rope. They then were chased to the village hall, cussed at and mistreated on the way, particularly by the gypsies. At that time a messenger arrived from Semlin requesting workers for a Russian commando. After these were selected and dispatched, the rest of the prisoners was divided into three groups. The first one consisted of 64 men, women and children. They were told that they now were taken home; but instead they were taken to the knacker's yard, horribly tortured and herded into a room. The local Serb Tošo Vujanić then threw a hand grenade into the room, which tore apart many of the occupants. Those still alive were butchered or beaten to death with hatchets. During this massacre, conducted under the command of a Kommissar and a female partisan, the butchers sang partisan songs. A local record names the following participating Serbs from India: Belić, Ivica Vujanić, Tošo Vujanić, Dujo Vujanić, Braco Vujanić, Jovo Kovačević and Vlajko Jojić.

On November 18th, 1944 more ethnic Germans, particularly older people, were incredibly tortured and murdered. The eyewitness reports are of such a fiendish cruelty, that it was decided not to publish details, paying respect to the victims and their families. The ones responsible for this barbarity were Miloš Kovačević, Sava Živković, Ljubo Stojić, Vlajko Jojić and Tošo Vujanić.

Semlin/Franztal (Zemun/Zemun-Novigrad)
At Semlin, a suburb of Belgrade (28,000 inhabitants, thereof 8,350 Germans), immediately following the occupation, the partisans arrested hundreds of ethnic Germans. Of the ones they murdered during the night of November 3rd 241 victims are documented by name.

The local records read as follows: "The first unit of the partisans came from Beschania. Three days after their arrival posters appeared in the entire city announcing that on October 29th, 30th and 31st, all Germans had to report for work to the 'Salzamt'. Anybody not following this order would be shot immediately, without a court martial. A great panic broke out among the Germans that had stayed at home." Responsible citizens as they had always been, the majority of the Semlin and Franztal Germans reported to the Salzamt. With very few exceptions none of them survived the trip. An eyewitness reports: "When I arrived the next day I found over 700 people crowded together in a small space; men, women and adolescents, but mainly older people. Since I was delivering milk for a municipal institution,

I was taken out of the Salzamt by the Serbian manager. In the night of November 3rd all those, that had reported to the Salzamt, disappeared."

A woman, who used to bring food to one of the persons held, on November 4th, 1944, did not find anyone, only big piles of their clothing in the hallway. The next day an ethnic German Franztal worker, who had not reported to the Salzamt, was told by a non German coworker at the electricity plant: "Last night they took your fellow-countrymen past this plant, stripped and two-by-two tied together." The electricity plant was situated at the Danube River. None was ever seen again.

After this occurrence the ethnic German Communists, under the leadership of Alexander Mettler, thought they could help their countrymen that were still alive in Semlin and Franztal. According to reliable sources Mettler went to Belgrade to protest against the partisans' actions in Semlin and asked for assistance. He was said to have gone to Moscha Pijade, one of the most influential members of the new government whom he personally knew from the time of the Communists' persecution during the reign of the Yugoslav monarchy. Mettler however was told to keep out of this matter if he didn't want anything to happen to himself. Mettler and his comrades in the Communist party were no longer considered important and they were just able to save their own heads.

Ruma (Ruma)

In November 1944 a similar bloodbath occurred at Ruma (13,400 inhabitants, thereof 6,950 Germans). During many nights numerous Germans were brutally murdered, initially at the Croatian Center (Hrvatski Dom) and later at the Rausch brick works.

A. Kreuzer reports: "As soon as the partisans moved into Ruma during the autumn 1944, they began a hunt for all ethnic Germans. The Germans from Ruma and surrounding communities, that had remained in the 'Autonomous Republic of Croatia' after evacuation of the German population, were rounded up and jailed in the Croatian Center. During the night a larger group of the partisan murderers, including a concertina player, arrived. They lined up in the second large hall. They all had daggers tied to the shaft of their boots or around the waist. The concertina player positioned himself in the doorway that led from one hall to the other. The ethnic Germans were ordered to lie down on the floor, closely together. When there was a deadly silence, the leader motioned to the concertina player, who then played a Kolo-dance melody, and the whole partisan group danced into the hall. The murderous gang trampled over the motionless German bodies, continually shouting and cheering while they stabbed the humans under their feet until they had finished their butchering. During the next two nights the same blood orgy was repeated with new groups of victims. Each morning German women had to wash the blood from the walls and floor."

Some reasonable Serbs apparently protested to the new rulers against the mass murdering in the center of Ruma. At any rate, the order came to discontinue the mass killing in the Croatian Center. Now the ethnic Germans were only herded together into the Croatian Center and, after midnight, stripped and chased to the Rausch brick works. The hands of each two prisoners were tied together with wire. At the brick works they again had to lie face down. The executioners stepped on the bodies of the victims, illuminated their necks with flashlights and murdered them with a bullet. This process lasted until there were no ethnic Germans left alive. The corpses were covered with lime.

A young man from Ruma was also shot in the neck, but not dead, only unconscious. After the murderers left the scene he recovered consciousness and being on the top layer of the dead, was able to free himself. In spite of his wound he could flee into a cornfield and make his way across the border to Hungary.

Main Source References 3.1

Arbeitskreis Dokumentation, *Leidensweg der Deutschen im kommunistischen Jugoslawien*, Vol. I – IV. Editor: Donauschwäbische Kulturstiftung München, 1991–1995. Abbr.: LW I … LW IV.

Arbeitskreis Dokumentation, *Verbrechen an den Deutschen in Jugoslawien 1944–1948. Die Stationen eines Völkermordes*. Editor: Donauschwäbische Kulturstiftung, München, 3rd edition, 2000. Abbr.: VDJ.

Schieder, Theodor et al., *Dokumentation der Vertreibung der Deutschen aus Ost-Mitteleuropa*, Vol. V: *Das Schicksal der Deutschen in Jugoslawien*. Editor: Bundesministerium für Vertriebene, Flüchtlinge und Kriegsbeschädigte, Bonn 1961. Abbr.: Dok. V. Identic reprint: Deutscher Taschenbuchverlag (dtv reprint 3274), München 1984, and Weltbild-Verlag, Augsburg 1994.

Sources 3.1.1

Zerne: Elisabeth Bürger, LW I, 163–170; Margarethe Themare, Dok. V, 215. *Palanka:* Heimatausschuss Palanka, Palanka a. d. Donau, Sindelfingen 1986; LW I, 526 ff.; Josef Kampf, Dok. V, 219 ff., LW II, 236–248; Sophie Haas/Hans Reck/Peter Wilpert, LW II, 528–536; Dok. V, 287–293; Anna Volk/Anton Scherer/P. F. LW III, 422–427; *Obrovac:* Fabian Walter, *Obrovac*, Neu-Ulm 1971, 44 ff.; LW I, 545–548; *Towarisch:* Michael Hausmann, LW I, 553 f.

Sources 3.1.2

Zerne: LW II, 237; *Batsch-Brestowatz:* Franz Wesinger, LW I, 469 f.; *Rudolfsgnad:* Lorenz Baron, LW III, 214 ff.; *Mitrowitz:* Wendelin Michels, LW I, 716 ff.; *Schowe:* Ludwig Ziwich, LW I, 572 f.

Sources 3.1.3

Groß-Betschkerek: Ivan Invanji, in: Franz Roth (Editor): *Beiträge zum Geschichtsbild der Donauschwaben* (Donauschwäbische Beiträge Nr. 97), Salzburg 1995; LW III, 65. *India:* Valentin Oberkersch, India, Stuttgart 1978, 326; LW I, 699–702; LW II, 732 ff. *Kolut:* Josef Willand, LW I, 424.

Sources 3.1.4

Georg Wildmann, LW I, 385–389; Enikö A. Sajti in the weekly "168 óra" (9.9.1991); Karl Ottenbacher, LW II, 559 f.; Márton Matuska, A megtorlás napjai, ahogy az emlékezet megörizte, Budapest o. J. 267 ff.; Tibor Cseres, Vérboszú Bácskában, Budapest 1991, 104–137 and 182 f.; Georg Wildmann, LW III, 336–339; 447–451.

Sources 3.1.5

Georg Wildmann, LW I, 612; LW III, 111; VDJ, 266 f.; Matthias Merkle, *Märtyrerbischof DDr. Philipp Popp*. Private publishing, Heilbronn/Frankenbach 1985; Vladimir Geiger, Nestanak Volksdojcera, Zagreb 1997, 105 ff.

Sources 3.1.6

VDJ, 97–99; Milovan Djilas, *Krieg der Partisanen* (War of the Partisans), Memoirs 1941–1945, Molden/Wien 1978, 574 ff.; LW I, 610–612, 670; Martin Reinspecht, LW II, 404 ff.; Helene Rajal, LW III, 324 f.

Sources 3.1.8

Milovan Djilas, *Krieg der Partisanen*, 572–574; Wendelin Gruber, *In den Fängen des Roten Drachen*, 113; Georg Wildmann, LW II, 390 f., 395, 62–68; VDJ, 101 f.

Sources 3.2.1 Banat

Sources 3.2.1.1

Deutsch Zerne (Nemačka Crnja)
Elisabeth Bürger, LW I, 163–170; Margarethe Themare, Dok. V, 215 ff.; Josef Kampf, Dok. V, 219 ff., 236–248; LW IV, 95–102; VDJ, 94 f., 258.

Charleville, Soltur, St. Hubert
Adam Hess, LW I, 148–157; LW IV, 79–95; VDJ, 107, 258.

Kubin (Kovin)
Franz Schenzinger, LW I, 244–248; Johann Fischer, LW II, 137–148; LW IV, 224 ff.

Ernsthausen (Banatsko Despotovac)
Ladislaus Schag, LW I, 172; LW II, 251; Elisabeth Flassak (daughter of L. Schag): LW II, 250; LW III, 509; S. Gärtner, LW II, 256; LW IV, 110–119.

Homolitz (Omoljica)
Michael Adelhardt, LW I, 226 ff.; LW III, 155 ff.; LW IV, 178–191.

Pantschowa (Pančevo)
Matthias Merkle, LW I, 284 ff.; LW IV, 288–307.

Zichydorf (Veliko Plandište)
Peter Singer, LW I, 363 ff.; Jakob Faul et al., LW II, 122–128; LW IV, 416–424.

Sources 3.2.1.2

Sources: Regional Liquidation Camp "Milk Hall" at Groß-Kikinda

Franz Schmidt et al., LW I, 204 ff.; Rose Mullarczyk, LW I, 206; Michael Hess, LW II, 329 f.; Peter Groß, LW III, 173–175; LW IV, 152–158; VDJ, 102 f., 259; Peter Binzberger, *Die Kikin-*

daer Donauschwäbische Gedenkstätte, private edition 2002. Siniša Jakonić: *ZLOČINI Miloševićeve Tajne Policije*, published December 2002, 132–139.

Sources: Regional Liquidation Camp "Stojković Telep" at Werschetz (Vršac)

Ingeborg Seidl/Helmut Frisch, LW I, 355 ff.; Sebastian Gotre et al., LW II, 44–59; Robert Hammerstiel, *Von Ikonen und Ratten. Eine Banater Kindheit* 1939–1949, Wien/München 1999.

Sources: Regional Liquidation Camp "Old Mill" at Groß-Betschkerek (Veliki Bečkerek, Zrenjanin)

Michael Kristof, BA, Ost-Dok. 2, No. 397 and LW III, 141 ff.; Walter Neuner, LW II, 217 ff.; Dr. Wilhelm Neuner, LW I, 187 ff. and Dok.V; Hans Diwald, LW I, 193 ff.; Adam Feketitsch, LW II, 231; LW IV, 68 ff.; Anna Rischar-Gajdics/Hedwig Lambrecht-Kaiser/ Lydia Junger-Lickfeld/Dietmar Prokle, *Modoscher Heimatblätter*, Nos. 109, 138, 139, 140, 164.

Sources 3.2.2 Batschka

Sources: Sombor (Zombor)

Martin Reinspecht, LW II, 402 ff.; Georg Wildmann, LW I, 608 ff.; Helene Rajal, VDJ, 98/99.

Sources: Batsch-Brestowatz (Bački Brestovac)

Franz Wesinger, LW I, 467 ff.; Eva Ruckober et al., LW II, 480–487; LW IV, 469–480; Anton Affolder, *Brestowatz* (Donauschwäbische Beiträge Nr. 56) Freilassing 1971.

Sources: Palanka (Bački Palanka)

Heimatortsausschuss Palanka, LW I, 522 ff.; Heimatortsausschuss Palanka, *Palanka an der Donau*, Sindelfingen 1986, 511–531; Dok. V, 287–293; LW IV, 658–670; VDJ, 263–265.

Sources: Klein-Ker, Kischker (Bačko Dobro Polje)

Nikolaus Dietrich/Johann Lorenz, LW I, 499 ff.; Nikolaus Dietrich, LW II, 608 f.; Johann Lorenz (Editor), *Unvergessenes Kischker* (Donauschwäbische Beiträge Nr. 38) Freilassing 1960, Karlsruhe 1980; Dok. V, 381 f.; LW IV, 607–616.

Sources: Werbass (Vrbas)

Karl Mengel, Report, Deutsches Bundesarchiv Bayreuth, Ost-Dok. 2, Batschka IV/4, 8 pages; LW IV, 765–776; Karoline Zepp, BA Bayreuth and LW II, 602 ff.; VDJ, 112 f.

Sources: Hodschag (Odzaci)

Peter Rakitsch, LW I, 461 ff.; Theresia Haltmayer, LW II, 467 f.

Sources: Filipowa (Bački Gračac)

Georg Wildmann/Josef Pertschi, LW I, 473 ff.; Georg Wildmann, LW III, 678–681; Dok.V, 265–269; Paul Mesli et al., *Filipowa – Bild einer donauschwäbischen Gemeinde*, Vol. VI: *Kriegs- und Lageropfer*, Wien 1985, 43–49; LW IV, 523–539.

Sources 3.2.3 Syrmia

Sources: India (Indjija)

Valentin Oberkersch, LW I, 701 f.; Valentin Oberkersch, *India – Deutsches Leben in Ost-syrmien 1825–1944*, Stuttgart 1978, espec.: 320 f., 326–329; LW IV, 832–837.

Sources: Semlin/Franztal (Zemun/Zemun-Novigrad)

Franz Zöller, LW I, 665 ff.; LW IV, 876–885; Nikolaus Hefner et al., *Franztal 1816–1944*, Salzburg 1984, 197–211.

Sources: Ruma (Ruma)

A. Kreuzer, LW II, 755 f.

Chapter 4: Deportation of Laborers to the Soviet Union

4.1 Stalin Demanding Deportations – in Violation of Human Rights

In late fall 1944 Stalin demanded from Romania and the territories of Hungary and Yugoslavia, which he had occupied at that time, to make available German laborers for the reconstruction of Russian areas destroyed during the war. The process started at Christmas 1944 even though it was only during the Yalta Conference, February 4th–11th, 1945 that Stalin obtained the approval of the Western Powers to receive from Germany a portion of its allocated war reparations in the form of labor. This agreement by the Allies to the "faite accompli" gave Stalin a quasi-legal base for the German "reparation slaves" from the Southeast European nations – even though this act was a human rights violation.

The whole chapter is based on eyewitness reports of Danube Swabians who were deported from Banat and Batschka and survived. Seven reports can be found in the official documentation of the Federal Republic of Germany, Bundesministerium für Vertriebene, Flüchtlinge und Kriegsgeschädigte, published by Schieder, Theodor (et al.): *Dokumentation der Vertreibung der Deutschen aus Ost-Mitteleuropa*, Vol. V: *Das Schicksal der Deutschen in Jugoslawien*, Bonn 1961, pages 295–344. Many other reports were gathered by Martin Reinsprecht and published in: Arbeitskreis Dokumentation, *Leidensweg der Deutschen im kommunistischen Jugoslawien*, Vol. II: *Erlebnisberichte*, pages 923–976, published by Donauschwäbische Kulturstiftung München, München/Sindelfingen 1993. The accurate and extensive investigations of Karl Weber, published in *Leidensweg ...* Vol. IV: *Menschenverluste – Namen und Zahlen*, München-Sindelfingen 1993, permitted a very exact calculation, how many Danube Swabians were deported form Yugoslavia to the Soviet Union and how many died there.

The military administration of the partisans made available to the Russians at least 12,000 Danube Swabian civilians from the West Banat and Batschka (8,000 women and 4,000 men) who were forcibly shipped to the mining and industrial areas in the Ukraine. The women were between 18 and 40 and the men between 16 and 50 years of age. There were at least eight trains, four from the Batschka and four from the Banat and each had up to 45 freight cars which were stuffed with up to 45 persons to a car. These transports, routed via Romania, took place during frigid winter weather and lasted about three weeks.

The Agony of Farewells and Brutality of the Transports

It was during the Christmas days of 1944 that the ones selected by the local partisan/communist functionaries had to leave all their loved ones, spouses, children, relatives and friends. They were forced to march with their baggage, often long distances and under strict military escort, to the collection camps. There, some of them were checked by Russion doctors, other were not, before chasing all of them to railway stations. The uncertainty of their own future was only matched by the anxiety about the loved ones left behind. During frigid temperatures the work slaves were shipped in cattle cars that were locked from the outside. There was no space for movement, ability to sleep only in a sitting position and running the risk of freezing to death while asleep. Food supplies were almost non-existent and people had to survive on what little they could bring along. The lack of water was particularly painful since it was often withheld for sheer sadistic reasons. In the crowded space and absence of all hygienic facilities, bodily functions could only be taken care of with greatest difficulties. In addition, they had to suffer the mental and emotional anxiety of not knowing where they were going and when this trip was going to end. The first casualties occurred already during the three-week trip.

Catastrophic Accommodations and Difficult Working Conditions

In Russia the tightly guarded billets initially often had neither windows nor doors. The premises were fenced in by barbed wire. Considering the notorious Russian winters, heating material was inadequate and often completely lacking, hygienic facilities insufficient, no warm water for washing and toilet facilities catastrophic. Epidemics and infestations started to erupt.

The food supply consisted almost entirely of lumpy, sour-tasting and hardly digestible bread as well as cabbage or flour soup without any meat or fat. The food had to be picked up from kitchens that were up to three kilometre away. The dishes consisted of rusty tin cans. Sometimes they were forced to exchange good clothing against torn and lice-infested military garb.

Extremely hard work had to be performed under all weather conditions. The work targets were usually set much too high. While bread rations were adjusted to the work requirement, they were still insufficient. In addition to the heavy work load, the long distance to the work stations entailed long arduous marches, even during snow storms. The women too had to perform hard labor, many of them below ground, down deep in the coal pits. Twelve hours and more daily, including Sundays, were mandatory, in winter at 40 degrees Celsius below zero (= – 40 F) in wet and torn clothing.

The High Mortality Rate of Humans at their Best Age

Even though Danube Swabian men and women were used to hard physical work, many could not endure the working conditions in the mines, at the railroad and construction sites. Undernourishment, humidity, rain, cold, excessive work hours and the excessively long distance marches led to the total exhaustion of many. Men in particular, who had to work the hardest, soon suffered from dystrophy. The additional insecurity of ones own fate which often turned into hopelessness, homesickness, longing for the loved ones at home and anxiety about their well being, soon led to the great mortality rate. When you consider that only the strongest age groups with a natural mortality rate of almost zero were deported, one can get an idea of the martyrdom the dead and living had to endure.

The slave labor in the Soviet Union resulted in the loss of life of at least 2,000 Danube Swabians. That is about 17 percent, including 1,100 men and 900 women. For those who were able to survive, the term of the slave labor lasted up to five years.

The first repatriation of the very sick and unable to work started towards the end of 1945. At that time many had already died. One of the first repatriation trains went to Yugoslavia where the returnees were promptly put into camps, most of them into the death camps.

It was only during the last two years of their stay in Russia, 1948 and 1949, that the conditions improved. Food was adequate and working conditions more bearable. At the end of 1949 the Russians dissolved the camps and shipped the deported to Frankfurt an der Oder, in East Germany. The last to leave had spent five years of hardship in the "workers paradise".

Upon their Return – the Bitter Truth

After their arrival in Germany the discharged slave workers had to learn that they could not return to their homeland and that their dependents, their children, parents and grandparents suffered a fate worse than their own. Bit by bit they found out who of their family and relatives did not survive the genocide perpetrated by the Tito-regime. Almost all temporarily orphaned children were shipped to unknown children homes and unknown locations in Yugoslavia. It took many years before they could be located (if at all!) and reunited, with the help of the Red Cross. Many of the younger ones no longer recognized their parents and had partially or totally forgotten their mother tongue. Every third of the deported women had to find out, that her husband was lost in the war, and she stood alone in the world.

Almost all of the slave workers suffered from health problems. Many, after their return to Germany and confronted with the loss of their loved ones and their home, were overcome and passed away.

The survivors, particularly those who, after their flight or expulsion, settled in Germany and Austria organized themselves into "hometown societies". These societies compiled rather exact statistical documentation of the fate of their former communities and inhabitants. Knowledgeable observers determined that the life span of surviving slave workers was much shorter in comparison to those who did not suffer those hardships.

4.2 "Life and Suffering under the Red Star" – an Eyewitness Report

In the *Modoscher Heimatblätter* no. 155, 156 and 157 Anna Bernauer née Zettl gives an account an how her family was torn apart, on her inhuman forced labor in the Soviet Union, the ethnic re-education and suffering of her small son till he finally found his way back to his parents. Here are excerpts of this heart-wrenching personal experience.

"On the second Christmas holiday 1944, at six o'clock in the morning, the police drummer was already making his round and announced that all German women between 16 and 40 years of age have to report to the city hall at eight o'clock. At four in the afternoon they already took us away. At the church, my dear mother stood with my little boy. She wept bitterly as we were led past as if she knew that we would never again be re-united. Aside from a few brief moments when we stood in the locked railroad cars I never saw my mother again. For five years I had no news from my son, didn't even know whether he was still alive or not."

The writer reports further that they were chased to the provincial capital Betschkerek, via Stefansfeld, and there temporarily locked up.

"New Year's Eve we were again chased through the streets of Betschkerek to the railroad station. Along the way we were spit upon, yelled at, pushed and beaten. The train moved very slowly, and when it came to a halt I saw the church steeple of Modosch. At daybreak family members appeared: parents, grandparents and children. Word was passed around and they brought straw, clothing, bedding and food. First the Russian guards did not let them to the trains, but they pushed forward and finally, with the help of some packs of cigarettes, they let the cars containing the Modosch women be opened and the items passed over to them. But the children, that wanted to join their mothers, were not allowed to approach.

There were four trains with about 60 cars each and it was a blessing for the people locked inside that the Romanian engines still had not arrived and the trains remained at Modosch for several days. Thus most of the prisoners could obtain a few things for their long frigid trip into the unknown. The Serbian partisans tried to prevent the supply of the prisoners, however the Russians, who had already taken control of them, stopped them. Then we left the Modosch train station. There were heartbreaking scenes that I shall never forget; parents, grandparents and children clung to the railroad cars, crying and screaming. The partisans and Russians beat them with fists and rifle butts till they fell back and the trains could move forward. He, who never experienced it, can probably never understand how it feels to be torn brutally away from your children, parents and grandparents and not knowing where one is being shipped to. It was terrible. I never saw my poor mother again.

The train moved very slowly through Romania. It stopped occasionally, but the doors were never opened. At Ploesti, we received, for the first and last time, some food for the 15 days trip. At the Russian border we were transferred since the Russian railroad was of a different gauge.

January 18th, 1945 we arrived at Kriwoi Rog in the Ukraine. It was terribly cold. The five, six houses in the camp were all wet inside. The very next day after our arrival we had to start working. It was very hard, strenuous work; loading and unloading gravel, bricks, coal and carrying railroad tracks etc. Our Russian female guards, armed with rifles, constantly yelled at us to work faster. There were days when we thought we could no longer go on.

We were often told we could go home, but these were always just lies. One evening we had to stand in formation in the courtyard. New officers arrived and inspected our hands and feet. They too said we could go home, but it wasn't true. The next day we were loaded an trains and taken to Dnjepropetrowsk. There we Modosch women were again divided. The camp I was assigned to had barracks. It was a large camp and surrounded by three layers of barbed wire, just as in Kriwoi Rog. We were treated like bad criminals.

During our stay in Russia we were never paid for our work. But our sleeping accommodations at Dnjepropetrowsk were good; we had plank beds. At Kriwoi Rog we had iron beds, but no mattresses and only wire and two women had to sleep in one bed; we always slipped an top of each other. A few days after our arrival we had to report for medical examination. We had to disrobe completely and, one at the time, enter a large room in which our 13 lieutenants were sitting. They were laughing and cracked suggestive jokes – only to degrade us.

The second day we were in Dnjepropetrowsk the Russians placed a large barrel with salted herring in each corner of the courtyard and told us we could eat as much as we wanted – and some did and died. Thus we lost our Modosch compatriot Perenz Leni and Pockemüller Anna from Pardan. We told them not to eat from the barrels since the salt was bad, but their hunger was stronger.

In 1946 I became so homesick that I had a breakdown. I was unconscious for two days and two nights. The nurse, from Transylvania, later told me that I wept a lot and always called for my child.

During the summer of 1946 they called for volunteers who were willing to work straight for twelve hours and then have 24 hours off. I noticed that the Russians sent those home that could no longer work. Therefore, I volunteered for the hard work in an iron mill. The first thing we did every evening, when we came home, was search for lice. Later I followed the advice of a Russian and used kerosene. While my head had a kerosene odor, I had no more lice.

In 1946 many of our deported men died; they often just keeled over and died.

I don't know why, but women were able to endure better. Many inmates suffered from lack of vitamins, had large sores an their backs which were very painful – but they still had to go to work.

The winter of 1946 was very cold and many suffered from frostbite, as they did in other winters too. I was among them; my toes and heels in particular were affected. The water pipes were frozen and for six days we had no water. For cooking we brought water from the river Dnjepr, but there was no water for washing. Sometimes we had no bread for three to four days.

In January 1947 we were supposed to go to a medical examination, but who were the physicians? They were our 13 officers! We were told to listen carefully. They told us who was going home and therefore immediately relieved of work. We were supposed to recuperate and eat well. (I was one of them.) But the food became progressively worse and we always were fed last. The so-called soup was only hot water and I noticed I became worse day by day. I knew I could not survive on that food and I was getting weaker by the day. At the end of January a nurse told me to sell what jewelry I had left otherwise I would not be able to make the trip home. I still had two rings and a set of earrings and sold the latter. With that money I could buy oil, sugar and bread. Thereafter I felt better and the nurse saved my life with her advice.

In May 1947 we actually departed from Russia. For the entire trip through Poland all we had was one loaf of bread, nothing else. When we crossed the bridge to Frankfurt/Oder we fell onto our knees and thanked God that we had left the Soviet Union."

In the following report Mrs. Bernauer writes that even during the first few weeks in East Germany she was close to starvation. Not having any news from her husband, who was also deported to Russia, nor from her child and parents she became despondent and lost her will power. It took three weeks of great efforts and help by the Engel couple, where she was supposed to help in their household, to get back an her feet and regain her will to live. Gradually she learned of the terrible fate of those who stayed behind in Yugoslavia.

"Meanwhile I learned that my dear mother had died in the Yugoslav camp. I had longed for her. I heard nothing from my son. On September 12th my husband Joschi found me. On the 15th we were already on our way to Graz, Austria. I didn't feel well.

Yearning for my child made me ill. But it was important to have Joschi at my side, I was no longer alone. We did not know where our boy was, not even whether he was dead or alive; the same about my father. After we finally made contact with my father, he wrote us that he also was searching for little Joschi, but could not find him either. He finally succeeded in 1949. He was now in contact with him and we also established letter contact. Our son, like so many of the Danube Swabian children, was in various children homes. The intent was to re-educate them and the frequent moves to other camps was supposed to make them lose all their traces. The Communists did not want to relinquish the children. They had made already considerable progress in their re-education; many children did not recall anything about their background and did no longer want to be Germans. Now our Joschi could speak only Serbian. He was indoctrinated to hate everything German. 'Druze Tito' was his idol. He went to school only when he felt like it; usually he was only tending hogs. Finally, on November 10th, 1950 we could hold our child in our arms; by that time he was twelve years old. He was part of a children relocation transport and we could receive him at the Austrian-Yugoslav border.

My husband and I were, of course, happy to have our son back. However, we had no idea of what was ahead of us. He did not want to attend school and did not want to learn. His father was very patient with him and every evening tried to teach him. But the boy tore up the papers and threw them at his feet. He continuously rebelled and stated that only 'Druze Tito' could command him and nobody else.

Two months went by and the situation did not improve. Then my husband said to me: 'You know I never beat the child, but my patience is coming to an end.' One evening they were doing math together and the youth screamed at his father: 'You do it, I go back to Tito.' Thereupon my husband took the strap, administered some strokes and said: 'As long as you only think of picking fights, steal and have a big mouth, you'll get the strap three times a day.' My husband and I endured much and we no longer knew what to do with our child. These were the results of the long separation and brutal ethnic re-education.

We emigrated to the United States, but everything stayed the same. One day when we were in church, my son told me, in front of all the people: 'If you think I am staying here, you are mistaken, I am going back to Tito.' On the way home my husband said to me: 'When we get home you fix the meal, we eat and then you pack Joschi's suitcase. Give him 20 Dollars and he can go wherever he wants to, I don't want to see him here anymore.' It hurt me very much, I wept a lot, but packed his suitcase and my husband showed him the door, telling him to go and only come back when he was willing to change. Your mother and I were never fighting with each other and we don't want to do it with you either. When he was outside my husband locked the door. Our boy sat on the stairs for two hours, contemplating. Then he knocked at the door and said: 'Father, let me in.' The boy explained that it was difficult for him to change because he was educated so differently under Tito. However, he was going to try. I believe deep down he suffered much more then he let it be shown. Nobody can imagine how the boy, and we as well, suffered. But slowly things were improving. He also served two years in the military. There he discarded everything that was troubling him due to the Tito-education. He wanted to become an engineer and he succeeded.

I also want to mention that later on the two Joschis got along quite well. They were one heart and one soul. My son now loved his father very much and when the father became very ill, the son came every evening to visit him. I too have an excellent relationship with my son. Almost every day he comes; he is happily married, has two married daughters and three grandchildren."

Chapter 5: Total Expulsion and Transfer to the Camps

"Austreibung", expulsion, was the customary expression of the Danube Swabians for the final removal from their homes and the complete evacuation of the ethnic Germans from the German villages. This was the result of the ruling of the "Anti-Fascist Council of the People's Liberation of Yugoslavia" (AVNOJ), the preliminary legislative board of the partisans. The ruling was issued on November 21st, 1944. In an "ex-judicial ruling" it declared the ethnic Germans "enemy of the people" and decreed their loss of all civic rights. Then it ordered the total expropriation of all their movable and immovable possessions. Deprived of property and all rights they could be chased out of their homes and interned in Camps.

Thus, total internment could be accomplished. 167,000 Danube Swabians were affected. The ones able to work came into work camps, the unable to work: mothers with infants up to two years of age, children up to 14 years of age, adults over 60 and infirm were shipped to the six liquidation camps in the Vojvodina, two in Slavonia and two in Slovenia. The expulsion was carried out between the end of November 1944 and August 1945.

In the Batschka, the Neusatz/Novi Sad county was the first to be "ethnically cleansed" in this manner. Its ethnic Germans were chased out of their homes between December 2nd–4th, 1944 and immediately divided into categories. The able-bodied remained mainly in the local camps or were transferred to the central civilian camp at Neusatz. The unable to work had to start their trek to Jarek within one to two days. Jarek originally housed about 2,000 ethnic Germans and was completely evacuated. It served, after December 2nd, 1944, as a concentration camp for the South Batschka.

Considering that the mass expulsion in the Banat also started at the beginning of December 1944 one can justifiably describe it as the "December wave" of internment. The next wave took place in the South and West Batschka, just before and after Easter 1945. The Middle Batschka followed about May 25th. The ethnic Germans of some West and North Batschka communities were completely expelled between the end of June and the end of August 1945. The usual "modus operandi" of the expulsion in the rural communities, mainly or totally inhabited by ethnic Germans, was as follows:

Partisan commandos secretly encircled the community and suddenly, beginning at one end of the village, began to chase the unsuspecting and unprepared inhabitants from their homes. They were chased to the village pasture at the edge of town where three to four thousand villagers were awaiting their screening: the separation of the able-bodied from those destined for the death camp. If a child was two years old or less, both mother and child went to the death camp. But if the child was older than two years, it was torn from the mother and shoved to a grandmother or other relatives or neighbours. The mother went to the work camp, the two years old or older child with the transport to the liquidation camp. Many a mother tried to smuggle herself over to her children.

The following description of the expulsion in Filipowa is a typical example of what happened in hundreds of villages. Rita Prost-Pertschy describes her expulsion experience on March 31st, 1945 as a ten years old girl:

"Saturday before Easter the women were baking for the Easter holiday when they heard loud cries and sobbing from the street. To their horror they saw people being chased from their homes at the lower end of the village. Hastily my mother put on several layers of clothing and my sister's new coat. Then we collected food in a blanket, but it was too heavy for me, so I threw half away and ran into the house to find lighter items. When I got into the courtyard, the partisans were already in front of the gate. They shouted: 'Napolje! Brze, brze!' We did not understand those words, however, when they started beating us with their rifles, we knew it was a situation of survival. They were beating mother, but she did not hurt too much since she wore several dresses.

A long line of people was moving past our house and we were shoved into the line. We now realized we had to leave our home forever. The women cried and prayed to God. The partisans chased us like cattle from the village to the pasture. There people were lying crowded together like a herd of animals. Here we spent the first day.

At daybreak they took every second woman and chased her into a house. When the women came out again, crying, they no longer had their bundle and no more jewelry. Also part of their clothing was removed. We met our aunt; she only had the empty baby buggy left. She had to put the baby into it without any bedding. When night came we had to search for a place to sleep. The partisans chased a group of 20 to 25 people into the courtyard of a house where we had to sleep in the open. The next day it started all over. Back to the street. People were robbed again of everything they had. This continued for three days and nights. We were sitting on our bundles in the dust and dirt and found out that people were even shot. (In Filipowa two men and a woman were shot.) I shall never forget these days, full of tears and sorrow. However, sometimes they were also full of hope, when we were told we could go home tomorrow.

The nights were particularly difficult. The children cried because they were hungry and freezing. Dogs were barking all night, being hungry and left alone in the houses. A few days later they were all shot. During the night you could hear the women crying and praying. While we still were under the stars of our homeland and the wind was still the same; however everything else had changed. I was particularly sad during the nights. I was longing for my father and sisters. We did not know where they were.

On the last day when the plundering started again, it was my mother's turn. The partisans dragged her from the column and into a room. When I wanted to hold on to her I was slapped in the face. I felt no pain since my fear for her was greater. I was happy when I saw her emerge alive. But this joy did not last long. Mother was ash-pale and her body shook. When she wanted to say something to me, blood streamed out of her mouth. Blood also dripped from her ears. Her gold-covered teeth were broken out and the earrings torn from her ears …

The next day started with a murder in front of our eyes. At daybreak we were chased to the railroad station. In front of us walked a man who continually laughed. I could not understand this. Our situation was anything but laughable. He wanted to join our row. When one of the partisans saw this, he came to us in a rage and shouted at the man, who continued laughing. The partisan beat him with his rifle butt, however, the man continued laughing. His wife tried to pull him back, but then the rifle cracked and the man sank to his knees. The blood spurted in a high ark out of his body and his face turned pale. But his mouth continued to laugh. At that moment, I developed a fright of uniforms and weapons which will stay with me for life. The women had to dig a hole right then and there into which he was dumped, his body still warm.

We were thinking of Easter, but it was not a time to think about celebration. We were stuffed into cattle cars. The partisans did not care whether families stayed together. The cars were sticky from the wet straw on which hundreds were shipped days before, going in the same direction. We were crowded with no place to lie down. When the train started moving, I was glad the doors were shut … We did not know where this trip would take us. But we sensed we were going farther and farther away from our homes. When, after many hours of torture the doors were opened we saw that we were shipped to the Gakowa liquidation camp."

This is how a purely German speaking community was extinguished – 182 years after its settlement. Additional shocking reports of the expulsion of ethnic German inhabitants can be found in LW II and III.

The expulsion of ethnic Germans in the cities took place in a somewhat different manner. In the cities like Sombor in the Batschka, ethnic Germans lived among Hungarians and Slavs and thus had different ethnic neighbours. These were supposed to notice as little as possible of the expulsion of their ethnic German fellow citizens. Therefore they were "collected" in secret actions during night. The author of this chapter, Dr. Georg Wildmann, had to personally experience one of these nightly actions when, on March 13th, 1945, he, not yet 16 years of age, was taken away from his hometown Filipowa, together with a larger group and interned in the barracks of the central camp at the Bezdan street in Sombor which was the capital of the Batschka province.

"It was during the last week in March – or early April 1945. We were lying, tightly cramped together in our barrack, which had no sleeping facilities, only some straw. We all were exhausted from the day's work in the city, tormented by lice and hungry; nevertheless, we fell asleep. During the night we were awakened, chased out and escorted by the partisans into the city. The fear that this could be our last march was constantly with us. A long line of horse-drawn wagons stood in the darkened street. Each four of us were detailed to one wagon, a grouchy coachman and a partisan were our companions. Towards midnight we proceeded to the first German houses. The partisan chased the occupants, that had already gone to sleep, out of their beds. Weeping and only skimpily dressed they stood in the street where another partisan took over and led them away. Inside the house our partisan companion told us in Hungarian: 'If you take anything, we'll shoot you down like dogs.' On the kitchen table stood a freshly baked cake. Nobody touched it. The partisan ordered us to take the still warm bedding and throw it onto the wagon. He cleaned out the closets; on the wardrobe he found an identity card. 'So', he said, 'he was a member of the 'Kulturbund' ('Cultural Society'). He'll be put on the black list.' We proceeded along the street. More and more wagons came together. A commotion in front of a house, apparently belonging to a German. We took only underwear inside and stacked it up. Filled up whole rooms – a house full of underwear. Then we proceeded to a house that had only bedding – with our shoes we stood on sheets, blankets and pillows then a house full of clothing … and had a first inkling of how many thriftily acquired and guarded belongings were trashed during the first night of the 'collectivism'."

Sources:

Rita Prost-Pertschy, *Das Heimweh der Simon Rita* (The Homesickness of Simon Rita), Sersheim 1994, 54–57; Anna Niklos-Nyari, *Nachruf auf verlorene Jahre. Eine Heimatvertriebene erzählt,* Karlsruhe 1991, 40–61; Paul Mesli/Franz Schreiber/Georg Wildmann, *Filipowa – Bild einer donauschwäbischen Gemeinde,* Bd. 6: Kriegs- und Lageropfer, Wien 1985, 92–109, 114–118; Georg Wildmann, VDJ, 144 f.; Juliane Supper, LW II, 170–173; Marianne Himmel, LW II, 514 f.; Jakob Diel, LW III, 452 f.

Chapter 6: Central Civilian Internment and Labor Camps

Overview

The internment of the Danube Swabians in Yugoslavia in central civilian labor camps began October 1944; the internment of the Gottscheer and German Unter-steirer took place at the end of the war. By August 1945 all communities of Yugoslavia were "cleansed" of their ethnic German inhabitants. Only Germans married to other nationalities or the few that had joined the partisans were spared from confiscation of property and internment.

In their process of the complete annihilation of Yugoslavia's ethnic Germans, the Communists established three types of camps: work camps, central civilian camps and "special camps". The latter served as liquidation camps for those unable to work.

In July and August 1945 the central camps and work camps reached their maximum capacity of about 120,000 civilian internees, of which over 100,000 came from the Banat and Batschka. They consisted mainly of marginally able-bodied men and women.

There were ten central camps in the Banat, nine in the Batschka and one in Syrmia, and about 200 work camps under the jurisdiction of the central camps. Almost each community with more than 200 to 300 German inhabitants maintained a work camp, consisting mostly of empty, pillaged German houses. The situation was somewhat different in Slavonia, therefore central, work and extermination camps of that region are presented together.

The central camps were set up primarily in existing barracks or former factories. Some were filled with several thousand internees in cramped facilities. These camps served, particularly in the Banat, during the "bloody autumn 1944" as the partisans' torture and execution stations.

The central camps allocated laborers for its work camps. The food provided for the forced laborers was usually completely insufficient. Starting in spring 1946 Slavs and Magyars could "buy" laborers for a day, month or longer periods (payable to the camp's commander; the prisoners did not receive any remuneration). For those lucky ones, it was often a life-saving opportunity. The condition in the central camps often resembled those in the liquidation camps. This is borne out by the fact that about 12,000 men and women, mostly of able-bodied age, perished between the end of 1944 and the beginning of 1948.

6.1 The Central Camps in the Banat

(LW III, 696–698; VDJ, 127 f.)

"Milchhalle" at Groß-Kikinda/Kikinda (LW III, 698 f.; VDJ, 127 f.) Already by the middle of October 1944, immediately after the take over by the Russians and partisans, it became a torture and murder camp for over 1,000 defenseless civilians. Subsequently, it was the central camp for the northern part of the Banat until the end of 1946.

"Alte Mühle" at Groß-Betschkerek/Zrenjanin (LW III, 699 f.; VDJ, 128) It was probably the most gruesome execution camp for the Germans during the *bloody autumn 1944* and later gradually became a central camp until May 1947.

"Stojković-Telep" at Werschetz/Vršac (LW III, 700 f.; VDJ 128) The town Werschetz, in the South Banat, was also notorious for the murders committed there. After the killing orgies of the *bloody autumn 1944* came to an end, it served as a central camp.

"Stockhaus" at Weißkirchen/Bela Crkva (LW III, 701 f.; VDJ, 128). This building too, was used for the torture and executions of hundreds of victims, before it was transformed into a Southeast central camp of the Banat.

"Schuschara/Šušara" (LW III, 702 f.; VDJ, 129) On December 24th, 1944 the whole village was declared a central camp for the German civilians of the surrounding area. For a time, children, old and ill civilians were housed there as well. It existed until spring 1947.

Karlsdorf/Banatski Karlovac (LW III, 702 f.; VDJ, 129) Established April 27th, 1945; it contained also children and old people until October 1945, when they were transferred to the liquidation camp Rudolfgnad. At Karlsdorf 1,000 occupants, including 400 documented by name, died of starvation.

"Fischplatz" at Pantschowa/Pančevo (LW III, 703 f.; VDJ, 130) This camp was established November 1944 and dissolved February 22nd, 1948. The conditions in the overcrowded barracks were horrible and led to diseases and epidemics. The commander, a cruel female named Radojka, indulged in torturing the defenseless victims.

Banat-Brestowatz/Banatski Brestovac (LW III, 704 f.; VDJ, 130) November 1944 – Early 1948. This camp contained, among many others, several thousand inhabitants of the city of Pantschowa, incapable to work, until October 1945, when they were shipped to the liquidation camp Rudolfsgnad.

"Seidenfabrik" at Kubin/Kovin (LW III, 705; VDJ, 130 f.) Towards the end of 1944, after termination of the murderous "Action Intelligentsia", this silk spinning mill was made into the central camp for the surrounding communities. It contained about 600 detainees. Commander was Silača Drašković.

Mramorak (LW III, 705 f.; VDJ, 131) By the end of April 1945 all those inhabitants of Mramorak, not yet interned, were put into several houses, together with children, ill and old people from the surrounding area. Beginning November 1945, children, old and sick people were all shipped to the liquidation camp Rudolfsgnad.

6.2 The Central Camps in the Batschka
(LW III, 756–759; VDJ, 132)

Neusatz/Novi Sad (LW III, 759–764; VDJ, 132 f.) Already in November 1944 the notorious central camp Neusatz was the first of its kind established on the swampy banks of the Danube River in the South Batschka.

Initially it contained able-bodied men and women from the South Batschka region. After additional central camps were created, it became the main "trading center" for this modern slave-trade and engaged in a continuous exchange of inmates with other central and liquidation camps. The sick ones were shipped to the liquidation camps and exchanged for still somehow usable workers. From here, many were selected for the deportation to Russia at Christmas 1944.

Even though the camp had a steady occupation of 2,000, it consisted only of two windowless barracks and a notorious "bunker" of six square metre. For even the slightest trespass, inmates were thrown into the waterlogged structure. For many the long ordeal of standing in the water was fatal.

The numerous mistreatments and murders without court proceedings, even though the war was over, induced Dr. Wilhelm Neuner, formerly Oberlandesgerichtspräsident (equivalent to president of a state appeals court) and also internee at the camp, to send written complaints to the ministry of the interior at Belgrade. These complaints were secretly smuggled out of the camp. For his courageous actions he was locked into the "bunker". He then was passed from camp to camp, but continued his written complaints and was eventually expelled to Hungary. The camp is said to have been closed during the last days of March 1948, when its occupancy was down to about 400. There are no records of how many of the inmates have perished.

Palanka/Bačka Palanka (VDJ, 134) The central camp Palanka was set up in November 1944, containing 14 to 15 years old boys and 60 to 70 years old able-bodied men from its surrounding area. Eventually it grew to an average of 600 internees.

Sombor/Sombor (LW III, 766–768; VDJ, 134 f.) The town of Sombor, as already mentioned in a previous chapter, turned out to be the "turn-table" for the persecution, internment and murder of the Germans in the West Batschka. It was established in November 1944 and also had jurisdiction of the central camps Hodschag, Apatin and Filipowa.

Thousands of ethnic Germans were stuffed into the lice-infected barracks, often mistreated, insufficiently fed and forced to work weekdays as well as Sundays. Whoever became sick was immediately sent to the death-camp Gakowa which was established on March 12th, 1945. The first camp commander was Rajko, the second one Dusan Kurepa. Both were cruel sadists, the second one even worse, he personally committed at least 13 murders. He sent for his victims, beat them almost to death and then cut their throat. The camp was one of the last to be closed sometime in March 1948.

Apatin/Apatin (LW III, 769 f.; VDJ, 135) This town was originally inhabited by 12,000 Germans. During the winter the local camp, under the overall jurisdiction of Sombor, suffered from starvation. The camp commander Mito Volić was particularly cruel. His deputy, Milivoj Beljanski from Sombor, took girls from the camp into his apartment and raped them. Later he was demoted and dismissed. His successor tied women to trees, whipped them until they became unconscious and threw them naked into the cellar. His specialty was to electrify naked women's breasts and genitals.

Hodschag/Odžaci (LW III, 770 f.; VDJ, 135) This camp too, fulfilled its purpose, particularly in the investigation and persecution of members of the *Kulturbund* (cultural society). Those arrested were never seen again.

Filipowa/Bački Gračac (LW III, 771–775; VDJ, 136) Because the liquidation camps Gakowa/Gakovo and Kruschiwl/Kruševlje were overflowing by mid-1945, this camp was opened between the middle of June to the middle of October 1945 for able-bodied, as well as those unable to work, of the Hodschag area. In this short time about 250 perished due to starvation and epidemic diseases. By October 1945, about 2,000 had died of starvation at Gakowa and since there were now openings there, those unable to work at Filipowa were shipped to Gakowa.

Seidenfabrik at Werbass/Vrbas (VDJ, 136) Towards the end of 1945 this former silk factory was established as a central camp for the Germans of the Middle Batschka. It also had jurisdiction over the relatively large work camps at Tschervenka, Kula and Weprowatz. The conditions there were worse than in a prison. Since there was no more work to be done in the fields as of December 1946, the camp commander made the inmates stand in formation from five to eleven o'clock during the bitter cold winter mornings. Then he let them sit till evening in the courtyard. The camp was most likely dissolved the beginning of 1948.

Sekitsch/Lovčenac (LW III, 776–778; VDJ, 136 f.) This used to be an entirely German community at the eastern edge of the German settlements and in January 1945 was transformed into a central camp for about 6,000 Germans. In October 1945 it was reduced to 1,500 inmates and was functioning as a work camp. Most of the rest were taken to the liquidation camps of Gakowa and Kruschiwl at about the time their inmates were dying in great numbers. Before they were shipped they were searched once more and deprived of their last miserable belongings. They even had to exchange any still somewhat useful clothing they wore for torn rags.

Stärkefabrik at Subotica (LW III, 778–780; VDJ, 137) This former starch factory was most likely converted into a central forced labor camp by the middle of November 1944. The 4,000 inmates were mostly Germans who earlier had fled to Hungary, but tried to return to their homes after cessation of the war. Upon crossing the border from Hungary they were immediately robbed of all their belongings. According to reports devastating typhus epidemics raged throughout the camp. It was most likely dissolved in January 1948.

6.3 The Central Camps in Syrmia

(LW III, 867; VDJ, 139)

Kalvaria at Semlin/Zemun (LW III, 867–872; VDJ, 139 f.) After the murderous stations in the villages India and Ruma were transformed into work camps, the central camp established on the Kalvarienberg (Kalvarien mountain) was apparently the only one of this kind. According to Hans Volk, it was a barracks area 100 metre × 200 metre, fenced in by high barbed wire. The inmates were Germans from the town of Semlin and the few Germans that did not flee from the eastern part of Syrmia. They had to sleep on bare wooden cots and forced to perform hard labor from 3 am till late at night. They were repeatedly and mercilessly beaten. The food was hardly any better than in the death camps: In the morning watery soup with some ground corn (maize), at noon soup with a few rotten potatoes or wormy peas and evenings whatever was left over from noon, with a slice of corn bread, without fat or salt – the same fare as in other camps. The central camp Semlin was evacuated in August/September 1945. As Hans Volk recalled, there were only about 150 men and 60 women that survived. These were shipped to the work camp in the nearby Bešania and in November 1945 after this one was also shut down, transferred to the death camp Mitrowitz/Sremska Mitrovica.

Reconstruction of the Railroad Belgrade–Slavonski Brod (LW III, 871 f.; VDJ, 140 f.) Hans Volk was present when, on April 12th, 1945, 660 men from the Kalvarienberg camp were picked to repair the railroad line Belgrad–Slawonski Brod. This notorious construction lasted probably till May 16th, 1945 about five weeks (including travel time to and from the construction sites). The food supply was completely inadequate and the work period punctuated by almost incredible killing episodes.

Here are some excerpts from Hans Volk's eyewitness report: "Daily several people passed away; on the way to Slakovci twelve sick were sorted out, shot and buried. When we moved on towards Semlin/Zemun and arrived there on May 25th, 112 out of 661 men were already dead and 20 more died during the following two days."

Georg König, another eyewitness from Filipowa, commenting on the fate of an 82 years old who could no longer walk well: "The partisans grabbed him, threw him into a lime pit where he burned, still being alive. Whoever could no longer walk was thrown into the ditch and beaten to death. About 20 men broke down, brutally beaten with carbines. I had to cover the graves with the dead and still alive, stamp on them and listen to the moaning of the ones still alive. The two partisans then agreed that the sick and weak should be beaten to death. Thus, about eight o'clock in the morning of May 2nd, 17 men were beaten to death with axes. From 480 men there were only 120 still alive. While we were 480 on April 20th, only 71 were left on May 8th."

Source reference

The descriptions and identification of the central civilian camps are based on reports of the surviving forced camp laborers. The major part of these reports are located at the *Deutsches Zentralarchiv* Bayreuth (Ost-Dokumentation 2). Their systematical evaluation was undertaken for the first time by the Danube Swabian "Arbeitskreis Dokumentation" ("Working Team Documentation"), published 1995 in Volume III of the series *Leidensweg der Deutschen im kommunistischen Jugoslawien* (The Suffering of the Germans in Communist Yugoslavia), which in more than 200 pages deals with the central civilian and the liquidation camps. This volume (abbr. LW III) is the main source reference for the previous summarized description. The same working team also issued the summarizing book *Verbrechen an den Deutschen in Jugoslawien 1944–1948* (abbr. VDJ), dealing with the same matter.

Chapter 7: The Liquidation Camps

Until the publication of the *Leidensweg*-documentation there had been no systematic description of the death camps which were an essential instrument for the execution of the premeditated genocide of the Danube Swabians in Yugoslavia.

The condensed descriptions in these pages are based on the incidents in the death camps as published for the first time 1995 in volume III of the documentation *Leidensweg der Deutschen im kommunistischen Jugoslawien* respectively in the *Weißbuch der Deutschen aus Jugoslawien 1995* (The tragedy of the ethnic Germans in Yugoslavia). They are the depositions of first person experiences of the survivors of the death camps. Most of the original reports are located at the Bundesarchiv Bayreuth (German Federal Archives at Bayreuth).

Eight Liquidation Camps for Danube Swabians in the Autonomous Province Vojvodina and Croatia (Slavonia), two Camps in Slovenia
(LW III, 707–893; VDJ, 125–127; 146–148).
In addition to the numerous local work camps and central camps the Tito-regime established a third category, officially called "special camps". In the Batschka, they consisted of the entire villages Jarek/Bački Jarak, Gakowa/Gakovo and Kruschiwl/Kruševlje. They were already established during the end phases of the war. In the Banat too, entire villages such as Rudolfgnad/Knićanin and Molidorf/Molin were designated as "special camps". For the relatively few Germans that did not flee from Syrmia, the silk factory at Mitrowitz/Sremska Mitrovica was converted into the notorious liquidation camp, whereas in Slavonia, sections of the villages Kerndia/Krndija and Valpovo were fenced in and made into death camps. The first liquidation camp was established on December 2nd, 1944 at Jarek and the last one, Rudolfsgnad, was closed in March 1948.

The two Slovenian liquidation camps Sterntal/Strnišće and Tüchern/Teharje, as well as the two Croatian camps Kerndia and Valpovo, were dissolved one year after the end of the war. The surviving inmates were expelled to Austria or to the Vojvodina. The camp Jarek in the Vojvodina was also closed one year after the war ended and the inmates transferred to Kruschiwl; Syrmian Mitrowitz and Molidorf, two years after the war and the internees of Molidorf were sent to Rudolfsgnad. Kruschiwl and Gakowa closed after about two and a half years (early January 1948) and their inmates sent to Rudolfsgnad – this largest liquidation camp was also the last one to close, March 1st, 1948. Thus three years after the war ended all camps were officially dissolved. At Rudolfsgnad, the remaining Germans were forced into mandatory three years "work contracts" outside their own home communities. (This means, the internment was converted into a banishment.)

Conditions at the Death Camps

The following examples are typical of the conditions in all liquidation camps. The inmates of the liquidation camps were usually those unable to work, people over 60, the infirm, children up to 14 years of age and mothers with children below two years old. These were usually already separated from the able-bodied at their home communities. The heart-rending scenes at these sites are described by the survivors in the depositions. We just want to mention here that all children over age two were literally torn from their mothers or relatives.

The mentioned villages in the Batschka and Banat which served as liquidation camps consisted of several hundred homes and were not fenced in, presumably because there was not enough barbed wire available. Therefore, they were closely guarded, around the clock, by the partisans or militia. The sentries were positioned every 100 metre. Leaving the camp was prohibited under penalty of death. The houses, built closely together as originally laid out by the Pannonian plans, had closed-in yards, but no front yards which made it possible to imprison the people in the houses as well. The houses, already completely ransacked, were, depending on room sizes, crowded with 15 to 20 occupants per unheated room or stable. As a rule, occupants had to sleep on the bare floor, often without even any straw or blankets. During daytime they also had to stay indoors. Due to the insufficient hygienic and sanitary conditions, they were defenseless against the flees and lice, brought along by the soldiers, which was particularly painful for the older people.

Food was scarce and often withheld for days. When available, it consisted mainly of ground up corn or flour soup, barley or pea soup, but without any salt or fat and a little coarse corn bread. It is noteworthy that the executive committee of the people's assembly of the autonomous province Vojvodina decreed in December 1945 that the bread for all camp inmates had to be made of corn flour without any wheat flour added.

Since no food was delivered to the camps until the middle of 1946 and the attempted begging trips by children and mothers with babies to the neighbouring villages of the Magyars and Slavs was severely restricted, the predestined annihilation by starvation of the inmates proved to be very effective. The death tolls increased rapidly.

Initially, the camp management made no efforts to provide any medical service. The one or two Danube Swabian physicians among the internees in the various camps had no medications with which to treat the sick and feeble. Personal hygienic and sanitary facilities were utterly insufficient for the overcrowded camps. Starvation diets, dystrophy and lack of vitamins weakened all to diseases. Consequently, by late autumn 1945, malaria, typhus, dysentery etc. reached epidemic proportions. The buildings which contained the sick became death houses. The winter months of 1945/46 were the worst in the liquidation camps, the last of which existed until March 1948.

The facilities in which the internees were contained had no heating even during the frigid winter months 1945/46. The use of any kind of fuel such as wooden fences or empty sheds were prohibited. No blankets were provided and their only protection against the bitter cold was the clothing they wore or the few covers some were able to bring along. It was not until the spring of 1946 when DDT powder was shipped from the USA that the lice problem could be contained and the death rate drastically reduced. The use of DDT powder, however, was only decided, when the partisan guards were about to contract the diseases and a countrywide epidemic envisaged. A further improvement of the conditions took place when the partisan guards were replaced by the militia or regular military.

The burial of the poor deceased was miserable and undignified as was their suffering and dying. When disposing of them to the mass graves they were roughly thrown onto wagons like dead cattle. The farewell by the still living family members was indescribably painful. As a rule there was no clerical assistance and relatives were not even allowed to attend the burial. The dead were thrown, usually naked (as ordered by the camp management), into the pits.

The Camp Victims – Horror Balance Sheet

Based on thorough research, presented by Mr. Karl Weber in volume IV of the named documentations, the extent of the perished victims in the liquidation camps, including the work camps and central civilian internment camps, are:

Civilians, interned in Yugoslavia from October 1944 onwards: 166,970.
Of these *perished*:
1944: 1,500; 1945: 21,832; 1946: 20,275; 1947: 4,075; 1948: 765;
(males: 16,878; females: 25,987; children: 5,582. *Total: 48,447*)
36,000 (figures rounded off) of these perished at the following liquidation camps:

Molidorf/Molin	from Sept 1945	to Apr 1947		3,000
Rudolfsgnad/Knićanin	Oct 1945	Mar 1948		11,000
Jarek/Bački Jarak	Dec 1944	Apr 1946		7,000
Gakowa/Gakovo	Mar 1945	Jan 1948		8,500
Kruschiwl/Kruševlje	Mar 1945	Dec 1947		3,000
Mitrowitz/Sremska Mitrovica	Aug 1945	May 1947		2,000
Kerndia/Krndija	Aug 1945	May 1946		500
Walpach/Valpovo	May 1945	May 1946		1,100

These are low, conservative figures. They are based on the investigations and compilations by the communities which, after their flight and after the war settled in their new home countries.

Since up to 70 percent of the victims could be accounted for by name and are documented in volume IV of the before-mentioned series, the averages of the casualties could be calculated.

They are very reliable figures. These somber numbers confirm the fact that 90 percent of the victims lost their lives long after World War II had ended.

The physical and mental anguish, which the victims had to endure up to their death, cannot be adequately expressed in words or print.

The mass graves were purposely made unidentifiable. Only in the late 1990s some half-hearted efforts were made to make the mass graves at Rudolfsgnad/Knićanin in the Republic of Yugoslavia and those at Kerndia in what's today Croatia visible by markers.

For the general public, up to this day, the genocide of the ethnic German citizens of the former Yugoslavia has remained a "non-event". Nor have any of the murderers, several of whom are still alive today, been charged in any courts.

7.1 Liquidation Camps in the Autonomous Province Vojvodina

Camp Molidorf/Molin (Banat)
Established September 1945 for the ethnic Germans of the North and Middle Banat.
Original Size of community: 1,200.
Number of internees: 5,000–7,000.
Duration of camp: September 1945 to April 1947 (20 months).
Casualties: about 3,000 (2,012 documented by name).
Main cause of death: starvation, typhus, malaria.

The ethnic Germans of Molidorf had to endure the sadic brutality of the local partisan chiefs even before the establishment of the death camp. In addition to the looting by the Red Army, partisans and particularly the residents of the surrounding Serbian communities, they immediately began with the arrests and torture of ethnic German men and the rape of women. Mayor Georg Haverkorn and four men were brutally beaten to death. At Christmas 1945 58 women and eight men were deported to Russia.

Between September and November 1945 the Yugoslav authorities began cleansing some 20 local work camps of men and women unfit for work, children and mothers with small children who were herded, in long marching columns, into the Molidorf death camp. The community, which originally had only 1,200 inhabitants, was stuffed with 5,000–7,000 occupants.

The camp administration often withheld food for days. Breakfast usually consisted of boiled water with ground corn (maize), no fat, nor salt. Lunch was always pea soup, also without fat or salt. Dinner: 150 gram corn bread, no fat. The hunger drove the inmates to catch and eat the cats in the village and, during the nights, to make their way into the neighbouring villages e. g. Torda and Hungarian Zerne to beg for food. Whoever was caught by the partisans was either brutally tortured or immediately executed.

In addition to the starvation and scurvy, the infestation with lice led to the demise of many inmates. The end came always the same way: The feet began to swell, then the face and after a few days, death.

The ones still able to work were separated from the totally unfit and had to perform hard labor, day or night. Whenever the church bells rang they had to report for work. The shifts often lasted up to 20 hours. They also had to carry all the wood, corn flour for bread and the entire provisions for the camp from the railroad stations of the neighbouring communities. Many had to carry loads of up to 30 kilo, with insufficient clothing and bad shoes along snowy and icy roads. They were slave caravans. Whenever somebody broke down, which happened frequently, sympathetic men or women, who wanted to come to their help, were beaten with rifle butts and brutally mistreated.

Camp inmates had to suffer not only from starvation and lack of other necessities, but also from continual torture and mistreatments. These mistreatments were carried out not only by the camp commander and the guards, but also by Serbs who came into the camp and picked out their victims. In one instance, Marianne Haberkorn, received repeated bloody beatings by her former farm hand who shouted: "Now we subordinates are the masters."

The camp commander was a sadist. His name was Danilo Kesić and supposedly he came from Banatski Dvor. Here is an example of his sadistic actions: On February 18th, 1946 at five in the morning he chased 30 women, without any reason, into a water ditch where they had to remain for half an hour in the icy water and mud. Then they were chased to work, in their dripping clothing. They were given no food and after work, at about 17:30 o'clock, they were chased back. Three of the women were so weak they collapsed. The first two were left where they fell and died the same night. The third was able to drag herself into the village. The first two women were 25 and 27 years old and left behind three small children. Seven other women became seriously ill.

According to statements of Dr. Jenö Heger, himself an internee who was allowed to practice as camp physician between January 1st and February 22nd, 1946, the health condition of the inmates was extremely bad. There were no sanitary installations, people had no soap or other cleaning materials to keep themselves clean. Rashes and other skin diseases were widespread. Among the infectious diseases, particularly typhus has to be mentioned, since it spread rapidly because of the weak body resistance of the inmates. During his position as camp physician, the daily mortality rate was between six and seven.

In view of the hopelessness of their situation and the inhuman torment, more and more inmates risked their escape to Romania. During one of such attempts a young woman from Kesić was killed. Since Dr. Heger could no longer tolerate the barbaric punishment of women and the reckless use of fire arms by the camp commander, he filed a complaint against him and also fled to Romania.

Dr. Steiner, from Zerne, who temporarily functioned as camp physician, tried to help the sick, but his possibilities were very limited. The only medications available were some aspirin, quinine, carbon dust against diarrhea and a skin cream against skin diseases. Cold compresses were the general treatment against all diseases.

There were no mass graves at Molidorf. 24 old men, designated as grave diggers, had to dig, in addition to the graves required during the day, additional holes as a reserve for the next day. The dead were sewn into old blankets and buried without any ceremony.

Taking Dr. Heger's daily mortality figures as a base, the extended number of the casualties for 20 months would be about 4,000. Mr. Karl Weber's estimate of 3,000, is also within the same proximity. 2,012 are documented by name in volume IV of the documentation series *Leidensweg der Deutschen im kommunistischen Jugoslawien.*

At the end of April 1947 the partisans dissolved the Molidorf liquidation camp and transported the inmates to the camp Gakowa in the Batschka. Only about 300 younger inmates who were still able to work, in spite of all the mistreatments, were retained and used for agricultural work in the Molidorf area.

This place of horror was totally destroyed by a flood during 1955/56 as if nature wanted to extinguish all memories of it.

Camp Rudolfsgnad/Knićanin (Banat)
Established October 10th, 1945 for ethnic Germans unfit for work, particularly of the Middle and South Banat.
Original size of the town of Rudolfsgnad: 3,200.
Number of internees, average: 17,200 average (maximum: 20,500).
Duration of camp: October 10th, 1945 to mid-March 1948 (29 months).
Casualties: about 11,000 (7,767 documented by name).
Main cause of death: starvation, typhus, malaria.

Overview
The large "special camp" Rudolfsgnad was located at the edge of the ethnic German settlement area of the Banat. Traffic-wise it was well-situated and easy to control since it was positioned at the point where the river Theiss flows into the Danube. Of the town's 3,200 inhabitants, 900 did not flee.

Before all the camps in Yugoslavia were officially dissolved in 1948, all their remaining inmates were transferred to Rudolfsgnad. There all remaining ethnic Germans were conscripted into three years "work contracts", mostly serving in areas outside their home territories, e. g. the mines of Serbia and Kosovo and the marsh areas of Baranja, Batschka and around Pantschowa. For about three years they were not allowed to leave the assigned places, i. e. as from 1948 to 1950 they still were not really free but banished people.

The health conditions, illnesses, treatments and mortality statistics were well documented by Dr. K. F. With 11,000 deaths Rudolfsgnad had the highest mortality rate of all the camps.

Immediately after its occupation, Rudolfsgnad experienced the furor of the persecution. Responsible were the commanders *Rado Perz* of Perles and *Lazo Milenković* of Tschenta. Under their command, on October 16th, the Danube Swabians *Jakob Werth*, *Franz Hess*, *Franz Metz* and *Michael Wacker* were tortured, shot and hung from acacia trees. *Johann Drumm*, out of desperation, hung himself. *Anton Karl*, 78, was shot for no reason. Milenković wanted to execute all Rudolfsgnad men, but was prevented from doing so by Russian officers.

On December 27th, 1944 47 girls and women as well as 20 men were deported to Russia as slave workers. On April 14th, after the village was completely ransacked, the Rudolfsgnad inhabitants had to leave their houses. Then all the women and children were concentrated in the school building and the men age 14 and up in the Kindergarten. The gypsy *Gajo*, also known by the names *Arandjelski* and *Bočarac*, commanded the guards.

As of October 10th, 1945 the Tito-regime interned thousands of ethnic German civilians, predominantly senior citizens, women with children and children whose mothers were shipped to Russia and concentrated them in the now empty houses. The camp was guarded by about 80 armed militia.

The arrivals, dressed with only minimal clothing were crammed into the empty houses, usually 20 to 30 to a room. They had no blankets and were forced to lie on the floor which was only barely covered with straw. During the entire period of the camp's existence and up to its dissolution in March 1948, the straw was never changed nor replaced.

Nourishment consisted of ground corn soup, polenta (maize) mash, corn bread and tea, no salt. Even babies and feeding mothers received nothing else or any additional rations. Initially, the usual camp soup was ladled out, but already in the winter 1945/46 it was given out scarcely and the inmates received only about two kilogram raw ground corn per month. Soon there were no more wooden fences, barns or fruit trees left. The inmates had to cook their own meager rations which they tried to augment by adding edible grasses or clover to fill their empty stomachs. They gulped down anything they could get their hands on.

Klara Deutsch, at that time only 13 years old, records: "People became blind or insane because of starvation, or they just lied down, went into a stupor for a few days until they fell asleep for good. The worst off were the ones that became insane. They screamed day and night; many walked around aimlessly, could not find their way home and died in the street." Stray cats and dogs were butchered, even dead ones were eaten. The sufferings from diarrhea are indescribable; they drained the last strength from their bodies and also led to other diseases. Once hit by diarrhea or dysentery, there was rarely a recovery. That winter thousands died.

These conditions forced people to desperate attempts to slip out of the camp and beg for food in the surrounding villages, inhabited by other nationalities. The Catholic priest Johann Nuspl, formerly priest at Tscheb in the Batschka, remembers that during one of these begging trips four women and five children were shot by the guards. The ones caught were usually locked into the cellar, called the "bunker", received almost no food but instead fierce beatings which some did not survive.

Cooking in the camp's kitchen resumed in spring 1946 and was considered a comfort not known for many months. The soup consisting of peas and barley was, for those that survived this terrible winter, the essence of delicacy. Beginning 1947 the food rations were somewhat improved; however, for the emaciated inmates hardly noticeable. As of May the restrictions on receiving packages was eased for the Serbs and non-camp internees. Also, many who had related or acquainted Serbs, could occasionally benefit from these relaxed restrictions. The Care program and the International Red Cross relief actions were supplying some camps. Now even packages from America arrived, sent by relatives who learned of the misery at Rudolfsgnad, father Nuspl reports.

Beginning May 1946 a "softer touch" in the elimination started at Rudolfsgnad as in other camps as well, apparently directed by higher authorities and due to political considerations. Now parcels could be shipped directly into the camp. The larger aid program, initiated by Peter Max Wagner and his Danube Swabian Aid Society of Brooklyn, started towards the end of 1946. The first phase of large-scale parcel shipments from the USA probably reached the camp around Christmas 1946.

Starting spring 1946, Serbs and Hungarians in the surrounding area could "lease" camp inmates for work, at a rate of 50 Dinar per head. The Germans were often shamelessly taken advantage of by their employers. Nevertheless, the inmates eagerly competed for this slave work since they received at least some food whereas there was almost nothing to eat within the camp. For many this outside work opportunity was a lifesaver. Also, starting in spring 1946 and particularly in 1947 many inmate workers took this opportunity to escape. At an opportune moment they sneaked away, searching a way to cross the border into Hungary or Romania. It was always a life threatening undertaking.

The heroic endeavors of the camp physicians and nurses, who themselves were internees, to fight against diseases and the epidemic were mostly in vain. The deplorable hygienic conditions, the meager rations, lacking salt and vitamins contributed to the spread of the epidemic. The physical and mental deterioration of the humans robbed them even of the strength to defend themselves against the infestations of lice, mice and rats that suddenly appeared in large numbers. Where the rats didn't find anything to eat they started to gnaw not only at the dead but also the defenseless living. The mortality rate reached its peak in February 1946.

Finally, the spread of the epidemic alarmed the authorities and a medical commission arrived to investigate. Quarantine was declared and the camp was sprayed with DDT powder. The group of physicians and nurses, risking infection themselves, worked selflessly to fight the epidemic and to save the humans. Nevertheless, many succumbed. In April 1946, after the epidemic was eradicated, the quarantine was lifted and the camp received a "clinic" for adults, a "children clinic" and a "children home". There the food was somewhat better than in the camp.

The "homes for the aged" were virtual dying places. Father Johann Nuspl, a camp inmate himself, was allowed to visit the homes in Molidorf as well as Rudolfsgnad twice a week. He writes about his visits: "The sick and dying were lying on the floor which was covered with a thin layer of straw, tightly crammed together and separated only by some loosely placed tiles. Dirty bowls with rotten food leftovers, pots serving as spittoons, unwashed bed pans, dirty rags etc. were scattered among the sick and dying; many in their own feces. This was the last chapter of our people's tragedy. I had never seen our people in such misery and downcast as here, however, at the same time so heroic. Most of them died composed and god-devoted. I remember with awe and reverence the people in these homes."

The partisans' treatment of the ethnic German children is one of the saddest chapters in the chronicle of the Yugoslav liquidation and slave labor camps. One has to keep in mind that the initial occupants of the dying camps consisted of boys and girls under 14 years of age.

Lorenz Baron, assistant to electrician Weissmann who had to install electric lighting in the so-called "children home", writes: "Upon entering the home one could hear a monotonous hum. It was the song of the children dying. Every room of the large building was full of defenseless, dying children. Not able to express any feelings myself, I climbed up the ladder and installed the fixtures. Some of the skeletons below me were still able to move somewhat and followed every move I made. Some then fell back, their gaze still focused on me – and were dead. Nobody showed any compassion, knowing that we ourselves could be the next to die."

The same author writes also: "We went daily to the pump well to drink water. There the children were sitting and catching each other's lice. Almost all had the scabies, pussy corners of the mouth and the cheeks of some were already rotten off, the teeth exposed like on a skeleton. Most were quietly weeping and listless, yet, the groaning of the poor children could also be heard outside the house."

During the summer 1946 the authorities then began to allocate groups of children to government children homes in order to assimilate them as "good citizens" into the national fold.

The camp administration and militia, belonging to the camp guards, were housed in the town hall. Some followed their orders off and on, others, however, were very evil. Franz Apfel, 14 years old, was caught going begging, beaten unconscious by the guards and, presumed dead, dumped into a manure pile. Regaining consciousness, he mustered all his strength to free himself and crawl to the next house where, with some help, could get back to his family.

As camp commanders were recorded Gajo (Arandjelski or Bočarac), a partisan woman Zlata and finally Čeda Stamatović (VDJ, p. 163).

Leaving the camp was strictly forbidden. Dr. K. F. recorded eleven executions in 1946 and three in 1947. In spring 1947 two men cutting down a tree were caught by a policeman and shot. Out of desperation eleven inmates committed suicide. Every death and cause was recorded. The month of February had the highest mortality: 1,346. February 4th had the highest daily number: 72. Total deaths during the existence of the camp (October 10th, 1945 to March 1948) were over 11,000.

The first mass graves were dug at the village cemetery. Due to the floods in spring 1946 no more dead could be buried there, but had to be moved to the Teletschka hill, about two kilometre south of Rudolfsgnad.

Camp Jarek/Bački Jarak (Batschka)
Established December 2nd, 1944 as a concentration camp for the unfit to work of the South Batschka.
Original number of inhabitants of the community Jarek: 2,000.
Number of camp inmates up to 15,000.
Duration of camp: December 2nd, 1944 to April 17th, 1946 (16.5 months).
Casualties: at least 7,000 (5,240 documented by name).
Causes of death: typhus, dysentary, exhaustion, dystrophy.

This community consisted of about 350 houses and was entirely ethnic German. Fortunately most of the inhabitants fled before it was captured by the Red Army and the partisans. Only 54 persons stayed behind. The entire community was declared as the first "special camp" for those ethnic Germans of the South and Middle Batschka that stayed behind. It was planned for the unfit to work of the regions Palanka, Neusatz/Novi Sad, Schabalj/Žabalj and Titel as well as some communities of the Kula region. The liquidation camp Jarek was also a collection point for the ethnic Germans from the Batschka and Syrmia who were put to work and survived, completely exhausted, the notorious Syrmia work projects, such as the rebuilding of the rail link Belgrade–Bosnian Brod.

At times the number of camp inmates numbered as many as 15,000. It was dissolved April 17th, 1946 and the survivors were transferred to the liquidation camp Kruschiwl. During the existence of the camp at least 7,000 civilians became mortality statistics of the mistreatments, starvation and epidemics. Mr. Karl Weber registered 5,400 by name. The victims came from 75 communities, predominately from the South and Middle Batschka as well as from Syrmia.

The peculiarity of the mistreatments of the Jarek camp consisted in the virtual confinement of the inmates to their lodgings. They were only allowed to come into the street to receive their scarce and almost inedible meals, for which the church bells were rung.

According to the hometown chronicle of Futok, the meals were dispensed from

19 kitchens. About 500–600 persons were served by one kitchen. New arrivals, however, received their first meal only after the eighth day. Normally three meals a day were served. Breakfast consisted of ground corn boiled in water; lunch was usually a soup, some barley or peas, also boiled in water, occasionally bugs included and 200 gram of coarse corn bread. Dinner was again soup.

The first camp commander who came from the neighbouring village Katch was relieved of his command because he was too humane. In his place came Jana Dragojlović from Banoštor, Syrmia. She was young, but very much dreaded and considered sadistic. She usually rode on horseback, attacked unsuspecting women and children, pulled them by their hair, whipped them, had them tied to trees and beaten untill blood flowed from their noses and mouths. Her usual comments while perusing the daily list of the dead was: "Not enough have died, more have to die." When she was rotated she remarked to the incoming commander: If he was going to annihilate 7,500 Germans within five months as she did, there won't be any left.

The guards were considered more sadistic than in other death camps and more trigger-happy. According to Katharina Frank they received for each kill a special furlough or other bonus. Katharina Haller had to witness how her own father was murdered. He was gunned down while trying to get a few potatoes from a nearby field.

Fritz Ilg also reports: "Daily the partisans came since some of us still had good clothing. We had to give everything away, while being beaten. An old man used to ask: 'Why are you beating me? I gladly give you my shoes, you don't need to beat me!'" Susanne Harfmann tells of three women who were murdered while coming back from a begging trip: "The three women were lying only 50 yards from the village; they were riddled by bullets. Next to each was a small bundle with food for themselves and their starving children."

Among the clergy interned at Jarek were also Kornelius Weinmann, Franz Klein, Karl Elicker and Kaspar Kopping. They were selected for particularly rough mistreatments by the partisans, ridiculed, beaten and had to perform the worst jobs.

Martha Müller describes the appalling conditions at the infirmary: "The sick were lying on the floor on a bundle of straw and waiting to die. They all had diarrhea and the lice were crawling over their faces. As soon as they were dead we took them out to the horse stable. The camp commander Jana repeatedly jumped on their chests and shouted: 'You Swabian, have you kicked the bucket?'"

Peter Wilpert, at that time six years old, talks about a somewhat older boy who climbed over fences to be with his mother who became insane and was tied to a post. "Her gaze was staring into a void. Her son sat in front of her, weeping silently. Even though I was younger then he, I sensed that it was his greatest pain to realize his mother did no longer recognize him. For me it was a heartbreaking scene."

Martha Müller was appointed head of the "children home". She relates: "The children were left to fend for themselves, neglected, dirty and lice-infested. They were sitting or lying around in the corners, usually in a state of shock. Nevertheless, they continued trying to break out of the home and go begging to the neighbouring town Temerin, an attempt that often was fatal. There was nothing we could do to prevent the mass dying; they were too weak and starving. One day they were still playing in the yard, the next day they were dead on their bundle of straw. Maybe it was a blessing that many a mother does not know how her child had to die. I repeatedly had to witness that the last words of children were: "Mother, please give me a piece of bread."

Many of the inmates coming from the village Bulkes in April 1945 collapsed since they arrived during a period when no salt was available. Ten to twelve inmates succumbed daily due to starvation, diarrhea and exhaustion. No medicine was available. The physician Dr. Hans Müller and pharmacist Öhl, both inmates themselves, tried to help and concocted some heart drops from a mixture of herbs. Even though they were not effective, they nevertheless had a psychological benefit and people were grateful.

Katharina Haller describes the misery and dying in Jarek: "Wherever you looked, you saw people shrunk to a skeleton who were trying to pick the lice from each other's body. They were lying on their straw bundles, conscious or unconscious and waiting for death to arrive. Most of them had sores over their entire bodies. Children had oversized heads and stomachs and one could count each bone. Some slept and died, others were struggling desperately with death. They couldn't help one another since everybody was helpless."

When Agathe Prohaska visited her great grandmother who was dying in the horse stable, the latter whispered to her: "My child, the dogs are biting at my feet." When she checked she saw that the rats were gnawing at her great grandmother's toes even though she was still alive.

Karl Weber, who was eleven years old at that time, relates his feelings about the dying children: "They died without their mother and without loving care, medical help or compassion. We were so stoic that we felt no sorrow about somebody's death. On the contrary, we were relieved that another crybaby disappeared. Everybody was concerned only with his or her own survival." Many of the surviving children report that, after having been witness to so many miserable deaths, they could no longer shed any tears, even at the death of their own family members. They were completely devoid of feelings and in a state of shock.

The last journey of the dead was equally inhuman. The daily removal of the many corpses had to be done with primitive means. A rack wagon was the hearse. The corpses were thrown into the wagon, one on top of the other, like the disposal of dead stray animals. In the mass graves, they were dumped, nude, in layers of up to five deep and then covered up. Family members were not allowed to be present, nor any clergy.

The Bulkes community has exact documentation on the perished occupants of the former hometown Bulkes. According to these records the chances of survival at the death camp Jarek were as follows: for children up to and including 14 years of age only about 50 percent. Adults from 50 to 54 years old about 30 percent and from 55 to 69 about ten percent; older ones practically nil.

Camp Gakowa/Gakovo (Batschka)
Concentration camp for the unfit to work, primarily for the Middle and West Batschka.
Original number of inhabitants of the town of Gakowa: 2,700.
Number of camp inmates: 17,000.
Duration of camp: March 12th, 1945 to beginning January 1948 (33 months).
Casualties: Approximately 8,500 (5,827 documented by name).
Main cause of death: starvation, typhus, dysentery, malaria.

Overview
On March 12th, 1945 the two neighbouring communities Gakowa and Kruschiwl, situated near the Hungarian border, became the two large death camps for the ethnic Germans of the West Batschka. The 6,000 ethnic Germans of Apatin were the first inmates. Between March 13th and October 17th, 1945 the unfit to work from 24 communities of the districts Apatin, Hodschag/Odžaci and Sombor were interned in these two camps.

In the year 1931 the community of Gakowa had 2,692 souls, 2,370 were ethnic Germans. By the end of 1945 17,000 were crammed into the completely emptied houses of the community. Already during the first ten months approximately 4,500 had died or were murdered.

Since both death camps were not fenced in by barbed wire and watch towers, they were guarded by patrols and sentries, placed about 100 yards or more apart. The camps were surrounded by fields and meadows. Due to this arrangement it was at times possible to sneak past the sentries and go begging or to attempt escapes. The camp commanders punished such attempts with executions, incarcerations, beatings and witholding of food, which many victims did not survive.

The daily camp ritual was as follows: The still somewhat able-bodied were chased out by the guards and divided into work teams. Under guard they had to work in the surrounding fields, perform work in the camp or push carts around the area to collect anything burnable for the kitchen.

For about a year, lasting to May 1946, there was, according to the impression of the inmates, a definite annihilation program by starvation, exposure to cold and further aggravated by unforeseen epidemics. During that time the guards were particularly cruel. About half of the 8,500 victims died during the "months of death": November 1945 to March 1946.

According to reports of inmates the first commander was a Slovenian partisan named Kos, he was cruel. The second one was a partisan from Syrmia, Grabić, called "Shuzo". During his command the guards were most gruesome. From June 1946 the successor of "Shuzo" was Stevan Bradić, who practised a milder control.

The attempted escapes from Gakowa to Hungary started rather early. However, more frequent and larger escapes began with the loosening of restrictions and the replacement of the cruel guards. Relatives, friends and other helpful compassionate minorities also aided the escapees. Most of them continued their flight to Austria and Germany.

Beginning late autumn 1946 and lasting into fall 1947, the so-called "white escapes" were tolerated by the camp commanders. The term "white escapes" was used in contrast to the previous "black escapes" which were prohibited and severely punished.

The use of DDT powder in March 1946 also brought an end to the "months of death". The replacement of the partisan guards by a militia in May to June 1946 also reined-in the worst of the wanton physical mistreatments which, at that time, were also officially prohibited. Apparently the hard annihilation policy was replaced by a "softer" elimination process.

Now the forsaken children were taken to government education centers with the intent to reeducate them ethnically an to become "young pioneers", model fighters for communism. Four of such transports of children from the Gakowa camp are known to have taken place.

Starting May 1946, people outside the camp were allowed to bring or send packages to camp inmates. However, there was no mail service, only the receiving of packages was tolerated. American food donations could be distributed such as powdered food for undernourished children. American CARE packages began arriving by the end of 1946, shipped by the Danube Swabian Aid Society of Brooklyn and American relatives of camp inmates.

The neighbouring camp Kruschiwl was dissolved on December 10th, 1947 and their inmates transferred to Gakowa. By the middle of January 1948 the last inmates of Gakowa were moved to the Banat liquidation camp Rudolfsgnad.

Peculiarities of the Gakowa Camp
The primary reason for the rapidly growing mortality was due to starvation which became more acute by the middle of October 1945.

Josef Thiel narrates: "During the winter 1946 the news was passed around the camp that a horse died outside the camp. My sister and I as well as a cousin slipped out of the camp, cut off large pieces and brought them back to the camp. Since there was almost no firewood the meat had to be eaten half-raw. The cousin died from it. Whenever a dog or cat was found it was caught and eaten."

During the summer and early spring 1945 the first epidemics such as malaria, dysentery and dystrophy began to appear and caused numerous deaths.

Chaplain Matthias Johler voluntarily came to the Gakowa camp to look after the spiritual welfare of the inmates. He himself became sick with typhus and was bedridden for four weeks. Here is an excerpt from his diary: "December 1st, 1945. The Almighty took also my sister-in-law. The funeral is supposed to be today. Deep

114

in thought and worrying about the young orphaned children I went to the cemetery to see if the grave had already been dug. Upon entering I noticed two girls, shivering, trembling and weeping bitterly. They were looking for their mother. They tell me that a cart was passing by their house and picked up their mother. It was the cart, picking up the dead. 'Now we are all alone', lamented the older, eleven years old. 'Only me and my sick little four year old brother who is at home.' I ask: 'And whom are you holding in your arms?' She replied: 'That's my little brother, ten months old', and presses him, covered in a piece of cloth, to her shaking bosom; he was dead."

In January 1946, at a time when half of the crowded inmates in most of the houses were ill, the camp leadership decided to order an extensive regrouping, according to able-bodied persons, children of four to fourteen years of age, and the infirm. This was taking place precisely an the three days of the winter's most violent snowstorms. It was apparently done on purpose to expedite the annihilation. Eye-witness Eva Schmidt, née Knöbl of Filipowa writes: "People were just chased out into the street and some had to remain there all day during the snowstorm; half of them were already ill with typhoid. Many of the ill were pushed around in wheel-barrows. One had to get the impression that this was intentionally done to expedite the mortality rate – the mass dying started promptly after these three days."

"A buggy went from house to house to collect the dead who were loaded like pieces of firewood. Those who could not be collected were pushed to the cemetery on a wheelbarrow. This manner of transporting the dead was a daily occurrence. Mothers pushed their dead children out into the street, children their mothers. Some corpses were sewn into a piece of linen, but most had only their faces and waists covered since there was nothing available to cover the entire body. At the cemetery the dead were piled up in the mass graves like logs. The priest could only utter a general blessing. No family members were allowed to be present."

During the period of March 5th to April 4th, 1946 Wendelin Gruber relieved the chaplains Johler and Pfuhl who were ill. In a discussion with the camp commander he was able to obtain the permission for the inmates to go to church on Sunday evening, after completing their allocated work duties. He was, however, not allowed to conduct any service. But he disregarded the order and did preach on March 24th. The church was too small to hold all the people; many were standing outside. The church bells rang and someone played the organ. During the service they repeated the solemn promise that, should they survive, to make an annul pilgrimage and should they be able to get back their homes and possessions, to build a church in the honor of the mother of Jesus Christ. The Danube Swabian annual pilgrimage to Altötting (Germany), taking place since 1959 is the redemption of this promise.

The Chaplains Johler and Pfuhl, after their recuperation continued to look after the religious needs of the inmates, a heroic achievement, considering the persecution of the clergy by the communists. In January 1946 the camp administration attempted to prohibit further clergy activity in the camp. Nevertheless, the clandestine activity continued. On October 30th, 1946, however, both chaplains were also thrown into the camp as inmates.

The fate of the children was deplorable, writes Chaplain Paul Pfuhl. "When a child fell ill it was taken to the so-called children hospital. This term, however, is misleading. While it had some beds, they were too few and often three to four children had to share one bed. These children hospitals were the saddest site in the whole camp. Reduced to skin and bones, they were too weak to call for help and even their weeping was feeble. Their eyes conveyed unspoken sadness, like those of a wounded animal – and an accusation for the injustice perpetrated upon them. One had to muster all one's strength to leave without shedding tears."

Camp Kruschiwl/Kruševlje (Batschka)
Established as a concentration camp for the unfit to work of the West and North Batschka.
Original number of the inhabitants of the village of Kruschiwl: 950; thereof 900 ethnic Germans.
Average number of camp inmates: 7,000.
Duration of camp: March 12th, 1945 to December 10th, 1947 (33 months).
Casualties: 3,000–3,500 (2,100 documented by name).
Main cause of death: starvation, typhus, dysentery.

The village Kruschiwl was only four kilometre from the Hungarian border. On March 12th, 1945 it was designated as the liquidation camp for the Danube Swabians of the West and North Batschka. Between April 15th and 17th, 1946 it received a significant increase in inmates due to the transfer of survivors from the Jarek camp. About 100 persons, mainly old people and children, were crammed into each house.

The camp Kruschiwl was particularly notorious for the cruelty of its guards and series of public executions, ordered by the commanders. After being able to escape in 1946, *Therese Schieber* reported the following events: "On April 1945 we were forced to hand over all money, watches, rings, earrings, jewelry and items of value. On April 13th at four o'clock in the morning we were called out into the street and the process lasted until five o'clock in the morning of the 14th. We all had to stand there during that time, including women with babies.

Two women, *Theresia Peller* and *Rosalia Langbein*, were found to have hidden some change. Mrs. Langbein implored the partisan not to shoot her since she had a five month old baby. In vain, both women were executed. As a deterrent for the others, the corpses were left in the street until the next day.

On April 24th, 1945 *Anni Schreiner*, a 16 years old girl from Sonta, and the 31 years old *Elisabeth Piry* were taking meals into the field and then went to Stanischitsch to beg for food. They were betrayed and upon return to the camp arrested and locked in a cellar. Like criminals they were taken before the camp commander and

116

given a short tongue-lashing. A partisan, Hungarian, was ordered to execute them; however he refused. The next partisan's rifle misfired and a third was called. He first shot and hit Mrs. Piry who fell down; then he shot at the girl, but she was only slightly wounded. She walked towards the partisan and implored him to spare her. However, he dispatched the girl with a bullet into the head. The three grave diggers, who were present, were ordered to put the two women onto a cart and take them to the cemetery.

On the way Mrs. Piry regained consciousness, asked for some water and for her child. The six years old daughter was walking along and praying next to the cart. The mother told her to remain brave and tell her father what was done to her. The partisan guard at the village entrance noticed that Mrs. Piry was still alive and notified Djević Stanko the camp commander who mounted his horse and rode to the cemetery. There he ordered the gravediggers to put the gravely wounded but fully conscious woman next to the dug grave, shot her in the head and pushed her with his boots into the grave."

The two guard teams were notoriously quick with cruel beatings. Mrs. Schieber writes: "Women before being beaten had to disrobe so that the whips and belts hit their bare bodies. Just before Easter several women were caught sneaking out of the camp to beg for food for their children. First they were thrown into a cellar and then brought to the guard house where they had to disrobe. In the middle of the room were two chairs, with the partisans sitting around them. Always two women had to kneel down and grasp the chairs with their hands. Then two partisans began beating the bare backs of the women. When the two were tired they were relieved by two others. The women's backs were bloody and became festered. Most of them died of their wounds. Only the 'third generation' of camp guards, mostly Moslems, was somewhat more humane."

The cold winter temperature was also one of the premeditated procedures to reduce the number of camp inmates. According to Stefan Mutter, "during Christmas and New Year 1945, the partisans repeatedly chased us during the nights barefoot across the yard and we had to stand for two hours in the snow until we were stiff from the cold. Then they chased us back into the camp.

Most of the people became gravely ill. I myself suffered from an inflammation of the joints. Another draconian edict was that no heating of the inmates' houses were allowed."

During the autumn 1945 a typhus epidemic spread throughout the Kruschiwl camp, as it did in the neighbouring death camp Gakowa. Over ten people succumbed daily to this disease.

Another major factor, in addition to starvation and epidemic diseases, was the lack of personal hygiene and washing facilities, which caused infectious skin diseases. This problem and the bites of fleas and lice affected particularly children.

The dead were collected daily by a cart which at times had to make two or three trips a day.

Camp "Svilara" ("Silk Factory") at Syrmian Mitrowitz/Sremska Mitrovica (Syrmia)

Conversion of the former silk spinning mill "Svilara" to a concentration camp for able-bodied and unfit to work ethnic Germans of Syrmia.

Established: beginning August 1945.

Number of internees: average always exceeding 1,200.

Duration of camp: beginning August 1945 to May 1947 (21 months).

Casualties: about 2,000 (1,033 documented by name).

Main causes of death: starvation, typhus, and dysentery, freezing to death.

The city of Mitrowitz is situated at the southern border of Middle Syrmia, directly at the river Sawe. Until October 1944 it had about 3,000 ethnic Germans. Already towards the end of 1944, after capturing the city, the Partisans established near the jail a central internment camp for the Danube Swabians of the middle Syrmian region. In April 1945, after the retreat of the German and Croatian military forces from the western frontier area of Syrmia, additional Danube Swabians from Syrmia were added. (It was only on April 12th, 1945 that the Partisans occupied Wukowar.)

The central camp in the "Svilara" was established at the beginning of August 1945 and was henceforth fully occupied by ethnic German inmates from Syrmia, Batschka and Banat. At about the same time the Partisans dissolved the central camp Kalvarienberg near Semlin. In contrast to the liquidation camps of the Batschka and Banat, the internees at the Svilara contained not only unfit to work but also mainly able-to-work Danube Swabians. Most were needed for work in the City itself, however, many also were conscripted to work on the farms and in the Vrdnik coal mine.

The term *liquidation camps* is justified because, as evident from the personal experience reports, the inmates were supposed to be killed by whatever means.

The "Svilara" was set up in a complex of buildings of the former silk spinning mill. It was an area fenced in by barbed wire of about 150×80 metre, near the river Sawe. The internees were housed in the two-story main building of 50×10 metre. The windows were bricked up except for tiny openings. Due to the scarcity of space additional plank beds had to be made to accommodate over 1,000 internees. Children were separated from the women and housed in a different building.

As far as camp food was concerned, *Hans Volk* gives the most detailed description: "The bread that was delivered from outside the camp up to October 1945 was fairly palatable. Initiaily, the bread, that was baked inside the camp, was made of wheat, then corn meal and coarsely ground, finally only of coarsely ground corn (maize). At first, the smashed and crumbled ration was 250 gram, then 200 and finally only 150 gram. The rations, however, were often not fully allocated; some received only two handful crumbs – all only slightly salted. In the morning we received a quarter to one half liter "Einbrennsuppe", a watery flour soup. At noon and in the evening bean or pea soup.

Katharina Vogel, who was interned with a group on November 25th, 1945, found the following health and hygienic conditions at her arrival: we were told to find a roof over our head, anywhere. As we entered one room, we were breathless. Only the ones, who saw the dirt, misery, the sick and helpless, can imagine the misery. People were lying on plank beds or an the bare floor, without any blankets, unable to wash themselves. The stench was almost unbearable. Many were shriveled down to skeletons; most so weakened by starvation and disease that they could not get up anymore."

A certain *Jelovac* from Semlin was the responsible camp commander. Chief of the guards (the "Dežurni") was the 22 years old *Drago* from Lačarak, a feared sadist. He mistreated many camp inmates in his "torture chamber" of the former administration building until they were unrecognizable, most did not survive the torture. Among the guards there also were cruel individuals. *Katharina Geislinger* recalls: "I remember the names of two of our butchers who hailed from Sremski Jarak. They were the brothers *Stevan* and *Stanko Jovanović,* both about 27 and 28 years old. I knew both from my childhood years since they went to school with my brothers."

The liquidation process of the camp leadership during the winter 1945/46 included the additional method of killing off the ethnic Germans by exposing them to humidity and letting them freeze to death. Katharina Geislinger: "One day in January we were detailed to unload a barge with wood at the river Sawe. This heavy work which lasted 14 days had to be carried out barefoot, as specifically ordered.

For food we only received cabbage soup. For the work at the Sawe River the partisans selected ill people that had no shoes and could not survive the six kilometre round trip to their place of work and back. The result was a mass perishing.

Particularly during this winter season we had to stand every morning outside, in formation. Woe to the sick that did not immediately come outside. The guards, armed with truncheons, beat and kicked the poor helpless to the exit. Some were only able to make it by crawling."

Traudie Müller-Wlossak who speaks Serbian very well confirms that this was a planned liquidation. In December 1945 during a visit of a man in civilian clothing and apparently with political authority she overheard him asking the camp commander while marching along the row of beds: "How much longer will it still take until they are all finished? I am surprised that so many are still alive."

The Svilara camp also included a camp for children. It was situated about 400 metre away from the main camp in a house, previously German-owned. If the children were up to two years old, their mothers could stay with them. *Anna Borosch* was allowed to visit their children and she reports: "I was led to a house where all children were together, the small ones and the sick. The older ones were taken somewhere to work. Many were already dead and the ones alive only skin and bones. I saw only misery and distress. The little ones played amidst excrement. My older boy (twelve years old) was lying an a plank bed – half-dead. His joy was great when he saw me. His diarrhea was getting better, he told me. I said: 'Be good and eat only a small piece of corn bread, but repeatedly so you get used to it.' I could not say more since tears were rolling down my cheek and I had to leave. I quickly hugged them all one more time."

Some time after, the camp leadership found out that due to the mass dying many children had become orphans. One day they were picked up by trucks. Nobody knows where they were taken.

Starting the middle of November 1945 dysentery and typhus epidemics broke out in the camp. When the number of sick increased they were taken to a house which they named "sick house". Since they could not defend themselves against the lice and maggots, they slowly died off.

During the dysentery epidemic many of the afflicted rotted away, literally, while being alive. *Käthe Sentz*, pharmacist from Lowas who was detailed to care for the sick, writes that her care consisted basically to "drag the dead from the rooms".

Reports about doctors, who were rather reluctantly allowed to work, are rather sketchy. Apparently there were only two, also inmates, whose attempts to help were tolerated. Such help, however, could mainly be only symbolic since no medications were available. One was a German prisoner of war, the other a Danube Swabian, *Dr. Franz Ehrlich*. He even had a room at his disposal. How little he could help is documented by the statement of Hans Volk, that during the epidemic, the terminally ill were taken to a shed from which nobody returned to the camp.

Dr. Ehrlich kept a diary, which also had an entry of the death of his wife. The camp leadership ordered him to destroy the diary. He refused, saying his duty as a physician requires he keeps a Journal of his activities. That evening he was picked up together with a nurse, taken to the Sawe river, tortured, beaten to death and at dawn tossed into the river. The two corpses floated to the banks and were found by local people. According to Hans Volk, it was Drago who, together with an accomplice, committed the murders. Both were arrested and taken away. They did not return but apparently were not punished. This incident took place probably in April 1946. Whether this terrible event led to the replacement of the military by the militia cannot be confirmed, however, the change in the camp command resulted in a certain improvement of the inmates' situation.

With the outbreak of the epidemic the daily mortality rate increased rapidly. In January 1946 about ten to twenty died daily of starvation, illness or mistreatment. At the end of December 1945, there were 1,200 inmates in the camp. By the end of March 1946, there were only 350 left. Specifics: At the beginning of December 1945 72 women fit for work from Sekitsch (Batschka) were taken to the Svilara. By the end of March 1946 only twelve were still alive. Of the 69 women, who arrived on December 15th, 1945 from the work camp Betschmen (Banat), only eleven. Of the 17 from Karlsdorf 13 died at the same time.

As these figures show, most of the some 2,000 victims died during this period. 1,033 are recorded by name in volume IV of the documentary series *Leidensweg der Deutschen im kommunistischen Jugoslawien.*

7.2 Liquidation Camps in Croatia

Walpach/Valpovo (Slavonia)
Established: May 1945 for the internment of the ethnic Germans of Slavonia and other parts of Croatia.
Housing: wooden barracks fenced by barbed wire.
Number of internees: up to 3,000.
Duration of camp: May 1945 to May 1946 (twelve months).
Casualities: 1,000 – 2,000.
Main causes of death: dystrophy, dysentery, typhus.

Overview
Relatively few ethnic Germans settled in the central Croatian area around Zagreb; on the other hand, eastern Slavonia, which always was part of the core area of Croatia, by 1944 had a Danube Swabian population of over 70,000. Adding those of the Baranja, which presently belongs to Croatia, the total was 85,000 persons. Since most of them were evacuated before the communists took over, the newly formed People's Republic of Croatia (a federal state of Yugoslavia) had to apply the AVNOJ resolutions of November 21st, 1944 only to a fraction of the original ethnic German population. As far as the execution activity was concerned, it was considerably less gruesome than in the neighbouring Autonomous Province of Vojvodina.

Initially, the communist rulers of Croatia tried to rid themselves of their ethnic German citizens by interim internment and expulsion transports from their country. After all, these were, according to the AVNOJ proclamations of November 21st, 1944, completely deprived of civic rights and their properties confiscated. The pre-planned expulsions of the ethnic Germans were further confirmed by subsequent expulsion resolutions. According to *Vladimir Geiger* such resolutions were issued by the departments of internal affairs in the regional committees or municipal peoples liberation committees. Apparently, Josipovac and Valpovo were established as interim collection camps in May 1945.

Short Term Central Camp Oberjosefsdorf/Josipovac
Josipovac is situated about ten kilometre northwest of the City of Essegg/Osijek near the river Drau and had originally over 1,000 ethnic German inhabitants. This is where the first central camp for about 3,000 Germans from the entire Slavonian area and part of Bosnia was established. It existed from May 1945 to July 10th, 1945.

In contrast to the liquidation camp Svilara/Mitrowitz, the events in Josipovac did not have the appearance that it was planned to annihilate the inmates, although, sporadic murders, mistreatments and unjust punishments did occur. The commander *Tepić*, according to *Tscherny*, was a malefactor. The inmates were used primarily to work in the fields that needed to be attended to.

After the war one tried to get rid of the ethnic German fellow countrymen in the area of the emerging Federal State of Croatia (Republic of Yugoslavia), by deporting them. At that time this probably would have been the most humane solution if the transports had been handled in a more civilized manner. On July 8th, 1945 a rail transport with some 3,000 inmates was sent off. Nobody knew the destination. For two days they stood in overcrowded cattle cars at Leibnitz in South Styria (Austria), where they were driven off the train by their inhumane guards which then immediately left Austrian soil. Two days later the camp was dissolved and the few that had stayed behind were chased into the liquidation camp Valpovo, 16 kilometre away. It was a miserable trek, even drinking water was withheld during the searing heat.

Temporary Camp Velika Pisanica

After the successful expulsion of 3,000 camp inmates from Josipovac to Austria on July 8th, 1945 another attempt was made on July 22nd, 1945 to expel 1,800 persons by rail from Valpovo to Austria. About 70 to 80 persons were crammed into each cattle car. However, since the British occupation authorities in Carinthia refused to admit them, the transport had to return and after several days of aimless movements ended up at Velika Pisanica near Bjelovar in East Slavonia. The same happened with two further transports.

This camp, already overcrowded with interned Croats (Ustaschas, intellectuals and clerics), had no space for the unplanned ethnic Germans' arrival. For weeks they were held in the open market square, exposed to rain and bad weather. The two German priests were locked up with eight Croatian clerics in a pigsty. At least 6,000 ethnic Germans arrived within a few days, most of them were refused entry to Austria by the British. Some were returnees who had fled from the partisans in October 1944. Food supply was insufficient and more than 100 people died. Finally the disenfranchised ethnic Germans were shipped to the liquidation camps Valpovo and Kerndia on August 10th, 1945.

Liquidation Camp Valpovo

Walpach, mostly called Valpovo, by its Croatian name, is situated 26 kilometre northwest of Essegg/Osijek, in the lowlands of the river Drau. Originally the community contained a minority of about 400 ethnic Germans. The ethnic Germans of Slavonia and particularly those of the Essegg area were interned in the existing ten barracks which were fenced by barbed wire. According to *Josip Globočnik*, this camp was in operation up to June 15th, 1946.

According to Geiger Josipovac was officially named as a "collection camp", whereas Croation documents refer to Valpovo as "radni logor", i. e. "work camp". The Autonomous Province Vojvodina named camps which contained the unfit-to-work, meaning children, old age and infirm as "camps with special status". They were meant to be "liquidation camps", since the death of the inmates was intentional.

In this book, the camps Kerndia and Valpovo are included in the sub-category "liquidation camps" since – after the abortive expulsion attempts – they had the same objectives as in the Vojvodina: internment until death or some other disappearance. According to camp commander *Globočnik*, Valpovo had a flow of able-bodied inmates: They went out into work camps and came out of work camps. Thus the occupation of the camp had a steady 3,000 inmates. The small children and old people were left to die and the camp management and higher authorities were perfectly aware of that. The nourishment did not deserve this name and, together with indescribable sanitary conditions, the plague of lice, and frigid temperatures eventually had to lead to epidemics. Effective measures to combat the foreseeable epidemic scale of deaths were taken only in spring 1946, when the typhus epidemic began to threaten the surrounding areas.

The former camp commander Globočnik, in a statement summarizes: "Today, after 52 years, I have come to the following conclusion: Although, after the war, there was a great lack of food and medications, much more could have been done for the camp inmates, if only there would not have been incapable and hateful people in the ministry for internal affairs and other offices."

During the one year existence of the Valpovo camp, it registered, according to the detailed count of the local Catholic parish, 1,015 deaths, listed by names. Michael Hantler counts, together with the short-term camp Josipovac victims, also by name, 1,215 casualities. The Valpovo parish, for example lists 49 deaths on January 21st, 1946. Valpovo may have been, de jure, a work camp, de facto, however, it was a liquidation camp.

The barracks had no window panes, they were therefore boarded up; there was no light nor heating. People were lying on the bare bunks and floors, without straw and crammed together like sardines in a can; whoever could not find any space had to sleep under the sky in the inner courtyard which, during rain, became a mud field. But even inside the barracks, also dark during the day, rain came down through the leaking roofs. Men and women were separated by a fence.

The following *camp commanders* are mentioned by name: *Relja, Pšemislav Pospišil* and, starting the end of November 1945, the 23 years old partisan captain *Josip Globočnik*. Pospišil was his deputy. Since Relja was a heavy alcoholic, the inmate *Stefan Pfaff* took care of the camp administration. Globočnik had to rely on Pfaff's experience and a hate/love relationship existed between the two. The camp was under the jurisdiction of the ministry of interior at Zagreb, a handful of militia constituted the interior guard and a group of the Narodna Odbrana secured the camp from the outside.

Nourishment did not include sugar, nor salt or fat. Breakfast consisted of leaf-tea or sloe-tea, at noon a thin watery soup and in the evening again soup, occasionally laced with potato peels or bean shells; sometimes even a few noodles. Bread was made of coarsely ground corn (maize) or pollard. Daily ration was 100 to 150 gram.

They went to *work* at six o'clock in the morning, in torn clothing and the feet wrapped in rags or barefoot. Those able to work, including 13 and 14 years olds, were used for wood cutting in the forests within a radius of 30 kilometre of the Drau lowland. The inmates gladly went to work as unpaid slaves or leased workers to the farmers that were waiting at the gate. The camp management charged between 50 and up to 110 Dinar for them. The often very friendly and kind farmers gave them a hearty meal and frequently also some food to take along for their family. They were life-saving gifts.

The *hygienic conditions*, due to the primitive latrines and lack of washing facilities, were catastrophic. The *health condition* of the inmates became progressively worse due to the lack of food. After one month, many became ill with dysentery. This was the reason why, eventually, *Dr. Hartel*, the ethnic German Valpovo community physician, was allowed to visit the camp twice a week. However, he too was almost powerless, since there were no medications whatsoever at his disposal. When, at the beginning of 1946, there was an outbreak of typhus and up to 100 people daily became ill, neither he nor the additional two physicians *Dr. Vile* from Essegg and *Dr. Pekić*, county physician from Vukovar, who were called in to assist, could help. They themselves became infected. The mortality rate, which was already high, increased even more due to the epidemic. It was only when the infectious disease spread to the Valpovo community and surroundings, that the health authorities of Essegg did initiate effective vaccinations. Finally, when, as of April 1946, barrels of DDT powder from the USA against the plague of vermin and sulfonamid pills from the UNNRA, against the infectious diseases began to arrive, did the epidemic cease.

The highest number of deaths per day, in February/March 1946, is recorded to be 32. The *dead*, about 20 to 30 daily, were put onto an open wide wagon and taken, in all weather conditions, to the cementery. Due to the rough road, corpses fell off the wagon and were collected on the way back. Over 1,000 inmates, reliably recorded, perished miserably at the Valpovo liquidation camp.

The catholic priest *Peter Fischer*, even though ridiculed and interfered with, was allowed to conduct *religious services* and participate at funerals up to December 1945. In January 1946, after the holding of religious services was forbidden, and anticipating detention at the notorious prison Stara Gradiška, he was, with the help of Croatians, able to escape to Austria. His reports are very informative.

Camp Kerndia/Krndija (Slavonia)
Established: August 15th, 1945 for the internment of the rest of ethnic Germans of Slavonia and other parts of Croatia.
Original size of town: 1,672 inhabitants.

124

Number of internees: up to 3,000.

Duration of camp: August 15th, 1945 to middle of May 1946 (nine months).

Casualities: at least 500, probably much more (101 documented by name in volume LW IV).

Main causes of death: starvation and typhus.

Because of the close interrelationship of the events during the persecution of the ethnic Germans in the Slavonian region, it is appropriate to mention the civilian camps with partial central functions in Slavonia, including the central work camps Podunavlje in Baranja and Tenje near Essegg, together with the two liquidation camps in Slavonia. Thus the actions against the ethnic Germans become more transparent.

Kerndia was previously an ethnic German community, just like the liquidation camps in the Batschka and the Banat. Situated about 35 kilometre southwest of Essegg, it had, beginning October 1944, more than 1,300 ethnic German inhabitants. Except for six families that stayed behind, all of them (luckily) fled on October 27th, 1944 to the West. Most likely the reason for its selection as a death camp was its relatively small size and that the ransacked houses were mostly empty.

On August 15th, 1945 the arrivals from Velika Pisanica were chased, on foot, from the railroad station to Kerndia. Additional arrivals brought the camp's total ethnic German internees up to 3,000. They themselves had to fence in their camp with barbed wire.

Theoretically, their daily rations were (in gram): bread 200, flour 20, salt 5, oil 5, peas 40, corn flour 80 or potatoes 100. However, this was rarely complied with. The corn bread was, most of the time, only half-baked.

Camp commander was the forest worker *Ivan Tomljenović*, and assisting him a gypsy as a political commissar. He personally murdered a three-member family. The guard unit consisted, according to *Peter Seiler*, of twelve to fourteen partisans; four of them were females and considered as beasts. During a drinking orgy at the outpatient station, the guards murdered at least three persons, namely *Rosalia Loher*, a *Mr. Schmidt* and a 14 years old boy. They also wounded several more.

As far as medical services are concerned, there was an outpatient station, headed by a former female goose tender. However, she did have Aspirin and ointment at her disposal. Some time later, the surgeon *Dr. Kirchbaum*, also an internee, was added. The latter, however, died of typhus. Then once a week a veterinarian came to act as a physician; but he also had very few medical supplies. January 1946 the mass dying started. A typhus epidemic broke out. Here too, a desinfection program with DDT powder took place in March/April, otherwise all would have perished (and the epidemic spread over to the local population), according to Peter Seiler.

The precise death toll between August 1945 and middle of May 1946 is difficult to calculate. It should range between the minimum figure of 300 as documented by *Karl Weber* and *Peter Seiler's* estimate of 1,300. Due to the numerous scattered

German settlements in the Slavonian region, only few comparable personal fate reports are available.

Mira Knöbl – a Slavonian-German Anne Frank

A unique discovery gives a particularly informative picture about the fate of the internees at the Kerndia Camp: "Letters from Krndija", written by *Mira Knöbl*, born 1926. She experienced Kerndia, together with her father and during the nine months existence of the camp sent 40 letters to her mother, a Croat who lived outside the camp at their hometown Djakovo. These were forgotten and for 50 years in an attic. Discovered by Vladimir Geiger and published by him and *Ivan Jurković* they are available since 1994 in the Croatian language, titled "Pisma iz Krndije".

In a German-language postscript the publishers write: "It is somewhat of a Slavonian Anne Frank" (referring to the Jewish girl, who reported from the nazi concentration camp). *Goran Beus Richenbergh* adds: "Mira's letters are ... without doubt one of the most shocking testimonies of the genocide committed against ethnic Germans."

The Work Camp at the Puszta Podunavlje in Baranja

The ethnic Germans who were not released at the dissolution of the two liquidation camps Kerndia and Valpovo in May and June 1946, were transferred to the camp Podunavlje in Baranja. The commander of the camp and all subordinated Puszta work stations surrounding the camp, was *Andrija*, a Serb from Bjelo Brdo, a village located 15 kilometre east of Essegg/Osijek in Slavonia. He shot to death at least 22 people, mostly infirm, and women. Another commander was supposed to be a certain *Predrag*. He was also in charge of the state farm Belje in the Darda district of Baranja.

The work slaves in Podunavlje and environs numbered about 1,000. The camp was dissolved August 27th, 1946. The old and ill were transferred to the liquidation camp Rudolfsgnad in the Banat and the able-bodied to Tenje near Essegg.

Central Camp Tenje near Essegg/Osijek

The last central civilian camp Tenje in the Federal State Croatia of the Yugolsav Republic was located ten kilometre southeast of Essegg. It was established towards the end of August 1946. The commander's name was *Jovan Radić*. At certain intervals, early November 1946, about 130 persons were released to Austria; uniting family members may have been a reason, as well as the desire to chase them out of the country.

When the camp was dissolved on January 18th, 1947, the last inmates, numbering several hundred, were shipped to the liquidation camp Rudolfsgnad which existed for another year. There many of the newly arrived died of starvation.

It is very deplorable but characteristic for the arbitrary treatment of the outlawed ethnic Germans all over Yugoslavia, that in Slavonia, due to malicious denunciations, families that already had been released, were again interned during 1947; this time, however, to the most terrible liquidation camp Rudolfsgnad. They had to suffer there again until this camp was dissolved in March 1948, but many of them did not survive.

The dissolution of the Tenje camp completed the total elimination of the ethnic Germans in Croatia with the exception of those few married to non-Germans in mixed marriages who, according to the AVNOJ resolution of November 21st, 1944, were not persecuted.

7.3 Executions and Liquidation Camps in Slovenia

The executions in Slovenia had their own character. The mass murder of German prisoners of war, Serb Tschetniks, their own Slovenian soldiers and home-guard fighters, "bourgeois class enemies", potential political opponents and finally ethnic German civilians (Lower-Styrians and Gottscheers), represent a difficult to analyze but even bloodier case.

The *"Parliamentary Investigative Commission* for Postwar Murders, legally dubious prosecutions and other irregularities" of the state Slovenia under the presidency of Joze Pučnik determines in its 1995 interim report the following: "According to reports of community committees, statements of interrogated witnesses and statements which were published in news reports and other publications, there exist in Slovenia numerous mass graves in which, it is presumed, large numbers of persons were buried. The following grave sites were the most often named:

Tüchern/Teharje, the Hornwald of Gottschee (Forest of Kočevje/Kočevski rog), tank trenches near Rann/Brežice and Feistritz at the Sattelbach (Sotla river), Thesen/Tezno near Marburg/Maribor, Gutenhaag near St. Leonhard/Lenart, St. Heinrich at Bachern/Pohorje, at the Bachern/Pohorje mountain above Kötsch/Hoče, Sterntal/Strnišče (formerly Kidričevo) near Pettaus/Ptuj, air raid bunkers near Windischfeistritz/Slovenska Bistrica, Tepanje near Oplotnitz/Oplotnica, Karstcaves near Logatec, the Brežar abyss at Podutik, Zančan at Windischgratz/Slovenj Gradec, many mass graves in the surroundings of Cilli/Celje. The assembly of the Cilli community, in a special statement concerning the protection and temporary arrangement of the mass graves identified 29 sites.

The *Slovenian Opposition Demos* of that period, who also investigated, came to similar results. In addition, many ethnic Germans, who, after May 8th, wanted to flee from *Marburg* and were captured by the partisans, were thrown from the Drau Bridge near Marburg into the Drau river. The corpses were later swept onto the river banks. The true number of people who starved to death, were tortured to death, beaten to death or shot to death will probably never be determined. From later reports and summaries it can be concluded that about 6,000 German Lower-Styrians and Gottschees suffered a horrible death.

To answer the question who ordered the mass murders, the parliamentary commission came to the conclusion that the *responsibility* fell onto the KP of Slovenia (KPS), the Slovenian OZNA, the II. division of the KNOJ and sections of the partisan army of that time. The number of the murdered Slovenians, mainly "White Guard" members and Domobrances (who fought against the communists), is estimated to be 11,750.

All chiefs of the OZNA in Slovenia were members of the KP Slovenia. *Ivan Maček*, chief of the Slovenian OZNA, and his deputy Boris Kraigher, were members of the KPS *Politbureau.* It is presumed that the general instructions came from Belgrade *(Tito, Kardelj, Ranković),* but it is evident that the selection of the mass murder sites were "independent contributions of the Slovenian OZNA to the plan of the Yugoslavian Party which were carried out by the KPS in Slovenia".

Considering the result of the investigation, it is obvious how the responsibility for the annihilation of the estimated 6,000 Deutsch-Untersteirer and 1,000 Gottscheer was shared between the "top KP leadership" and the leadership of the Slovenien KP. The KP, respectively the OZNA of the State, executed the instructions of Belgrade.

A particularly gruesome method of killing was the firing into the abyss, caves and abandoned mines. The report of the personal chauffeur of Count Dr. Ferdinand von Attems, master of the manor of Windischfeistritz, describes a particularly gruesome mass murder.

Here is an excerpt: "The lives of all three *Attems family* members, the count, countess and oldest son, came to an end in June 1945. They were accused being supporters of the occupiers, and to have enriched themselves during the war. The real reason, however, was their wealth, which had to be confiscated. One night in June eleven covered trucks, containing shackled humans, arrived. At that time nobody knew who they were and where they came from. Later it became known that they all were, in addition to the Attems family, wealthy people, owners of large farms, tradesmen and merchants with their families. They were taken to an air raid tunnel about five kilometre from Windischfeistritz/Slovenska Bistrica where they were ordered to disembark: men, women and many young people. Nobody wore a uniform. Up to that point the trucks were covered with tarps, presumably so nobody would know what the trucks contained. The hapless victims had to disrobe and were chased into the air raid tunnel. The Partisans immediately opened fire and mowed down the ones in the back of the group. The ones in front may have only been wounded or not even that. Therefore, they tossed hand grenades after them and the tunnel entrance was immediately walled up" (LW II, 867).

Of all the locations where the internment, starving to death, executions of prisoners, ethnic Germans and "class enemies" were carried out, there are two that stand out and can be considered similar to the liquidation camps in the Vojvodina. They are the camps Sterntal near Pettau and Tüchern near Cilli. Additional work camps and internment camps were at the Castle Herbertstein/Hrastovec, at the seminary for priests at Marburg/Maribor, at the textile factory of Tüffer, at Thesen/Tezno and Bresternitz/Bresternica near Marburg/Maribor.

Liquidation Camp Sterntal (Strnišče) near Pettau/Ptuj
Established May 1945 for the internment and liquidation of ethnic Germans, Slovenian Domobrances (Home Guardsmen) and Weißgardisten ("White Guardsmen") who were fighting the Communists and potential enemies of the Communist regime.

Original purpose of camp: prisoner of war barracks during World War I and later housing for the factory workers of the nearby Aluminium factory.
Number of camp inmates: initially 3,000–4,000; later steady 8,000–10,000.
Duration of camp: May 1945 to October 1945 (six months).
Casualties: over 4,000.
Main causes of death: executions, starvation, dysentery, typhus and torture.

The barracks village Sterntal became the Golgatha of the ethnic Germans in the Lower Steiermark (Styria). According to *N. v. Preradovich* it had to be dissolved in October 1945 due to the protest of the International Red Cross.

J. K. born 1910, of Pettau reports on the number of internees and how the induction into the camp Sterntal took place. "In Pettau we were brought to the municipal jail. As a reception, we all received a beating. At night the same vehicle took us to Sterntal. There too the reception consisted of a beating. Here my whole family was together, however, the women in a women's section, separated from the men's section (all in barracks), by barbed wire ... I had to compile a list of the camp inmates (females and males). That's why I remember the number of approximately 9,500 inmates. I was not informed of the number of outgoing victims. A large number of inmates died of exhaustion, illness and beatings. Executions were carried out at the shooting range. At night you could hear individual shots or volleys coming from the range. The camp commander's name was *'Tine'*, he was the son of a saw mill owner near Windischgrätz."

The personal chauffeur of *Count Dr. Ferdinand von Attems*, owner of the Windischfeistritz estate, narrates: "The worst were the nights. Every evening the partisans appeared with long lists of names and every one who was called up knew what fate awaited him. They looked quietly at their acquaintances and friends then, with bowed head went to the door, their last walk. Half an hour later we heard the machine guns and knew that now they were relieved of their suffering."

The description by the old *Countess Fünfkirchen* from Oberradkersburg: "The mortality rate of the children and old people was horrendous. Daily you saw caskets being carried, one day I counted 16. (comment of the editors: It is questionable whether there actually were that many caskets available or whether they were corpses just wrapped in cloth.) Most of them died of starvation, particularly the poor children. When we initially arrived at Sterntal it was full of lovable small children. Then it became quieter and quieter. The children who used to jump around in the street could no longer run, no longer sit, no longer walk. They looked to us like flowers that were not watered and who all had drooping leaves and blossoms. Finally the poor children were only carried around and soon their short blooming life expired. The cause was the totally insufficient nourishment. There was almost no milk, the little there was, was mostly sour. Only three times a day did they receive a little food which, particularly for the very small one or two years old, was insufficient and they did not last long. It was a heartbreaking situation."

Every night people were taken away to be executed and new prisoners arrived the next day. The "dirty work" had to be completed before the new constitution was supposed to become effective. One can picture the situation which a participating "old-time communist" recorded and was published by *Zdenko Zavadlav*: "It was particularly 'old-time communists' they selected for this dirty work. We had to hurry up because the task had to be completed before the new constitution was to become effective and the camps had to be abolished. I was responsible for the inmates of the Sterntal camp ... According to the list we initially had to load and shackle 60 inmates together with wire; the same with the ones that came from the Marburg prison. Meanwhile, KNOJ men had dug ditches an the Bachern (Pohorje mountains) between Hoče and the Marburg cabin and forced the inmates to sing the German national anthem. It was a horrible picture. Was this really what we fought for? The inmates had to undress in front of the ditches. For them to do this we had to untie them and then retie their hands with wire. I was shocked about a minor daughter of a German. All had to sit on the edge of the ditch. Suddenly one of them jumped up and ran towards the woods, the KNOJ officer chasing him. A wild shooting started and suddenly the KNOJ officer fell down hit by a bullet. The inmate, however, succeeded to escape. After that incident the KNOJ men shot the inmates in their legs and ordered to open fire with machine guns. The inmates tumbled, by rows, into the ditch ... They kept shooting at anything that was still moving. The poor German girl also disappeared in the ditch. When it was all over, we drank Cognac."

The Sterntal camp, because of a protest of the International Red Cross, had to be closed by end of September 1945. A larger part of those inmates that survived the terror were shipped, in cattle rail cars, via Laibach and Assling/Jesenice to Carinthia. A smaller part, however, were sent to the municipal jails. There they suffered even more than at Sterntal. At least there they were hauled into court and one could call witnesses., The convicted were then shipped to work camps, particularly to Thesen near Marburg where most perished miserably.

Liquidation Camp Tüchern (Teharje) at Cilli (Celje)
Established for the internment and liquidation of the ethnic Germans, enemies of the regime and particularly the "White Guard" prisoners of war (indigenous soldiers serving with the German armed forces against the communists).

130

Number of inmates: intermittently 3,000–4,000.
Duration of camp: May 1945 to May/June 1946 (probably more than twelve months).
Casualties: over 3,000.
Main causes of death: executions, starvation, dysentery.

The camp Tüchern/Teharje, situated about four kilometre outside of Cilli, consisted of a row of barracks, along the road towards Austria and the rail line from Steinbrück/Zidanimost; it was built already by the Germans. An eyewitness reports that the camp was set up between May 15th and May 20th by the "State Security Agency" (probably the OZNA), 2nd battalion of the III. brigade, which arrived at Cilli May 10th–11th, 1945.

The camp was to serve as a liquidation camp for the ethnic Germans of Slovenia as well as for the "helpers of the occupiers", "class enemies" and potential enemies of the communist regime which was beginning to be formed.

Alois J. from Tüchern confirms this and states: "It was a camp for the opposition, for the opponents of communism, but particularly for children, women and sympathizers of the Slovenian Domobrances, and for the pre-war political parties. Many Domobrances were murdered." They were members and dependents of the Slovenian "Home Guards", while the "White Guards", commanded by their *General Rupnik*, fought with the Germans against the communist partisans.

The first who were executed were the Germans, then Slovenians. According to *A. P.* from Buchenschlag, the deep tank obstruction trenches, dug by the Germans, were filled with their corpses. "Behind the castle Bežigrad there were German tank trenches. All of them were filled with bodies of the liquidated ethnic Germans of the surroundings of Cilli who allegedly had dirtied their hands by collaborating with the occupiers, but also bodies of Slovenians accused of collaborating with the Germans. Above all it was a 'settling of political accounts'. Together with the ethnic Germans, merchants and dignitaries of Cilli were executed with their families at the swampy valley of Koschnitz (Košnica). According to *Jožica Widmar*, two large mass graves with about 350 bodies are located there.

Many of the ethnic Germans from lower Styria were first jailed at the Cilli prison. There the men, but also women, were tortured. Many of them were led away to never be seen again.

On June 6th, 1945, *Olga von Kottowitz* from Cilli was transferred from the Cilli prison to Tüchern. 'During my stay of six days at the Cilli prison we heard, how during the nights, individual inmates were beaten with chains. We heard their screams up to the second floor where we stayed. In the morning the blood was washed away with watering cans."

As far as the conditions at Tüchern are concerned, von Kottowitz continues her report: "We were ten or more people crammed in a small room. Some of us slept on the floor, some on plank beds. Day and night we were attacked by whole processions of bed bugs; my throat was all bitten up, some other inmates' heads were a sore wound. We were terribly hungry. For five weeks we received daily only dried vegetables, or, what was already an improvement, dustings of maize porridge, both cooked in plain water; very little bread. Everybody suffered from dysentery and many died. Many suffered from dropsy due to the starvation."

Young *Vilko Zibelki* was eyewitness to the cruel fate of many girls and women at the Tüchern camp. "I shall never forget, it was a Saturday evening, when the partisans picked out of the barrack where civilians were housed, ten girls and chased them to the camp staff office. Since the camp was illuminated I could see through the window of our barrack how the girls cried and wiped their tears. Soon thereafter we heard them screaming and imploring and the shouting of the soldiers. It was about one o'clock at night that we saw them again, being chased to the valley where they were shot to death. The same happened on the two following Saturdays."

The Tüchern camp also served as a *prisoner of war camp*. The long tortures which the "White Guardsmen" had to suffer before the ones that were still alive, were executed, make Tüchern probably one of the worst prisoner of war camps in military history. *Olga von Kottowitz* continues: "The sufferings these poor souls had to endure are indescribable. They were about 2,000 who sat out in the open behind barbed wire, legs crossed, an rough gravel stones, crammed together and bare chested, day and night, rain or shine. Nobody was allowed to stand up. The guards shot at anyone who did; the partisans took the dead out to the nearby forest where they were covered with earth. There the executions also took place. We did not see, but we heard them and were told so by the (good) partisans. Food was given only once every third day, consisting of dried vegetable, called 'barbed wire'. When I left the camp, less than 100 White Guard members were still there."

Reports indicate that in May 1946 some ethnic Germans were transferred from Tüchern to Marburg/Maribor and from there sent to Austria. Thus it is assumed that the camp was still in existence during May 1946.

Most important sources

Arbeitskreis Dokumentation, *Leidensweg der Deutschen im kommunistischen Jugoslawien*, Volumes I–IV. Editor: Donauschwäbische Kulturstiftung München, München/Sindel-fingen 1991–1995. Abbr.: LW I etc. (The volumes I–III were identically published by Universitas, München, under the title: *Weißbuch der Deutschen aus Jugoslawien.*)

Arbeitskreis Dokumentation, *Verbrechen an den Deutschen in Jugoslawien 1944–1948. Die Stationen eines Völkermords.* Editor: Donauschwäbische Kulturstiftung München, 3rd Edition, München 2000. Abbr.: VDJ. (This book summerizes at about 370 pages the four Volumes of *Leidensweg/Weißbuch*).

Schieder, Theodor et al., *Dokumentation der Vertreibung der Deutschen aus Ost-Mitteleuropa.* Vol. V: *Das Schicksal der Deutschen in Jugoslawien.* Editor: Bundesministerium für Ver-triebene, Flüchtlinge und Kriegsbeschädigte, Bonn 1961. Abbr.: Dok V. Identic reprints: Deutscher Taschenbuchverlag (dtv reprint 3274), München 1984, and Weltbild-Verlag, Augsburg 1994.

Sources 7.1

Sources for camp Molidorf/Molin (Banat)

Dr. Jenö Heger, LW III, 256 f.; Maria Euch, LW II, 285; Ingeborg Seidl/Helmut Frisch, LW I, 359 f.; Ernst Lung, I, 272 f.; Kornelius Weimann, LW II, 690 f.; Peter Heinrich, LW II, 332 f.; Karoline Bockmüller, LW II, 246 f.; LW III, 508; Anna Wilms, Dok. V, 370 ff.; LW IV, 25 Dok. V, 370 ff.; LW IV, 254–258. 4–258.
The longer version: LW III, 708–724; VDJ, 149–152.

Sources for camp Rudolfsgnad

Dr. med. K. F., LW III, 246–240 or: Dok. V, 496–512; Klara Deutsch, LW III, 187 ff.; Franz Apfel, LW III, 191–201; Lorenz Baron, Tiposkript 1994 or: LW III, 215–219, 222–225; Franz Janzer, LW III, 219–222; Dr. med. Jenö Heger, LW III, 256 f. or Dok. V, 374–376; P. Wendelin Gruber SJ, *In den Fängen des Roten Drachen*, Jestetten 1989, 111–131; Heimatbuch Weiß-kirchen, 283; Josef Jerger, LW III, 531–534; Elisabeth Kuhn, LW III, 530 f.; Franz Fillips-Renatz, *Donauschwabenkalender 1559*, 103 ff. and *Der Donauschwabe*, 20.2.1994. Peter Max Wagner and his Aid Society of Brooklin, LW III, 125–128.
The longer version: LW III, 724–755; VDJ, 153–169.

Sources for camp Jarek/Bački Jarak (Batschka)

Georg König, LW III, 383–391; Katharina Frank, LW III, 417; Katharina Haller, LW II, 703 or: Dok. V, 401–405; Fritz Ilg, LW III, 352–357; Friedrich Glas, LW III, 566–570, LW II, 704; Martha Müller, LW III, 654 f.; Susanne Harfmann, LW III, 358; Jakob Plees, LW III, 437 f. or: Dok. V, 395–400; Dr. med. Hans Müller, LW III, 412 f.; Agathe Prohaska, LW III, 660; Katharina Lauterer, LW III, 571–577; Karl Weber, LW III, 582–595; Georg Haug, LW III, 406–411; Agathe Dorth-Prohaska, LW III, 658; Elisabeth Lusch, LW II, 537.
Longer Version: LW III, 782–807; VDJ, 170–179.

Sources for camp Gakowa/Gakovo (Batschka)

Chaplain Paul Pfuhl, LW III, 271–285 or: Dok. V, 414–441; Chaplain Matthias Johler, LW III, 286–318 or: 442–485; P. Wendelin Gruber, LW III, 118–120, 318–322; Josef Thiel, in: Paul Mesli/Franz Schreiber/Georg Wildmann, *Filipowa – Bild einer donauschwäbischen Gemein-de*, Vol. 6: *Kriegs- und Lageropfer*, Wien 1985, 136 ff.; Anton Findeis, LW II, 415 f.; Konrad Gerescher, *Maisbrot und Peitsche. Erlebnisbericht aus einem Flüchtlingslager*, Münden/Scheden 1974, 141 f., and LW III, 560; Michael Brandt, LW II, 410; Maria Arbruster, LW II, 881 f.; Marianne Müller, LW III, 478; Magdalena Hirtling, LW II, 489; Maria Menrath, LW II, 477; Eva Spiegel, LW III, 328; Katharina Schreiber, in: Paul Mesli, a. a. O. 139; Anna Niklos, LW III, 556–558 or: *Nachruf auf verlorene Jahre*, Karlsruhe 1991, 92–94; Eva Knöbl, in: *Filipowaer Heimatbriefe*, Wien, Nr. 8 (1967), 12 f.; Eva Schmidt, in: *Filipowaer Heimatbriefe*, Nr. 12 (1969), 15 f.; Andreas Rack, LW III, 377–383.
The longer version: LW III, 808–849; VDJ 180–198.

Sources for camp Kruschiwl/Kruševlje (Batschka)

Therese Schieber, Statement, Bundesarchiv Bayreuth, Ost-Dok. 2, Nr. 400, partly published in Dok. V, 416 f.; and statement Nr. 401, partly published in LW III, 550 f.; Martin Mayer, *Erschie-ßungen im Kruschiwler Lager* (Shootings in camp Kruschiwl), unpublished manuscript 1994; Josef Kämmerer, in: Josef Klingler (Ed.), *Unsere verlorene Heimat Futok* (Donauschwäbische Beiträge Nr. 27), Freilassing 1958, 252 ff.; Stefan Mutter, LW II, 740 f.; Fritz Ilg, LW III, 424; Anna Volk, LW III, 424; Anton Wolf, LW II, 425; Anonimous author: Statement about the

names of the camp commanders of Kruschiwl, Bundesarchiv Bayreuth, Ost-Dok. 2, Nr. 420.
The longer version: LW III, 850–866; VDJ 199–207.

Sources for camp "Svilara" ("Silk Factory") at Syrmian Mitrowitz/Sremska Mitrovica (Syrmia)

Wendelin Michels, LW I, 716 ff.; Anna Borosch, LW I, 670 f.; Katharina Geislinger, LW I, 708; Hans Volk, LW III, 162 ff.; Traudie Mueller-Wlossak, *The Whip. My Homecoming*, 1982, (Germ. "Die Peitsche des Tito-Kommissars", 1987); U. L., in: Hans Schreckeis, *Wukowar – Alte Haupstadt Syrmiens*, Salzburg 1990, 170 f.; Dr. Eduard Herzeg, Abtsgmünd, 15 pages typoscript, 1995.
Long Versions: LW III, 872–884 and VDJ 208–218.

Sources 7.2

Sources for camp Walpach/Valpovo (Slavonia)

Josef Wagner, LW II, 81 ff., LW III, 471 ff.; Peter Fischer, LW II, 768, Dok. V, 534 ff.; Peter Seiler, Dok. V, 525 ff.; A. Z. from Brčko: LW II, 828 f.; Josefine Pirk, LW II, 798 ff.; Vladimir Geiger, *Radni logor Valpovo 1945 – 1946* (work camp Valpovo), Dokumenti. Issued by Volksdeutsche Gemeinschaft in Kroatien, Osijek/Essegg 1999, 443 pages, with German-language summary (431–441) and eyewitness reports in the German and Croatian languages; Maria Burger in Geiger 383 f.; Michael Jung in Geiger 387; Johann Stemmer in Geiger 388 ff.; Nikola Mak in Geiger 425 ff. (German translation by Oskar Feldtänzer); Josip Globočnik (camp commander) in Geiger 428 ff.; important: *Death count* by Michael Hantler in Geiger 335–354; mortality registry of the Valpovo parish in Geiger 259–333.
Longer Versions: LW III, 889–893; VDJ, 224–228.

Sources for camp Kerndia/Krndija (Slavonia)

Georg Tscherny, LW II, 816 ff.; Matthias Stolz, LW II, 119 ff.; Peter Fischer, LW II, 768 ff.; Anna Selenkowitsch, LW II, 800; Sophie Schadt, LW II, 787 f.; Josefine Pirk, LW II, 799; A. C. of Brcko, Dok. V, 522; Peter Seiler, Dok. V, 531; Katharina Vogel, LW III, 466; Vladimir Geiger/Ivan Jurković (editor), *Mira Knöbl, Pisma iz Krndije* (Letters from Kerndia), Zagreb 1994.
Long Versions: LW III, 885–889; VDJ, 219–223.

Sources 7.3

Interim report of the "Parliamentary Investigative Commission for postwar murders, legally dubious prosecutions and other irregularities" of the state Slovenia under the presidency of Joze Pučnik, published in the newspaper "Slovenec", September 23rd, 1995. Translated into German by Josef Ehrgott in the paper "Der Untersteirer", vol. 29 (1996), no. 1 and 2.

Sources for liquidation camp Sterntal (Strnišče) near Pettau/Ptuj

N. von Preradovich, LW II, 874–876; J. K. (born 1910 at Pettau), LW II, 878 f.; The personal Chauffeur of Count Dr. Ferdinand Attems, LW II, 866 f.; Helene Countess Fünfkirchen, LW II, 871 f.; Zdenko Zavadlav, LW II, 900; General contribution also: Stefan Karner, *The German-speaking ethnic group in Slovenia. Aspects of its development 1939–1997*, Klagenfurt/Ljubljana/Vienna 1998, 132–154.

Sources for liquidation camp Tüchern (Teharje) at Cilli (Celje)

Alois J. (from Tüchern), LW II, 882; Ivan Kamenšek (from Buchenschlag), LW II, 883; A. P. (from Buchenschlag), LW II, 884; Erika Ehrgott, LW II, 889; Jožica Widmar, LW II, 886; Olga von Kottowitz, LW 890–894; Vilko Zibelki, LW II, 890; Roman Leljak, LW II, 881 f.; Dok. V, 546, 574 footnote, 575.

Chapter 8: Crimes Committed against Children

The most cruel and most shocking chapter of the tragedy of the ethnic Germans in the communist Yugoslavia is the fate of the children. Their demise in the liquidation camps, caused by starvation and diseases is documented in many eyewitness and first person reports. The extent of the spiritual and mental anguish, however, can never be adequately described.

The later attempt of the Tito-regime to send the surviving children who had no parent or relative left in the camp to government children homes, subject them to a re-nationalization process and arbitrarily determine their ethnic identity, runs against the human rights and personal dignity. Fortunately for most of the children, this detestable crime had to be terminated at the beginning of the 1950s due to world-wide moral pressures, particularly those exerted by the International Committee of the Red Cross (ICRC) in Geneva. At that time, the ICRC, as well as world opinion, could resort to the United Nations Resolution of December 9th, 1948 according to which the forcibly transferring to another nationality was explicitly termed a form of genocide and condemned.

The torture of children was also programmed at the end of 1944 together with the internment of all ethnic German civilians. The children were, together with the old, the sick and those unable to work chased into the liquidation camps – also called "death camps", "starvation and dying camps". Particularly cruel was the brutal taking of children from their mothers since almost all young women were to be shipped as work slaves to Russia.

It is documented that 45,000 children, of up to 14 years of age, were interned and at least 6,000 (13 percent) starved to death. The percentage of children in the liquidation camps was very high. On April 30th, 1946, at the Rudolfsgnad camp there were approximately 18,000 inmates registered of which 8,288 were children under the age 14. For many children the care by parents or relatives was of short duration, since the death rate, particularly up to May 1946, was at its peak and the older people used to sacrifice themselves by giving their tiny rations to the children.

The terms "death camp", and "liquidation camp" are, indeed, justified. One example out of many gives clear evidence of that: At the death camp Jarek 171 of the 190 dead children of the village Bulkes (Batschka) died within one year. That's 42 percent of the 457 interned children from that village.

At the Rudolfsgnad camp 7,664 people out of 17,000 perished between October 1945 and December 1946. Of these 1,036 were children up to ten years old.

The rapid demise of older people, mostly grandparents and relatives of these children, separated from their parents, created a high percentage of orphans. These were then put into children sections within the camps. From there they were shipped to children homes in the Banat and the Batschka and from there split up to distant homes from Mazedonia to Slovenia.

Siblings were separated with the intention to make them forget their origin. This was mainly achieved with very young children. Those forcefully separated brothers and sisters met again only many years later – if at all – at Belgrad where the Red Cross organized the reunification transports. Most did not recognize each other any more and even spoke different languages. Very few, however, still spoke German.

Eyewitness Reports of the Children's Fate

Volume III of the documentation series *Leidensweg der Deutschen im kommunistischen Jugoslawien* (abbr. LW III) contains 53 reports (pages 475–666). They were written by men and women who experienced these events as children. The following are a few of these tragic experiences, which are recorded also in *Verbrechen an den Deutschen in Jugoslawien 1944–1948* (abbr. VDJ).

David Gerstheimer, born 1936 at Kischker/Batschka. Within a few months after being interned at the Jarek liquidation camp his mother, six siblings and grandparents died of starvation. David, at that time eight years old, was the only survivor and sent to a government children home for re-education and "Slavinizing" (LW III, 647; VDJ 244).

Father Wendelin Gruber S. J. (1914–2002), Filipowa/Batschka. He spent some time in the Gakowa death camp: "Afternoons I went to the children sections which were set up in the larger farm houses. There the children, between 20 to 30 in a room, were lying around, only on straw and scantily covered. Only skin and bones, sick, and with infected wounds. Nobody cared for them. The small ones cried and screamed pitifully – they were starving. Others were lying motionless; they didn't even have the strength anymore to cry. I went from room to room, always the same picture. A woman who took over as caretaker lead me to the room in the back. Carefully she pulled the cover from a pile of children. What a sight! 'Are they still alive?' I asked trembling. These little ones, in a row on rags are almost naked; skin and bones only. They were gasping for air with open mouths. The last thing the world can offer them. 'We pulled these out since they cannot digest food any more and are the first to die', was the reply" (LW III, 623; VDJ, 244 ff.).

Šuco, the almighty commander of the Gakowa camp, responding to the question what plans the communists had for the surviving children tells father Wendelin Gruber: "Don't worry, comrade Pope! Everything will be in order! Our Socialist State will look after the children. They now will be adequately fed and then housed in government children homes. A progressive kindergarten teacher has already arrived. She will now take over the responsibility for a good education. These children will be Tito's pioneers and brave fighters for our liberation revolution.

You will see, these fascist, capitalist children will become model members of the liberated working class and enthusiastic supporters of a better future" (LW III, 624; VDJ, 245 f.).

This programmed re-education which was supposed to awaken the hatred for their "fascist" parents was reported by most of the children. At the time of the reunification process there were children who did not want to go home to their "criminal parents".

Karl Weber, at that time eleven years old, reports of the tragic consequences of trying to go begging. "My friend Philipp was beaten to death during such a begging trip (on October 28th, 1945). It didn't take much, we were already half dead", said Karl Weber about the fate of his friend Philipp Bauer with whom he undertook several such begging trips (LW III, 588; VDJ, 246 f.).

At the Jarek camp, *Friedrich Glas* from Bulkes who saw two of his great-grandparents and two grandparents, as well as his two years old sister starve to death, was caught, together with his friend *Peter Kendl* slipping out of the camp to go begging. The two partisans took them to the guardroom. After a while they were led back to the place where they were caught and motioned to go away. After they made a few steps the guards then shot at them from behind. Fritz, who played dead, survived. The wounded Peter however screamed, after the guards had already started to go away. They returned and killed him with a bullet to the head (LW III, 566 ff.; VDJ, 247).

Suicides because of despair, fright and sense of shame after being raped also occurred. Not even children were spared from rape during the mass rapes at Deutsch-Zerne in October 1944. *Eva Bischof*, only nine years old, was cruelly raped by nine men. Her injuries were so severe that she lost consciousness and was unable to move. Thereupon her own mother, in desperation, hung her child and she hung herself (LW III, 238 ff.; VDJ, 248).

Juliane Wirag (1908) from Ridjitza strangled her twin daughters, born in 1944, because she could find no way to save them from slow starvation and then hung herself (LW III, 546; VDJ, 248).

Eva Butzschedel (1932), at Gokowa, relates one of the most tragic and touching experiences documented. Her mother was sick with typhus. "Day by day, the condition in our room and that of my mother became worse. We were praying intensely. Mother never stopped praying. God, however, had other plans for her. Her condition became worse and we saw death approaching. Everybody in the room already had high fever and nobody was aware of the others around him. When Monika, my sister, became aware of mother's imminent death she did not leave her side. She constantly called: 'Mother, you will not die, right? Mother you won't abandon us, right?'

She implored the Holy Mother: 'Wonderful Mother, please help our mother.' She continuously caressed mother and noticed that she became increasingly weaker. Her tears kept dripping down on the terminally ill as if she believed they would help save her from death. I think there is nothing worse in this world for a child than in such a state of loneliness, surrounded by death and distress to kneel at the deathbed of the mother, not being able to help in her struggle and having to watch how the hand of death slowly takes her away forever …" (LW III, 598–609; VDJ, 249 f.).

Karoline Bockmüller (1905), Deutsch-Zerne, Banat, describes the condition of the children section in a part of the Rudolfsgnad liquidation camp. "I had to visit this children camp and happen to enter a room which contained 30 to 35 children (from babies to 16 months old) whose parents had died. None of them could stand, let alone walk. They were just lying there or slid around the room on their bellies. The room was reeking of excrements. The children were crying, were pale and starving. Their bodies were smeared with excrement, which was partially dried to the skin. I fled from the room, weeping and asked the women whether there was anybody to look after these poor abandoned children. They replied they could not help since they had no diapers, nor towels, water basins, water, soap, practically nothing. They continually asked the camp administration for just the basic requirements, however received nothing, only the comment: 'The children should kick the bucket.' They also tried repeatedly to take away my grandchild and put it into the children camp, but I did not give her up. After she died I escaped from the Rudolfsgnad camp and went to Molidorf to look for my mother. There I was told that my mother and aunt had died of starvation in the camp" (LW III, 508; VDJ, 245 f.).

Peter Wilpert (1938) from Palanka/Batschka about the conditions at the liquidation camp Jarek: "Both grandmothers died within a week. After that I was, six years old, all by myself, terribly alone" (LW III, 654 f.; VDJ, 248 f.).

Katharina Weber née *Lauterer* (1935) from Bulkes/Batschka, at that time ten years old, was together with six of her schoolmates at the Jarek liquidation camp. Five of them died between September 1945 and February 1946. The sixth girlfriend died in October 1947 at the Subotica camp. The surviving Katharina was shipped to a government home (LW III, 572; VDJ, 247).

Anna Niklos-Nyari describes the sad passing away of an entire family at the Gakowa liquidation camp: "There was a young mother who lived in a room with her three small children. When her last child was struggling with death she said to the people in the next room: 'I don't know anymore for whom I should pray, mourn or weep first: for my husband who died in the war, my parents, my grandparents, brothers and sisters or for my children. What does the Almighty want to do with me? Haven't I suffered enough yet? Do I now also have to give up my last child?' She staggered back into her room and knelt down next to the dying boy. We stood in our own room and wept. If tears of compassion could have helped, the little boy surely wouldn't have died.

We heard the boy groan and for a long time I could not fall asleep. It must have been early in the morning when I woke up. Everybody around me was still asleep.

I looked into the neighbouring room. The little boy, lying on the floor, had his hands folded; I knew what this meant: The woman's third child had now also died. She didn't wake anybody, but kept watch and prayed all by herself. At that moment I saw her kneeling down, her gaze up to the ceiling and she started to talk aloud. Was she becoming insane? Her voice was humble: 'Almighty, you have taken all my loved ones to you. I hope you now won't forget to take me. Don't let me wait long, I am ready to die. I have only one wish: When Tito dies then let all the poor souls who were tortured, starved to death and murdered on his orders pass by his death bed, me and my children last. Only then should he be allowed to die'" (LW III, 557; VDJ, 247 f.; first report in: Anna Niklos-Nyari, *Nachruf auf verlorene Jahre,* Karls-ruhe 1991, 92–94).

Rescue Efforts

Promises of the Yugoslav representation in the USA were never carried out. It was all deception and delaying tactics. Endeavors of governmental, ecclesiastical, as well as the efforts of the welfare offices of the Red Cross in Germany and Austria, remained ignored by the communist Yugoslavia. Even the efforts of the International Committee of the Red Cross in Geneva remained without real success. There were not only problems with the Yugoslavian authorities; the allied occupation forces in Germany and Austria were not always understanding and often delayed possible support.

Finding the location and repatriation of the "lost children" entailed great efforts. The distribution of the publication *Kinder im Schatten* (Children in the Shadow) by Batschka writer Adalbert K. Gauss, in early August 1950 initiated some movement in the rescue of the children. Several organizations and individuals and particularly the International Committee of the Red Cross, after tedious struggles, achieved some success and, between 1950–1959, about 2,300 children could be re-united with their parents and relatives. Still, several hundred German children could no longer be found and meanwhile were "re-educated" and "Slavinized". They now live somewhere in the partitioned Yugoslavia. They may be lost, but never forgotten. It is one of the most tragic chapters of the Danube Swabian tragedy (LW III, 482–491; VDJ, 252–259).

Chapter 9: The Suffering and Dying of the Ethnic German Clergy

The Catholic and Protestant clergy was a highly respected profession by the Germans in the former Yugoslavia. During the persecution of the ethnic Germans by the partisan regime 37 of them were killed, mostly in a gruesome manner. The clergy of both denominations became martyrs for two reasons: 1. because they were declared ideological enemies of the Atheist dominated Yugoslavia and 2. because they belonged to the ethnic German population which was destined to be exterminated.

The short biographies of some of these murdered clerics are representative of the suffering and annihilation of this vocational group. More detailed descriptions are documented in the book *Verbrechen an den Deutschen in Jugoslawien 1944–1948* (Crimes against the ethnic Germans in Yugoslavia 1944–1948), pages 256–270.

Already in 1941, at the beginning of the Axis Powers' war with Yugoslavia, some clerics were taken as hostages and interned at Petervardein. With the battle fronts getting closer in 1944, most of the clergy refused to leave even though implored to flee. While some were initially spared from internment, others were ridiculed, forced to do menial work and tortured. Several were already murdered in their parishes immediately after the occupation as part of the annihilation process by the *Intelligenzija* campaign. For them death was a release from their sufferings.

Here are some particularly notorious examples of such suffering and murders.

Dr. Philip Popp (1893–1945), born at Beschania near Semlin, Bishop of the German-Protestant church in Yugoslavia and Senator of the Yugoslav Upper House, 1940. Dr. Popp was loyal to his German heritage and the Yugoslav nation. In those difficult times he was criticized by those not sharing his views, however, he preserved the independence of his church. When Croatia became an independent nation, he protested against the persecution of Serbs, helped them to flee and accepted them in his church without baptism.

Towards the end of the war, when the partisan army approached, he remained in his Agram parish. He was arrested in May 1945, court-martialed and condemned to death on false charges on June 28th, 1945. He was shot the next day. The Serbian Patriarch German in Belgrade described Bishop Dr. Popp as a just and loyal man. He died a martyr's death for the Danube Swabian Protestant church.

Adalbert von Neipperg (1890–1948), Count von Neipperg was born at Meran, South Tyrol, became member of Benedictine Order and served during the World

War II as priest who looked after the spiritual needs of the German troops at Windisch-Feistritz in Slovenia. He became a prisoner of war in 1945, refused the offer of freedom and remained with the soldiers as a medic and priest. At the notorious POW camp 233 at Werschetz/Vršac (Banat) he succeeded in obtaining additional food and performed religious services. The POWs (Prisoners of War) called him "Our Father". On December 23rd, 1948, the day before Christmas Eve, he was summoned to the communist staff headquarters and did not return. He was found the next day with his throat cut, tortured and murdered. His remains were transferred to the monastery chapel at Neuburg. The grave marker reads "Martyr of Love".

Anton Adam (1908–1944), born at Chicago Il, USA, died at Groß-Kikinda. He was the priest for the parishes St. Hubert, Charleville and Soltour. Father Adam was, together with 120 men, tortured and executed by machine guns.

Anton Berger (1884–1944), born at Kunbaja, priest at Tavankut. He was taken out of his rectory and disappeared. Manner and place of death unknown.

Josef Böckmann (1910–1945), born at Rudolfstal/Bosanski Aleksandrovac. Priest at Glamoč and Prijedor (Bosnia). Secretly executed.

Franz Brunet (1898–1944), born at Modosch (Banat), representative of the Belgrade Episcopal Administration at Groß-Betschkerek. Priest at Deutsch-Zerne. Was taken as hostage and executed by the partisans.

Julius Bürger (1885–1944), born at Kula (Batschka), priest at Podravska Slatina. Executed for keeping religious articles.

Valentin Dupp (1883–1944), born at Bukin (Batschka), priest at Tschurug. Even though he intervened on behalf of the Serbian priest during the Hungarian occupation in 1941, the son, a partisan, ordered him executed.

Josef Eppich (1874–1942), priest at Bittersdorf, in the province of Gottschee, Slovenia. Was killed on his way to visit sick people at one of the dispersed settlements.

Ferdinand Gassmann (1914–1946), born at Batsch-Sentiwan, Franziscan and missionary, took food to the Gakowa liquidation camp. He was arrested by the OZNA (Secret Police), condemned to death and executed.

Anton Haug (1890–1945), born at Srbobran (Batschka), priest at Tschonopel. After torture and starvation, died at the Svilara camp in Syrmia.

Theodor Klein (1879–1945), priest at Manoster/Beli Manastir, Dechant. Died after torture at the village inn.

Franz Klein (1879–1946), born at Neu-Werbass (Batschka). Lutheran pastor at Katsch/Kać (Batschka). Had a good relationship with the authorities and Serbian clergy. Looked after inmates at Jarek and Kruschiwl camps. Died of starvation.

Josef Knapp (1912–1944), born at Kathreinfeld (Banat), priest at Glogon. Before being executed with 46 men of the community, he admonished his companions to face death with faith and confidence.

Josef Kornauth (1872–1945), born at Sopron, Hungary, priest at Groß-Gaj (Banat). He died at camp Setschanfeld.

Wilhelm Kund (1880–1946), born at Oberschützen, Burgenland, Austria. Lutheran pastor at Pantschowa. In spite of prohibition to preach, torture and injuries he secretly prayed with the camp inmates of Rudolfsgnad. He succumbed to his injuries from torture at the camp prison.

Johann Nepomuk Lakajner (1873–1944), born at Osijek, priest at Ruma (Syrmia). He refused to be evacuated before the capture by the partisans and stayed with his community. He was said to have been tied to a wagon and dragged to death by the partisans.

Peter Müller (1884–1951), born at Szakadát, Hungary, priest at Filipowa/Bački Gračac. Arrested by the UDBA (Yugoslav Secret State Police) in 1948 because he was corresponding with former members of his parish (prisoners of war, refugees and deportees to Russia), he was sentenced to three years at the penitentiary. Since he was terminally ill, he was released after 20 months and died.

Stefan Müller-Majoros was priest at Neu-Palanka (Batschka). In 1944, forced by the partisans to walk to Hungary he was supposed to have died there due to the hardships he endured.

Josef Novotny (1909–1944), born at Vareš, Bosnia, priest at Plawing/Plavna (Batschka). Kidnapped by the partisans to Batsch, tortured to death at the cellar of the town hall and disposed of in the forest.

Fanz Plank (1885–1944), born at Tolnau, Hungary, priest at Alt-Siwatz (Batschka). Murdered by the partisans.

Emanual Retzer (1912–1944). Lutheran pastor at Heideschütz (Banat). Deported as slave worker to Russia and presumably succumbed to the hardships in one of the slave labor camps.

Michael Rothen (1895–1944), born at Groß-Betschkerek, chaplain at Weißkirchen, Zichidorf and Werschetz. He was tortured and murdered, together with 28 other ethnic German men at the notorious "Milchhalle" at Groß-Kikinda.

Michel Schaffer (1908–1945/46), born at Pantschowa. Lutheran Pastor at Laibach/Ljubljana, Slovenia. As an ethnic German and priest he was arrested in 1945, became ill while in jail and, after his release, died as a result of his incarceration.

Wilhelm Schäfer (1848–1944), born at Groß-Kikinda (Banat), priest at Tschestereg. Was interned with community inhabitants. Because of being a priest he was humiliated and tortured. He died in the camp.

Franz Schaffhauser (1919–1945), Franziscan. He is one of the 139 Franziscans who were murdered in Yugoslavia between 1941 and 1946 by either the Tschetniks or partisans.

Lorenz Scherer (1912–1947), born at Kula, Vicar at Tscherwenka (Batschka). Was deported as slave worker to the coal mines of Russia. Because of his faith esteemed but particularly mistreated. He died by exhaustion.

Josef Schmidt (1913–1944), born at Batsch-Monostor, professor for religion and youth counselor at Dubrovnik. As an "enemy of communism" he was murdered on the notorious "Death Island" Dakša near Dubrovnik.

Josef Schmidt (1876–1949), born at Weißkirchen/Bela Crkva, priest at Modosch (Banat). Because he issued documents (certificates of birth, matrimony) to members of his former Modosch congregation, he was admonished, then arrested and sentenced to two and one half years of detention. He died while in jail.

Adam Steigerwald (1876–1944), born at Heufeld (Banat), priest at Heufeld and Mastort. He offered physical resistance, when the German inhabitants of his parish Heufeld were expelled by partisans; so he was killed in the city hall.

Karl Unterreiner (1897–1944), born at Filipowa, teacher of religion at Palanka, Papal Honorary Chaplain, founder of Boy Scout groups and the Bonifatius Society at Budapest (Hungary). Arrested together with 100 German men and, after gruesome torture, executed in the forest near Palanka (Baschka).

Andreas Varga (1913–1944), born at Setschan (Banat), priest at Toba, chaplain at Werschetz and Weißkirchen. Tortured at the town hall, dumped into the basement, killed and disposed of.

Peter Weber (1884–1944), born at Groß-Kikinda, priest at Karlsdorf/Banatski Karlovac. Tortured by Red Army soldiers, during the "Action Intelligentsija" executed by the partisans.

Peter Weinert (1874–1945), born at Tschonopel, priest at Palanka/Batschka. Together with 1,200 ethnic German men chased to the central camp at Neusatz/Novi Sad, where he died. The regime had to consent to his burial in the tomb of the last abbot of Neusatz, with a large participation of believers.

Michael Werner (1883–1944), born at Batsch-Sentiwan, priest at Martonosch. Dragged, together with 21 ethnic German men by local Serbs to the basement of the town hall. There they were tortured, mangled with pliers, taken to Tschurug shot and disposed of in trenches.

Anton Weiss (1913–1943), born at Sarajevo, served as German military chaplain. Captured at Stalingrad (Russia) and executed by the Soviet Army.

Richard Weiss (1916–1944), born at Doboj (Bosnia), chaplain at Modritsch (Bosnia). Tortured and murdered by Tschetniks or partisans.

Chapter 10: Flight from the Camps

Already during the bloody autumn of 1944, when the atrocities of the partisans and their helpers started, the ethnic Germans that had stayed behind in the country began to realize that their trust in personal innocence turned out to be a life-threatening mistake. Some tried to flee to neighbouring Romania and Hungary. As the expropriations, expulsion from their homes and internment in camps began, the escape attempts increased considerably. Now it was clear even to the last optimists that the only thing that mattered was to save their own bare life.

Those who were detailed to work outside the camps, especially the ones that had to work in the fields, had the best chances to ecape. The stupidity of the guards was often their salvation: While the guards counted their slaves several times a day, they always arrived at different numbers. Sometimes, after some persons had fled, they nevertheless counted several more people than they had in the beginning; cursing vehemently they then gave up. This saved the fugitives from being pursued immediately and the remaining workers from the rage of the guards.

The fact, that the desperate people tried to flee, was, however, not unnoticed by the rulers and they increased the controls throughout the country and especially along the national borders. Apparently they even entered into an extradition agreement with Romania; so while, in the beginning of 1945, it was still relatively easy to find refuge there, later on many escapees who were captured during raids or at border crossings were returned to Yugoslavia. Those who fell again into the hands of the partisans were treated cruelly, often resulting in their demise.

10.1 Escaping from Yugoslavia

Johann Hebel of Gakova, an eyewitness who served as a gravedigger during his internment reports: "Whenever people were captured during an escape, the partisans finished them off right at the border. We picked up many such bodies and brought them back for burial at the camp cementery. Once we had a husband, wife and their eight to ten years old son. The parents were beaten to death and the boy's stomach slit open with a bayonet from top to bottom with his intestines hanging out."

Ernst Lung from Hetin, district of Modosch/Banat, reports: "During the autumn 1945 maize harvest, several ethnic German women and girls succeeded in escaping through the dense maize fields to Romania. These escapes disturbed the partisans.

As a retaliation, two internees, arbitrarily selected, had to gather their bundles, were chased across the railroad tracks and shot to death 'trying to escape'.

Despite further reprisals, threatened by the camp commander Kuljić, more and more inmates risked their flight. Thus, about 30 more Germans from the Deutsch-Zerne camp and others from Hetin managed to flee to Rumania. One night in January 1946, several Germans from the camp Deutsch-Zerne, among them Mathias Kaiser and Johann Hockl from Hetin, risked their escape. During this attempt one man and two women were stopped by a partisan patrol near the border. These three, including Mrs. Retzler from Stefansfeld, were initially badly maltreated, then shot to death and buried at the knacker's yard.

The internees, in addition to their desperation, suffered from hopelessness since at the beginning of 1946 the daily food rations were reduced to three watery soups, in spite of the imposed heavy work load. The enslaved internees preferred risking death during the escape rather than languishing in the claws of the partisans."

Johann Pudel tells about his escape from Kruschiwl/Batschka in 1947: "Our first attempt failed. We sold everything we had. There was an order, stating that all persons left behind in a room or house out of which inmates escaped, were to be executed for 'aiding the escapees'. In order not to endanger anybody and not to be betrayed out of fear, we began to move out during the night into a house where finally all 30 persons who wanted to escape were the only ones in the house. One night we sneaked out of the village, following a guide, past the guards and across the fields. We had to cross a brook, over a narrow, rickety bridge. We have a painful and sad memory of this bridge. There, a mother lost her three to four years old child. Not to give us away, she could not call out for the child. In addition, she had to look after her own mother and had hoped her child was with some other person in the group; however, it could not be found and presumably slid into the brook and silently drowned."

Magdalena Brenner from Filipowa/Batschka describes how she was taken to the Gakowa liquidation camp, together with her two youngest daughters (out of a total of seven) Viktoria (12) and Katharina (9) as well as two grandchildren and also the starvation, maltreatments, typhoid epidemic and the mass dying in that camp. She describes how the partisans, during a severe snowstorm January 14th–16th, 1946, chased all internees into the street to "resettle" them into a different street. Many of the sick were crawling on hands and feet since they were too weak to walk. The death toll escalated rapidly – exactly what the partisans intended. They even used the icy snowstorm for their sadistic murders.

Magdalena's husband Georg Brenner was a discharged soldier in Hungary and learned that a large part of his family was at the Gakowa camp. Together with a young man who had crossed the border several times as a guide for escapees and whose family was also at Gakowa, he went there to steal his family out of the camp.

During the mentioned snowstorm both men sneaked into the camp and Georg found his family, totally weakened by starvation and sickness. Sadly he had to realize that they were not fit enough to undertake the escape and initially wanted to return alone to Hungary. However, his daughter Maria was not to be deterred. In order to escape the terrible camp life and certain starvation, she insisted in accompanying her father, together with her five years old son, even though she had not yet fully recovered from her typhoid disease. They also took along the daughter Viktoria.

Magdalena Brenner now relates the escape of part of her family: "The evening of January 16th my husband, daughters Viktoria and Maria with her child Martin sneaked out of the camp. Their guide, a young man from Brestowatz, also took his family along. He was an experienced 'border crosser'. During the snowstorm it was easy to leave the camp unseen – but the route was very problematic. Once out of the camp they had to move through the high snow and storm towards the Hungarian border. For the weak camp inmates the going was terribly difficult. During the night they moved about aimlessly. Soon some could no longer cope with the strain. First the mother-in-law of the guide, then his wife died in the open field, about one kilometre from the Hungarian border. What to do now? The guide had enough problems of his own. He pointed out to my husband the direction to go and told him to keep moving.

My husband could no longer find the way he came from Hungary. The children stopped to rest for a while and he went to search for the right way. When he returned Maria was getting worse. My husband took her to a stack of maize stalks, about one kilometre from the border. Here they found shelter. Maria became progressively weaker and could no longer walk. She was exhausted due to the cold, her weak physical condition and apprehension. She died in the arms of her father. It was a distressing situation for my husband, Viktoria and little Martin. They prayed and had to accept the fate of her death. Outside the stack the snowstorm continued mercilessly and snow covered the maize shelter in which they endured their greatest misery and total loneliness.

My husband then got up again and resumed his search for the right way (when being sure about the route, he intended to pick up the children and flee across the border with his dead daughter), but was captured by a border guard. The guard wanted to take him along, however my husband told him that there were his children waiting for him. The guard went with him to the stalk pile. There my husband told him that he also had a dead daughter. Unmoved the guard replied 'we'll bury her' and forced everybody to go with him. The dead daughter had to stay behind. The indiscribable pain cut through the three hearts, however, they couldn't even weep anymore; the pain sealed their throats. All this happened even before dawn.

Three human beings out of a small group died in their desperate attempt to save their naked life. Nobody knows what ever happened to their beloved deceased. My husband, Viktoria and little Martin were chased to the headquarters at Rigitza.

There they were terribly maltreated. They had to disrobe down to their underwear and were locked up in the basement. After a few days they were interrogated and the verdict pronounced: execution by firing squad. When my husband asked why execution, the partisan said because he took his family out of the camp.

They were chased into the street in front of the headquarters and had to sit down into the snow. A partisan opened the window and aimed his rifle at them. At the last moment another partisan pushed him aside and closed the window. Then they were chased into the Kruschiwl camp. The trip to the camp was terrible, through the snow, cold and torture. After several months they were able to escape from Kruschiwl and came back to the Gakowa camp; unfortunately without the daughter Maria."

10.2 Setbacks in Rumania and Hungary

As the following two reports show, the ethnic Germans who succeeded in escaping from the camps and crossing the borders to Romania or Hungary, were still far from being safe. The governments of these neighbouring two countries were allied with Yugoslavia within the Communist Eastern Block. In addition, part of their population were "anti-fascistic" and followed the official "collective guilt of all Germans" propaganda. Also, unscrupulous individuals took advantage of the defenseless poor refugees to rob them of their last few belongings. However, it has to be stressed that there were also many decent Hungarian and Romanian people who helped the hunted fugitives. Thus it depended on the personal luck whom you encountered. But these unfortunate, harassed human beings definitely could only feel save, after further sacrifices and hardships, upon reaching Austria or Germany where they were officially accepted.

Herbert Prokle from Modosch/Banat, narrates in the *Modoscher Heimatblätter* how in March 1945 he fled, eleven years old, with his father from the local Modosch camp to Romania. His mother did not accompany them. The second son Dietmar, as a 16 years old classified a "man", had been shipped to the liquidation camp Betschkerek and, for that reason, she did not want to leave the country. However, she supported the escape of her husband and younger son since friendly Serbs warned them of an imminent tearing apart of families. Aside from many flight events, Herbert Prokle narrates the following:

"At the beginning of 1945 we refugees from Yugoslavia were in Romania still somewhat of a rarity, however, gradually more and more arrived. From former Modosch residents and other acquaintances we sometimes obtained news about my mother and brother who still were held in different camps of Tito. It was reassuring to know that they were still alive (contrary to thousands of other country-men, including close relatives); sadly, however, they themselves did not come.

In spring 1946 my father, by coincidence, met a countryman who was very courageous but at that moment rather distraught: As a German soldier he became a prisoner of war by the Russians and escaped several times, but was always recaptured. He did, however, not give up and eventually was able to make his way to Romania. Here he learned about the fate of the ethnic Germans in Yugoslavia and that his wife and small son were held there in various camps. He promptly proceeded to go to find them. Even though he spoke Serbian without an accent and had some Serbian friends who helped him along, it was still a tremendous risk. Discovery would have resulted in his certain and painful death. His courage though was rewarded. He found his wife and son, succeeded in kidnapping them out of the two different camps and brought them safely to relatives in Romania. The joy, however, did not last for long. His wife was arrested during a raid and sentenced to be extradited to Yugoslavia. She was held at the Temeschburg prison where Germans from Yugoslavia were collected and, in groups, returned. The two men struck a deal: If my father would succeed in freeing his wife from the prison, the other would go to Yugoslavia to bring my mother and brother.

Since the verdict was already entered and the extradition date set, my father had to give up his first plan to 'buy her out'. The people that were to be bribed would not be able to justify the discharge without causing suspicion and danger for themselves. Thus my father decided on another considerably more dangerous path. By bribing the guards he could visit the women and tell her of the plan to liberate her. He went to see her every day and always stayed a little longer, also giving the guards every time a higher tip. The prisoners were not held in cells, they could move around and had to work under supervision. The guards had gotten to know the daily visitor and showed their appreciation of the supplement to their meager wage by not being too strict in their supervision. His assured manner enabled my father to leave the prison with the woman and disappear in the crowd of the large city. When the escape was detected a large-scale search was undertaken, including searches at the railroad station and on the trains. But by then my father delivered the woman to her husband and they all remained hidden for several days.

When the woman learned of the agreement of the two men she strenuously tried to keep her husband from going back to Yugoslavia. She wept bitterly and did not want him to risk his life again, now that they just succeeded to be together again. However, he said: 'I gave Mr. Prokle my word and I am going. He also kept his promise.' It would have been understandable if he had not taken that risk, however, his word of honour was more important to him. Together we went to our relatives at Johannisfeld (close to the Yugoslav border) where I was supposed to stay until, as we hoped, the good man would return with my mother and Dietmar.

A few days later, just before dawn, there was a knock at the window and we excitedly jumped out of our beds – the nervous wait was over. I delightedly embraced my brother and could also welcome his friend Anton Ziel. However, my searching look for my mother was in vain. Our friend explained that she no longer was at the expected camp and nobody knew where she was transferred to. The venture was only half a success, but we, and particularly my brother Dietmar, are forever greatly indebted to the brave gentleman."

Paul Mesli, from Filipowa/Batschka, writes how about 1,000 people who successfully escaped from the liquidation camp Gakowa and thought to be save, were captured in Hungary and brutally chased back to Yugoslavia. Here are some excerpts from his detailed report:

"The flight from Gakowa to Csatalja in Hungary was successful. For six weeks we could already recuperate from the horrors of the camp and the flight. We felt like new-born humans even being in a foreign country. A young Hungarian family, who in the fall of 1944 was deported from Topola/Yugoslavia, took us in. They lived in a house that had been owned by an ethnic German in Hungary who fled from the advancing Russians and now homeless, must be moving around somewhere. The Hungarian family Varga was very kind to us and helped whenever they could. We in turn, worked for them on their farm.

For several days already the police started to engage in raids and arresting refugees who came from the Yugoslav camps. Varga Pista wanted to hide and protect us, however, the danger to him and to us was too great. We wanted to move on, to Austria. We sold the last of our clothing to collect the money for the trip. At six o'clock in the morning I stood, together with the entire Mesli-clan, in the courtyard and tearfully bid good-bye to the Varga family. We then proceeded to the Baratschka railroad station. By the time the train arrived there were so many refugees congregated that two additional freight cars had to be added so that everybody had the opportunity to travel along. Full of joy we bought tickets to St. Gotthard, the last stop before reaching the Austrian border.

The train entered the station and the passengers in the train could not understand why there was such a large crowd, about 250 refugees, standing at the station. After awhile though they began to shout: 'These are all Swabok (Swabians), war criminals, fascists! To hell with you all!' The station master, however, was very kind to us and cooperative. He saw to it that everybody managed to get on the train. The whistle blew and the strange rail-freight started to move. There were only smiling faces, full of joy and hope to soon be able to disembark in Austria.

After a short trip we arrived at Baja. Two policemen with drawn guns stepped in front of the engine while other policemen boarded the train and chased all of us off. From the station we were chased to the military barracks where hundreds of fugitives were already held in the courtyard. Why were all these people collected? Nobody gave any answer. Our begging for some food for the children was answered with cursing and scolding. We were about 1,000 people. By 10:30 in the morning we were told to pack up and start marching.

The reaction of the local population to our miserable procession was mixed. Some were spitting at us; others wanted to give us bread, money, food, but were driven off by the police. A farmer offered to drive the children and old people on his wagon, but was refused and cursed because he wanted to help the 'fascists'. Among us there were many sick and old people who could hardly walk. Meanwhile it began to rain hard and we were drenched down to our skin. It was terrible. Nobody knew where we were headed since we were all strangers and did not know the region.

The miserable column moved slower and slower; the people just could no longer walk. There were beatings and we were forced to continue. As we moved through villages, people, good ones and bad ones, lined the threets. Again farmers offered to drive children, the sick and old people. Since there was no other way, two were allowed to do it. On the open road a farmer with his horses came from the opposite direction. He stopped and looking at us he cried. He too offered immediately to drive the ones that could no longer walk. He was permitted to do so. When the guards realized that they could no longer move us on they stopped more farmers to drive the people. All farmers gladly complied.

Meanwhile we began to realize that we were taken towards the Yugoslav border. We had just began to hope that we escaped death in the camps, but now had to experience being driven back into annihilation. We implored the guards not to chase us back to Yugoslavia, but to let us proceed to Austria. They knew what was happening to us Germans in Yugoslavia, but they continued chasing us back. By the time we reached Gara it was already pitch-dark. The police was given search lights to keep an eye on us. Now we were moving straight towards the border. Outside of Gara the column was devided into smaller groups. The knowledge of being thrown back into Yugoslavia was paralyzing. It took us more than four hours to reach the border. We went through mud and water; we all dragged ourselves quietly and resigned to our fate. Suddenly we had to stop. Children and sick had to get off the wagons. Nobody was allowed to talk. It was pitch-dark and they kept chasing us, like cattle; even in the mud the policemen pushed us forward.

Suddenly somebody shouted 'stoj' ('halt' in Serbian). Shots were fired, bullets flew over our heads. We were at the border and the Hungarians pushed us over the line. However, the Yugoslavs pushed us back into Hungary and the Hungarians pushed us again over into Yugoslavia. Everybody was shouting and shooting. It was frightful. People screamed and wept and ran into all directions. Suddenly we were surrounded by partisans who chased us to another group that was already captured. The sufferings of the about 1,000 humans is indescribable. We never learned whether anybody was killed during this 'battue'.

After a short march we stood in front of a long train with damaged rail cars. We were chased inside and many immediately fell asleep. Partisans guarded the train the whole day. Reinforcements arrived at night. We were prepared for the worst. In the darkness the cars were emptied one by one and the people led away but not all in the same direction. We remembered that many of our countrymen were taken in that manner to dig their own graves and then shot. With such memories we awaited the next events.

Now it was our turn, about 180 people. One partisan in the lead, three in the back, we moved diagonally across wheat fields. There was again some shooting and commotions. We shuddered. They ordered us to be quiet and move faster. Suddenly we stood at the border, the partisans stayed behind and we moved on to Hungary. Both sides were again shooting over our heads. The group in front of us was stopped by Hungarian border guards, but we managed to cross over undetected. The groups that were stopped, were chased by the Hungarians again back to Yugoslavia, I do not know what finally happened to them.

Out of the danger zone we rested in the middle of the wheat field and, exhausted, fell asleep. At dawn we saw that we were near Csatalja. We split up into smaller groups and together with my clan we went to the Varga family."

On January 13th, 1947 Paul Mesli and his family renewed their attempt to reach the Austrian border. At the border town Körmend all fugitives were again captured at the railroad station and chased to army barracks. In groups they were led to the guard office. "We were totally robbed of jewelry, money and better clothing. In Hungary the helpless and exploited fugitives were again taken advantage of. Anybody could step on us, like on a worm, just as they pleased", writes Mesli. The following night they were led to the border and could cross over to Austria.

10.3 "Black" and "White" Escapes

From the end of 1946 to late summer 1947 apparently orders were issued "from higher up" to allow a certain number of escapes, presumably to get rid of the hated Swabians in this manner. This handling could particularly be observed in the Batschka liquidation camps Gakowa and Kruschiwl, situated very close to the Hungarian border; considerably less in other camps. However, it did not mean that these camps suddenly were open. As a rule the camp commanders handled the so-called "white escapes" in a way that only those were let go who could come up with some money to bribe them. Whoever had no money (and most inmates were already robbed clean), still had to take their chances with the life threatening "black escape".

Towards the end of 1947 the "white escapes" were completely cut off and the controls and punishments drastically stiffened again. So the "black escapes", with all the terrible risks involved, were again the only possibility to get out of Yugoslavia and its murderous camps.

During the period of 1944 to the closing of the camps in 1948, about 30,000 to 35,000 ethnic Germans were able to save themselves across the borders, corresponding to more than 15 percent of those who fell into the hands of Tito's partisans. It is not known how many escaped as "white" and how many as "black" fugitives. Nor do we know how many were murdered in the course of their flight attempts. By all means, these occurrences are one important aspect to reveal the ethnic Germans' fate who according to the Communist version just "disappeared" from Yugoslavia. And if this considerable number had not saved themselves by risking their escape, many of them would have been murdered in the camps thus increasing even more the total number of mortal victims.

Sources
Leidensweg der Deutschen im kommunistischen Jugoslawien, Vol. I–IV (LW I–IV):
Ernst Lung, LW I, 219; Johann Pudel, LW II, 56; Magdalena Brenner, LW III, 373 ff.; Paul Mesli, LW III, 391 ff.; Johann Hebel, LW III, 401 ff. and 838 ff. Herbert Prokle, *Modoscher Heimatblätter,* No. 68.

Chapter 11: Original Size and Disappearance of the Ethnic German Population in Yugoslavia

In 1941 about 541,000 ethnic Germans lived in Yugoslavia, thereof 508,000 Danube Swabians and 33,000 Germans of Slovenia. Up to October 1944 about 13,000 of them were killed as soldiers.

The Danube Swabians lived mainly in the Banat, Batschka, Baranja, Syrmia, Slavonia and, to a lesser extent, in Croatia, Bosnia and the capital Belgrade. The Slovenia-Germans consisted predominantly of the Gottscheers and of Lower Styrians.

Larger Communities and Dispersed Settlements up to 1944

About 70 percent of the 541,000 ethnic Germans lived in entirely or predominantly German communities, particularly in the Banat and Batschka where most of the Danube Swabians were domiciled. At the census of 1931 in the pre-war Yugoslavia more than 1,000 inhabitants in 115 localities stated to be of German ethnicity.

A small percentage of the Danube Swabians, namely in Slavonia, Croatia and Bosnia, lived in dispersed settlements.

In October 1944 the remaining 33,000 ethnic Germans in today's independent state Slovenia, whose numbers since World War II were greatly reduced due to political circumstances, lived mainly in dispersed settlements, except in Laibach, Marburg and Gottschee (which were predominantly German).

Remaining Ethnic German Population in Yugoslavia in 1948

About 245,000 ethnic Germans were evacuated or fled on their own initiative before the Tito-regime came into power. Around 95,000 were serving as soldiers in the German, Hungarian or Croatian armies. About 200,000 ethnic German civilians stayed at home and came under communist rule.

As explained in the foregoing chapters of this book, of the 200,000 people nearly 10,000 were murdered during the bloody autumn 1944 and around 12,000 were deported to the Soviet Union for hard labour (2,000 perished). In 1945 all remaining ethnic Germans, with exception of about 8,000 (mostly married with other ethnicities), i. e. approximately 170,000 were concentrated in labour and liquidation camps.

Early 1948 the last camps were closed. Deducting from the 170,000 interned persons the perished victims, the ones who escaped from the camps and the children who in 1946 were taken to "children homes" for their slavinization, the number of remaining inmates may be estimated to have been 70,000 to 75,000. And what happened to these ethnic Germans after the camps were closed in 1948?

Banishment, Reintegration and Legal Emigration

When the camps were closed, the people were not really free. They could not go back to their home communities nor could they choose any new domicile; they were forced to enter into two to three years labour contracts in unfamiliar localities, which they were not allowed to leave. This type of banishment lasted up to 1950/51.

Only after the hard labour contracts expired, the remaining ethnic Germans in Yugoslavia were theoretically free to change their type of work or move, however, where should they go? Their properties remained confiscated, their former homes were occupied by other nationals (almost exclusively Serbs) and these new settlers did not want the expropriated German owners coming back to their original communities. Even worse, the torturers and murderers were still there, some occupied important places in the Communist Party and others in public administration. The traumatized survivors of the camps could not feel safe; after the barbaric treatment they had suffered, they could no longer consider Yugoslavia their home country.

So the ethnic Germans considered their reluctant and still limitted reintegration in Yugoslavia only as a temporary arrangement and worked hard to save some money in order to be able to pay the high costs for a legal emigration as soon as possible. This is how and why most of the survivors of the camps left Yugoslavia between 1950 and 1960.

The following eyewitness report is a typical example of how the horrified remaining ethnic Germans felt and lived in Yugoslavia after the camps were closed.

Life after Rudolfsgnad – an Eyewitness Report

Rosalia Becker née Ziwei, together with her mother and her brother (her father had died as a German soldier), were forcibly transported from the camp to their new place of work without even being informed what was going on; much less they were asked about their opinion. In the *Modoscher Heimatblätter* no. 159 (pages 3297–3306) Rosalia Becker published the following report:

"In December 1947 we were among the first to be taken out of the camp. Selected were families who had young males of 16 years and older since these had to perform hard labour in the coal mines. As a start we were given some clothing to wear, used clothing from America. Then we were put into railroad cattle cars, their floors covered with straw and off we went into uncertain destiny. Nobody was asked whether we wanted to go, it was compulsory, just as everything in the past.

We received one loaf of 'maize bread', which had nothing in common with what was meant by bread since a stone could hardly have been harder. Our mother boiled a bottle of tea, made of vine twigs; that's all we had te eat and drink for the next two days. We took turns keeping the bottle on our bosom to prevent the tea from becoming frozen. Thus we could take a sip now and then. It was a long trip, two days and one night and in severe cold weather. At one time the train stopped and we were jubilant because we thought we had reached our destination; however, to our disappointment, only some of the cars were disconnected – they went off into a different direction and we also moved on again.

The second evening we arrived at Mirovo in the original part of Serbia. There we had to transfer onto open trucks to be taken to Rtanj (Rudnik) since the train did not go that far. There we were sitting in the open air, the cold wind blowing about our ears, driving slowly through the winter night and still not being treated huzmanely. All the more we were surprised to find warm food was awaiting us at Rtanj: pork stew with potatoes and fresh white bread. Food of which we only dreamed of for years at the camp. We could hardly believe that nobody became ill from eating such fat food that we were not used to any more.

After the meal we still had to go on by foot, however, there were German prisoners of war who had worked in the coal mines before our arrival and they had to help us get to the 'Sokolana' (gymnasium) since we could barely stand on our feet. That was the condition in which we, 60 families of about 200 people, almost frozen to death, arrived there around midnight. The large hall had straw on the floor and we could again sleep together, just like in the camp. However, each of us received a 'horse blanket' which, for us, was already a luxury.

The next day already the young boys received their work clothing, shoes and boots. Each of us few girls received a pair of sturdy, laced shoes of which even the smallest sizes were too large, but that did not bother us. Most important to us was that we again had whole shoes. With some rags wrapped around our feet they fit pretty well and we had warm feet. We slept at the gymnasium only for a few more days and received the meals from the Mensa (common mess hall) only during our stay there. Then each person received a tin cup with knife, fork and spoon and a piece of fish soap; each family was given also a tin hand basin. Each family was assigned one room in a 'Koliba'; these were small huts with three rooms, each with its own door to the outside. Thus three families could be accommodated. Each room had a small window, two beds and a small stove in the shape of a drum. The stove served for heating, cooking and, when dark, for illumination; one only had to open the small door. For a long time the only sitting furniture was a log. Now we also had to look after our own food supply. We received ration cards. Those working in the mines received the best cards; women and girls were entitled to less and whoever could not work, like my mother who was very weak from her stay in the camp, received very little.

My mother and I wanted to immediately start cleaning the room. The floor was rather uneven and we tried to even it out, but as we proceeded the floor started to lift. More and more pieces began to become loose and we noted that beneath there was a wooden floor. Then our real work began and ended only when we had removed the entire covering. Later we found out that the covering was not dirt, but sheep manure – the 'Kolibas' were previously used as sheep pens.

The second day already the boys began their work in the mines. They were divided into three shifts of eight hours daily. Saturday was a full work day, Sunday was free. They were told to take their lamps along when they went outside at night – to chase the wolves away. Supposedly they were afraid of light, which was not the case. In the winter they came down from the mountains and howled at our hut's door. We were often afraid they would tear down our door.

Women and girls were also detailed to work. The first two years were typical hard labour periods. Everybody had to perform whatever work he or she was given. I cannot remember that either I or my mother ever signed a work contract; perhaps my brother had to sign one since he was the main person in the family and he was selected for this work. However, with or without our signature, our opinions were meaningless; we were brought to this place and had no choice. We were not allowed to leave this place during the first few years. But compared to the camp we were relatively free since there was nobody standing behind us with a rifle. We were also paid for our work.

Most of the women and girls worked at the 'Separazia', which was the coal transfer station. Coal was transported from the mines by lorries on rails and then by funicular to Mirovo, since, as already mentioned, Rtanj had no railway connection. About ten connected lorries were pulled by a horse, led by my girlfriend Hanni whilst the 'Bäsl Liss' (Mrs. Lizzie) was the 'brake'. She was walking behind the lorries and when going somewhat downhill had to put a rod into the last wheel. That's how modern we were. My first job was to take the mine lamps from the 'Separazia' to the 'Lampara' to be filled and take them back again.

The German prisoners of war were soon released and allowed to return to Germany. Then Serbian soldiers were brought in from Zrna Gora (Montenegro). Also volunteer civilians from Slovenia and Croatia and moslems who came to earn some money. They all were young men without families, usually stayed about six months and then returned home; then new ones came. The cooking for them, about several hundred men, was done at the mess hall. For that they needed women and girls in the kitchen. How happy we were to work in the warm kitchen after having been outside in cold and wet weather. We were also allowed to eat all we wanted. There was, however, one disadvantage, we had to work seven days a week. The shift hours were from 5 to 13, from 13 to 21 and from 21 to 5. The night shift was the worst; two 80-liter pots of potatoes had to be peeled or large bags of beans to be cleaned, etc. Everything had to be prepared for the next day. Being 14 years of age I was the youngest of all, but looked only to be eleven and the women felt sorry for me.

The loving God must have held his protecting hands over our boys. None of our Danube Swabians was killed in the mines during the six years we spent there. However, the fear was always there. My brother Mischi was spring master and always had to walk in front and there was always danger. Once, during springing, he could not get away fast enough and the heat damaged his eyes. He could not see for several days, but, luckily, this was only temporarily and the accident had no further consequences.

Rtanj was actually only a work station; there was no town hall, no church, no post office, only a 'Uprava' (office building) and an 'Upravnik' who was in charge of all the workers. In addition to the volunteer workers who lived there for a limited period without their families, many Serbs from the surrounding villages came to work daily on foot across the mountains. Only very few Serbian families were permanent residents at Rtanj, in addition to our 60 Danube Swabian families. We had a normal contact with the locals and none of them were hostile. On weekends we had dances and we all got together at the 'Dom'. The Slovenes and Croats played also German music but since there were only few girls, they played mostly Kolo (a Serbian folk dance) which could be danced by the young men as a group.

In time our situation generally improved. New houses were built and we asked the Upravnik to give every family a small piece of land to plant some vegetables. He immediately agreed but gave us a slope full of rocks, probably thinking nothing would grow there anyway. But the Swabians showed him that where there is a will there is a way. All 60 families began with their work. First the stones were removed and then the hard ground was broken up. We were successful and everything grew beautifully. During 1949 the houses were completed and we could move from our sheep pens into the new settlement. The apartment had a kitchen with stove and we finally could do some normal cooking. The previous small stove could only accommodate one pot and we had to restrict our cooking to one-pot meals. In the kitchen we now even had a table and two benches and we also had a sleeping room. Well, after five years the situation became a little more humane. However, now we also had to pay rent.

Those of us who had relatives in America could now also receive packages. The brother of my Wajer-grandfather had emigrated as a young lad and we fairly often used to receive packages from him. But to obtain the packages we had to walk over the mountains into the city. At the post office everything was opened and they took away whatever they liked and we had no authority to say anything. But they left something over for us.

After the two hard labour years, we were allowed to travel to other parts of Yugoslavia, if we did have the necessary money. Whether or not we would have been allowed to move away I do not know. Where could we have gone anyway? The Banat and Modosch were no longer our homeland. Serbs were now living in our houses and they certainly would have been hostile. After these two years of hard labour we did not yet know of any possibilities to emigrate to Germany. Thus, for the time being, we continued to stay at Rtanj.

Since the 60 families were selected because they had sons 16 years and older suitable for work in the mines, there were only few small children, particularly since we came from the liquidation camp where most of the small siblings starved to death. Thus we had only few school-age children and these went to school with

Serbian children. Teaching was only in the Serbian language. I am in connection with many ethnic Germans who were at other locations in Yugoslavia and none had encountered any German school teaching after World War II, let alone knew of a German-language school. Nor have we seen or heard of a German-language newspaper.

It was only after some men were released from captivity to Germany and were searching for their families through the Red Cross did we learn that one could legally emigrate and we also received the address of the German embassy at Belgrade. First priority was given to people who had a husband or brother in Germany where they could find a place to live. At that time the refugee camps were still overcrowded. We applied for immigration at the German embassy, but by the time we received the reply it was too late. My brother Mischi (and all the other young men) was drafted for two years into the Yugoslav military and he had to start his term in fall of 1950. Therefore we were forced to stay until he was discharged.

It should be mentioned that our citizenship was also taken away at the time we were disfranchised, expropriated and shipped to the concentration camps. Thus we were stateless for five years, but when they wanted Mischi for the military we became automatically again Yugoslavian nationals. My mother and I now had to continue on our own with only very little money, which was not very easy. We planted maize and could even feed a hog – how proud we were of our achievement. I also found work in an office since, by that time, I had a good command of the Serbian language. Mischi was stationed at Rijeka at the Adriatic Sea. This was very far away and only rarely was he allowed a furlough to visit us.

I also want to mention that all the 60 families came from different villages, but we all had one thing in common: We survived the annihilation camp and this has forged a bond for life between us. We were like a large family. There were no fights, no envy and all were always ready to help. The friendships established at that time still exist to this day.

Meanwhile we renewed our immigration application to Germany and had no problem receiving the entry permits since my mother was a war widow. When after two years, my brother was discharged from the military we had everything ready, but there was still one hitch: To obtain the emigration permit from Yugoslavia, we had to relinquish the 'generously' granted citizenship at the beginning of his military service. For that we had to, of course, pay a fee. On December 23rd, 1952 we drove to Belgrade to deposit the money and with great joy, became stateless again.

I want to clearly stress that neither I nor anybody else wanted to emigrate to Germany for material reasons. We did not even know anything about the economic situation in Germany. The reason was – and in this respect I can speak in the name of all Danube Swabians who were in the Yugoslav liquidation camps – that nobody, I repeat, *nobody* wanted to stay even one day longer than absolutely necessary in this country where so many loving people, close relatives and friends were most brutally tortured, murdered and sadistically left to starve to death.

On February 8th, 1953 we arrived at the Piding receiving camp in Germany. Only now were we really free and very happy that the nightmare Yugoslavia was behind us."

Disappearance of the Ethnic German Minority in the Former Yugoslavia

More than 90,000 ethnic Germans of the former Yugoslavia did not survive the war and the genocide. Almost all of the survivors of the camps have left Yugoslavia. Counting these to the previously evacuated and escaped before the communists' takeover, about 450,000 ethnic Germans of Yugoslavia were rescued. Only Germans in mixed ethnic marriages and the few communists remained in the former communist Yugoslavia. The realistic figures of the Germans remaining in their homeland are, at the most, 12,000 to 15,000. Of these 10,000 to 12,000 are Danube Swabians.

The New Homelands of the Surviving Ethnic Germans of Yugoslavia

Most Slovenian Germans found their new homeland in Austria. According to reliable figures about 300,000 (or 70 percent) of the Danube Swabians from Yugoslavia settled in the country of their ancestors, Germany; another 67,000 in Austria, 25,000 in the USA, 10,000 in Canada, 4,000 in Brazil, 3,000 in Hungary, 2,000 in Argentina, 1,000 in Australia and about 3,000 in various other countries.

In the year 2001, about 170,000 (40 percent) of the 425,000 Danube Swabians who escaped the genocide were still alive. Counting their descendents, the total of Danube Swabians originary from Yugoslavia exceeds one million.

Chapter 12: Documentation of Human Casualties

The previous chapters described the gruesome atrocities committed against the ethnic Germans by the Yugoslav communist regime, resulting in the genocide of this significant part of Yugoslavia's population.

After their escape, the survivors of the Danube Swabian genocide organized "home town societies" in their new domiciles, particularly in Germany, Austria and overseas countries. This enabled them to establish reliable documentations of the tragic events and casualties, including names, times and places of their death. Over 60,000 names are recorded. This represents about 70 percent of the calculated victims. The following tables detail the numbers and localities of their demise between 1944 and 1948.

Banat					
CAMP	**VICTIMS BY NAME**	**ROUNDED ESTIMATED FIGURES***	**CAMP**	**VICTIMS BY NAME**	**ROUNDED ESTIMATED FIGURES***
Banat Brestowatz	335	400	Lazarfeld	25	
Banater Topola	24		Mastort	72	100
Betschkerek	201	1000	Modosch	20	
Botschar	32		Molidorf	2,012	3,000
Charleville	185	200	Mramorak	78	100
Elemer	21		Nakodorf	201	200
Deutsch-Zerne	46		Pantschowa	298	400
Ernsthausen	81		Pardan	16	
Etschka	12		Rudolfsgnad	7,797	11,000
Franzfeld	99	150	Schuschara	59	
Georgshausen	13		Setschan	58	
Glogon	16		Setschanfeld	185	200
Heideschütz	38		Sigmundfeld	48	
Heufeld	20		Soltur	15	
Homolitz	21		St. Georgen	60	
Jabuka	160	200	St. Hubert	12	
Karlsdorf	394	500	Stefansfeld	218	250
Kathreinfeld	336	400	Tschestereg	23	
Kikinda	668	800	Weißkirchen	71	100
Kubin	87	100	Werschetz	100	1000
Kudritz	298	300	Zichydorf	50	

Batschka

CAMP	VICTIMS BY NAME	ROUNDED ESTIMATED FIGURES*
Altker	27	
Apatin	261	300
Batsch-Brestowatz	33	
Batsch-Sentiwan	32	
Filipowa	221	250
Futok	36	
Gajdobra	19	
Gakowa	5,827	8,500
Hodschag	96	100
Jarek	5,240	7,000
Karawukowa	17	
Kernei	61	
Kischker	21	
Kolut	29	
Kruschiwl	2,103	2,800
Legin	64	
Miletitsch	18	
Neusatz	81	100
Palanka	28	
Schowe	21	
Sekitsch	309	400
Sombor	97	150
Stanischitsch	91	100
Subotica	42	100
Torschau	53	
Tschonopel	31	
Weprowatz	31	
Werbass	76	100

Baranja

CAMP	VICTIMS BY NAME	ROUNDED ESTIMATED FIGURES*
Albertsdorf	10	
Mirkovac	16	
Mitvar	60	100

Slavonia/Croatia

CAMP	VICTIMS BY NAME	ROUNDED ESTIMATED FIGURES*
Essegg	17	
Groß-Pisanitz	15	
Josipovac	38	100
Kerndia	100	500
Valpovo	393	1,000

Syrmia

CAMP	VICTIMS BY NAME	ROUNDED ESTIMATED FIGURES*
Irig	16	
Mitrowitz	1,033	2,000
Semlin/Franztal	277	500
Vodjinci	13	
Vrdnik	17	
Wukowar	23	

Others

CAMP	VICTIMS BY NAME	ROUNDED ESTIMATED FIGURES*
Belgrade	11	
Bor	26	

* Rounded off and estimated figures calculated on this basis.

Estimate of Camp Casualties by Area

AREA	ESTIMATE OF CASUALTIES
Banat	22,000
Batschka	22,000
Baranja	250
Syrmia	3,000
Slavonia	1,750

Total Casualties of all Ethnic Germans in Former Jugoslavia

	Danube Swabians	Germans in Slovenia	total
Civilians	59,335	4,300	**63,635**
Soldiers	26,064	2,700	**28,764**
total	85,399	7,000	**92,399**
rounded	**85,400**	**7,000**	**92,400**

Source: *Verbrechen an den Deutschen in Jugoslawien 1944–1948,* p. 312.

Total Casualties of Danube Swabians

(Lowest Limit Estimations)

Casualties		Banat	Batschka	Baranja	Syrmia	Slavonia/ Croatia	Bosnia	Serbia	Others	Total
Before internment after 1941	M	3,526	1,599	40	975	602	85	55	15	6,897
	F	332	247	10	326	90	20	10	5	1,040
	C	27	18		29	28	5	5		112
	T	3,885	1,864	50	1,330	720	110	70	20	8,049
During internment in Yugoslavia from Oct 1944 to March 1948	M	7,547	7,157	581	703	790	45	45	10	16,878
	F	11,822	11,322	806	824	1,058	70	70	15	25,987
	C	2,471	2,318	133	268	357	15	15	5	5,582
	T	21,840	20,797	1,520	1,795	2,205	130	130	30	48,447
While escaping from internment (probably many more)	M	33	33	11	15	5				97
	F	41	51	4	10	5				111
	C	6	12	4	5	5				32
	T	80	96	19	30	15				240
Total in the former Yugoslavia	M	11,106	8,789	632	1,693	1,397	130	100	25	23,872
	F	12,195	11,620	820	1,160	1,153	90	80	20	27,138
	C	2,504	2,348	137	302	390	20	20	5	5,726
	T	25,805	22,757	1,589	3,155	2,940	240	200	50	56,736
In the USSR during slave labor period	M	398	708							1,106
	F	427	461							888
	C									
	T	825	1,169							1,994
Outside of Tito's jurisdiction and outside the USSR	M	17	38	8	40	32	89	4		228
	F	22	57	6	54	37	54	4		234
	C	8	20		13	32	68	2		143
	T	47	115	14	107	101	211	10		605
Total civilians	M	11,521	9,535	640	1,733	1,429	219	104	25	25,206
	F	12,644	12,138	826	1,214	1,190	144	84	20	28,260
	C	2,512	2,368	137	315	422	88	22	5	5,869
	T	26,677	24,041	1,603	3,262	3,041	451	210	50	59,335
Soldiers	M	8,804	7,748	794	3,662	3,926	850	250	30	26,064
	F									
	C									
	T	8,804	7,748	794	3,662	3,926	850	250	30	26,064
Total of all casualties	M	20,325	17,283	1,434	5,395	5,355	1,069	354	55	51,270
	F	12,644	12,138	826	1,214	1,190	144	84	20	28,260
	C	2,512	2,368	137	315	422	88	22	5	5,869
	T	35,481	31,789	2,397	6,924	6,967	1,301	460	80	85,399

M = male
F = female
C = children
T = total

166

Chapter 13: The Facts of Genocide Committed against the Ethnic Germans in the Communist Yugoslavia during 1944–1948

The purpose of the following presentations of occurrences is to determine whether the persecution and expulsion of the ethnic Germans in the former Yugoslavia during the period of 1944 to 1948 represent a genocide as defined in the December 9th, 1948 Convention on the Prevention and Punishment of the Crime of Genocide of the General Assembly of the United Nations or if the above named events constitute "merely" crimes against humanity. It has to be examined whether acts committed against the ethnic Germans of Yugoslavia fit the genocide definition – this is called the "physical state of facts" – furthermore, it has to be examined whether it can be proven that the ones responsible had the intent to destroy the ethnic Germans as group – this is called the "mental state of facts". The latter is the determining factor for the state of genocide.

Clarification of this question is necessary for various reasons. If the fact of genocide is proven it will contribute a legal basis for illuminating the historical truth and will be of service to jurisprudence. It will give the legal administration a signal that action to proceed against the perpetrators and executors is required. It strengthens the politicians both morally and pragmatically in the execution of their obligation to enforce justice. It will force the perpetrating nations and their successor nations to hold the extent of their moral responsibility in front of their eyes. Last but not least, it gives the victims the satisfaction of acknowledgement, by international law, of their injustices suffered and enriches the dignity of their remembrances. Finally, the judical examination of a calamitous history based on the facts of genocide can contribute to safeguard the ethnic treasures of the world for its future.

13.1 The Convention on the Prevention and Punishment of the Crime of Genocide

In the Convention on the Prevention and Punishment of the Crime of Genocide, adopted December 9th, 1948, the General Assembly of the United Nations refers to its declaration in the Resolution 96(1) of December 11th, 1946 according to which genocide is a crime under international law, contrary to the spirit and objectives of the United Nations and condemned by the civilized world.

For footnotes see pages 182–184

Article I states: "The contracting parties confirm that genocide, whether committed in time of peace or in time of war, is a crime under international law which they undertake to prevent and to punish."

Article II gives a more detailed definition[1]: "In the present Convention, genocide means any of the folowing acts committed with intent to destroy, in whole or in part, a national, ethnical, racial or religious group, as such:

a. killing members of the group;
b. causing serious bodily or mental harm to members of the group;
c. deliberately inflicting on the group conditions of life calculated to bring about its physical destruction in whole or in part;
d. imposing measures intended to prevent births within the group;
e. forcibly transferring children of the group to another group.

According to international law historians, the Convention on the Prevention and Punishment of the Crime of Genocide of December 9th, 1948 codifies the International Law that was already in existence long before Word War II. Therefore, punishment for genocide, for acts committed before 1948, is by all means possible, notwithstanding the habitual prohibition of retroactive application of penal laws.[2] The protection of the ethnic diversity is such a great legal treasure for the community of nations that, in this case, a universal validity of this International Law is applicable; this means that not only international courts such as the Ruanda and the Yugoslavia Tribunals or the International Criminal Court may persue and punish the crime of genocide, but also national courts.[3]

Nevertheless, the Convention represents a significant progress since it defines in a more precise manner the term "genocide", and because it obligates the signatory nations to adopt the Convention into their national penal codes and enactment of penalties.[4]

13.2. The Physical State of Facts: Execution of Genocidal Actions in the Communist Yugoslavia according to Article II, a–e of the Genocide Convention

Genocide has been perpetrated if at least one of the acts, specified in letters a–e of article II, has taken place. The committing of such acts against members of the ethnic German group in Yugoslavia between 1944 and 1948 has been documented in the preceeding chapters of this book.

Letter a: Killing members of the group. The premeditated killing of members of the ethnic German population, particularly mass executions, took place immediately after the occupation of the Banat, Batschka and Syrmia during October and November of 1944. Up to the end of the war, 7,000 persons were murdered. Details are reported in chapter 3 of this book. However, further premeditated killings took place in all internment camps throughout the country.

Letter b: Causing serious bodily or mental harm to members of the group.[5] Forceful removal to work camps, hard labor and insufficient nourishment, without medical facilities, demeaning treatment, suffering from mental as well as emotional anguish because of lack of knowledge of family members' fate, are documented in chapter 6 of this book and fulfill the condition of letter b. This fact is reinforced by the internment of old age and ill people as well as children in concentration camps. There they were kept under most indescribable sanitary conditions, crowded and sleeping on bundles of straw, lack of adequate food, no heat and no medical care. They suffered from starvation, epidemic diseases, freezing temperatures as well as emotional distress, lonely and orphaned humans, as documented in chapter 7 of this book.[6]

Letter c: Deliberately inflicting on the group conditions of life calculated to bring about its physical destruction in whole or in part. To fulfill this condition it is necessary that the premeditated living conditions are conductive to lead to the physical destruction of the group. It will suffice to satisfy this condition if only a part of the group is subjected to inhuman conditions. Examples are internment in concentration camps, confiscation of property, factual slavery and, according to the opinion of the Federal Court of the Federal Republic of Germany and the International Ruanda Court, also the systematic expulsion of the group from its native homeland.[7]

The actions against the ethnic Germans of Yugoslavia also fulfill this condition specified in letter c of article II of the Genocide Convention:

– Based on the decisions of the Anti-Fascist Council of the National Liberation of Yugoslavia (AVNOJ) of November 11th, 1944 the ethnic Germans in Yugoslavia were collectively expropriated without compensation. Details are given in chapter 2 of this book.

– Furthermore, in Slovenia and Slavonia (which is part of Croatia) systematic expulsions took place by attempting to ship those Germans that had not fled before the communists took over, by rail to Austria. These attempts were only partially successful because the British occupation authorities refused to accept some of these train shipments. All these deportation measures were very cruel since the people were stuffed into cattle cars, without food or water. See sections 7.2 and 7.3 of chapter 7.

– Conditions of this letter c are also complied with by the fact that the premeditated internment in work camps and concentration camps of the group and the living conditions led to the total or partial physical destruction of the inmates. Of the approximately 170,000 interned people about 50,000 perished within the three-year confinement, as documented in the chapters 5, 6, 7 and 12.

Letter e: Forcibly transferring children of the group to another group. This alternative of the state of facts defined by the Convention on Genocide also has been met in the case of the ethnic Germans of Yugoslavia since many children who survived the liquidation camps up to 1946 (not only orphans but also those forcibly separated from their parents and close relatives) were taken to state institutions and systematically re-educated. See chapter 8 for details.

Conclusion:
As documented by the cited evidences, the "physical state of facts" condition of genocide committed against the ethnic Germans of Yugoslavia has been met.

13.3 The Mental State of Facts of Genocide: The Deliberate Intent of the Group's Destruction in whole or in part

The determining feature of genocide is established only by its mental components, according to which the perpetrator acted deliberately *with intent, to destroy* in whole or in part a national, ethnic, racial or religious group *as such.*

a. The mental component *to destroy*

Some of the international law literature assumes that the term *to destroy* means only the physical-biological destruction.[8] However, already since the 1950s, the interpretation has been that the intended destruction of the social existence of a group also qualifies as the state of fact of genocide. For simplification purpose one talks of a "narrower" and a "broader" interpretation of the concept *destruction.* Both interpretations play an important role in judging the crime of expulsion. Those that represent the "narrower" interpretation tend to consider the expulsion as a crime against humanity or violation against customary international law but not as genocide.[9]

However, one has to remember that according to the UNO Convention also crimes against humanity do not become statute-barred.[10] It has to be noted though that international law does not obligate a nation to enforce the rights of her citizens who became victims of international law violations against the perpetrating nation.[11]

The "broader" interpretation of deliberate destruction, which also includes the systematic expulsion of a group in its definition of genocide, is supported by the negotiations of the German Bundestag (Federal Diet) for the Federal Republic of Germany joining the Genocide Convention in July 1954 and the deliberations in the Bundestag to establish an appropriate Paragraph (220 a) in the StGB (German Penal Code) which includes the terms of the UNO Convention in the national German legislation. The reporting delegate Seidl (CDU/CSU) explained that the term *to destroy* was chosen after mature reflection because this word is a more comprehensive term which was supposed to include the group as a sociological concept.[12] The delegate Altmaier (SPD), in his speech explicitly categorized the expulsion of ethnic Germans after World War II as genocide.[13]

For the German parliamentarians of 1954 the systematic expulsions of ethnic groups fit the definition of state of facts of genocide.[14] The US Congressman Caroll Reece, in a speech in May 1957 in the US House of Representatives, also stated that the expulsion of the ethnic Germans includes the crime of genocide.[15]

In a more recent legal opinion *Felix Ermacora* (reputed expert at international law) in 1992, dealing with the expulsion of the ethnic Germans from the Sudetenland (since World War I part of Czechoslovakia, for centuries almost exclusively inhabited by Germans) stressed the thesis that the destruction of the social existence of a group is considered genocide.[16] In his judgement, genocide consists of a sum of acts which not necessarily leads to the physical extermination of people, but to the removal of a group from its ancestral home territory and to the destruction of its sense of unity. In his opinion, it is not only the expulsion of a group as such that represents an act of genocide but already their collective expropriation.[17] In the case of the ethnic Germans of the Sudetenland – and the same holds true for the ethnic Germans of Yugoslavia – expropriation and expulsion have to be considered one act.[18] If expulsion is part of a genocide, then the expropriation of private property is one as well, since the law of parts is determined by the law of the total. Expropriation in itself as part of the overall combination represents genocide character.[19]

Additional supporters of the "broader" interpretation are *Hans-Heinrich Jeschek*[20], as well as the German International law attorneys *Gilbert Gornig*[21] of the Marburg University and *Dieter Blumenwitz*[22] of the Würzburg University. The Bundesgerichtshof für Strafsachen (German Federal High Court for Crimes), in a decision in 1999 also adopted the same position.[23] A constitutional appeal against this decision was rejected by the German Bundesverfassungsgericht (Federal Constitutional Court) on December 12th, 2000.[24]

In its decision, the BGHSt (Federal High Court for Crimes) states that § 220 a StGB (of the Federal Penal Code) does not serve to protect the affected individual person's property rights but to protect the social existence of the persecuted national, racial, ethnic or religious group. The BGHSt stresses that the inhuman factor and injustice, in comparison to the crime of murder, is that the perpetrator or perpetrators do not see the human being in the victim but merely the member of the persecuted group.[25] Hence, the pertinent paragraph does not necessarily presuppose that the perpetrator wants to achieve the bodily annihilation, that is the physical destruction; it suffices that the perpetrator acts with the intent to destroy the group's social existence (the group *as such*), the social unity in its character and peculiarity and its sense of unity.[26]

A "broader" interpretation is also within the *spirit of genocide prohibition* since it specifically serves the purpose to protect the group as such. The existence of the group is not only jeopardized when the aggressor aspires to achieve the total (physical-biological) annihilation. The group is equally endangered when the characteristic features for its social existence such as the basis of unity and ethnic peculiarities are taken away by acts as cited in article II of the Convention of Genocide. Such is the case in systematic expulsion. Where members of a group are expelled from their ancestral areas and the basis of their physical existence is taken away through expropriation, the life of the group as such is no longer possible. The group does not distinguish itself only by its language and culture but also by its bond to a piece of soil on which it lives – its life thrives in its homeland. The intent to get rid of a population group that has become undesired can be achieved by destroying their social existence.

A "narrow" interpretation of deliberate destruction would not only run against the spirit of the Convention, but give all perpetrators the possibility to carry out the destruction of a group without running the risk it would be characterized an act of genocide.

In summary, it can be determined that the legal point of view of the Danube Swabians of Yugoslavia are in accord with the expert legal opinion of the highest judicial authorities of the Federal Republic of Germany and the legal view of renowned international law experts, namely, whoever acts with intent to destroy the social existence of a group, commits genocide.

b. The mental element *intent*

The perpetrator must act with the *intent* to destroy a group as such. The mental intent to destroy is the distinguishing feature for the crime of genocide. As long as the acts listed in article II, letters a–e are not based on the *intent* of the perpetrator to destroy a group in whole or in part, it is not considered genocide even though such acts are particularly gruesome. This factor distinguishes genocide from other crimes, such as crimes against humanity.

To prove intent it does not suffice that the perpetrator may foresee (partial) destruction of the group as certain result of his action; rather he must have destruction as primary intent.[27] In this respect, it is documented that the ethnic Germans were supposed to be eliminated just because they were ethnic Germans, as distinctly shown in chapter 2. In view of the supported interpretation that genocide has been committed also by social destruction of a group since such destruction is unavoidable by expulsion from their homeland, the principle "Whoever desires the expulsion of a group, commits genocide" is applicable. He does not see it merely as a result of his action.

Ethically, man is also morally responsible for the forseeable consequences of his actions. A wrong, committed indirectly remains his responsibility, just as the one directly caused.[28] Causing the expulsion the perpetrator cannot pretend he did not directly desire the resulting destruction of the social structure of the group.

Legally it is, however, not necessary that the physical or social destruction of the group actually occurs. According to article II of the Convention of Genocide it suffices that the intent to destroy is aimed at part of a group; however, it must pertain to a substantial, respectively selective or locally cohesive part of a group. The way the partisans or the commandos serving the OZNA selected their victims during the bloody pogroms in autumn of 1944 in the Banat, Batschka and Syrmia are indicative of their emphasis to destroy the leading faction of the Danube Swabians that had remained in their homeland. Chapter 3 deals with these events.

c. The mental element *as such*

The formula *group as such* represents a compromise by the UNO jurists. The two words are to indicate that the essential element of the crime is the premeditated attack on the existence of a group of humans, leaving open whether a specific motive is required. However, the following remains: "The victim is not attacked because of his or her individual identity, but because of his or her being part of the attacked group."[29] Because of being part of the group of ethnic Germans of Yugoslavia, even babies and infants were included in the alleged collective guilt. Accordingly they too were subjected to the fate of internment with all its fatal consequences.[30]

13.4 The Manifestations of the Tito-Regime to Eliminate the Ethnic Germans of Yugoslavia as a Group

The "physical state of facts" of genocide in the form of deportation of a small section, permitting the escape of an additional section and the physical liquidation of a larger section of the Danube Swabians has been documented in the foregoing chapters. The following explanation is intended to demonstrate the "mental state of facts", namely the clear intent to liquidate the group of ethnic Germans of Yugoslavia as an entity.

While it is sometimes already difficult to discover a crime, it is, of course, even more difficult to prove the intent to commit a crime. To substantiate the mental fact of genocide it is, however, essential to prove the intent to destroy, but the perpetrator(s) will rarely admit such intent; therefore, it must be admissible to deduct this intent through documented facts. Otherwise, great majority of crimes of genocide could not be established and prosecuted. Such decisive self-limitations surely were not the purpose of the authors of the Genocide Convention.

An explicit, written order by Tito, individual Politbureau-Members, or the Politbureau as such, to eliminate the ethnic Germans of Yugoslavia is, at this time, not known. The archives, as far as they still exist, particularly the Military Archive in Belgrade, are supposed to be accessible by 2005. By then perhaps additional evidence will be found. The intent of elimination by the supreme leadership of the Federated Peoples' Republic of Yugoslavia and her individual states can, however, already now be evidenced by the following documented statements:

1. *Milovan Djilas* in his memories describes, quite some time after the events, but with little inner distancing, the opinion process in the highest leadership body which led to the liquidation of the ethnic Germans: "In reality the Politbureau was only confronted with the problem of the Hungarian minority since the fate of the group of ethnic Germans was, so to speak, predestined. Our soldiers as well as the people were already so 'sick and tired' of our Germans that in the Central Committee the question of expulsion of the ethnic German population had frequently been raised. However, we could possibly have considered otherwise, had not the Russians, the Poles and Czechs already decided on the expulsion of their ethnic Germans and already partially started this action. We arrived at our position without negotiation, without discussion, as something that was justified and conceivable because of the 'German crimes'."[31]

Further statements of Djilas indicate that the Central Committee was from the very beginning, aware of the inhuman conditions applied during the process of internment of the ethnic German population. Even though occasional doubts were raised about the legality, the injustices and crimes were permitted to go on. Djilas continues: "Ranković later admitted that there were horrid conditions at the camps. Kardelj pointed out that because of these conditions we had lost the most productive group of our population. A large part of the land – if not the majority – that was split up after the war by the agricultural reform, really belonged to the ethnic Germans. I assume that the reason Tito kept silent about this was that he believed that this was the way it had to be."[32]

2. *Information of the Presidency of the Council of Ministers of the Democratic Federation of Yugoslavia, dated June 11ᵗʰ, 1945* (Br. 122 Pov)[33]: "The Yugoslav government is of the opinion that all ethnic Germans who are within the borders of Yugoslavia have to be resettled to Germany as soon as favorable technical conditions for such action have been created."[34]

The State Commission for the Repatriation of the ethnic Germans of the Ministry of Interior of the Federal State of Croatia, Zagreb, on July 7th, 1945 notified the regional committees of this decision and included detailed instructions (Broj 1/45).[35]

3. Since the Allied Occupation Forces in Austria and Germany considered the escaped and evacuated ethnic Germans as Yugoslav nationals and these agreed to their repatriation, their return to Yugoslavia was made possible.

Sreten Vukosavljević, Minister for Colonisation, of the "Democratic Peoples Republic of Yugoslavia" (DPRY), was informed of this fact and, on July 26th, 1945 he stated his opinion to the Presidency of the Council of Ministers of Yugoslavia in Belgrade: "In order to prevent a return of a large number of ethnic Germans into the Vojvodina or their accumulation at our borders with Hungary, it is my opinion we have to inform the Russian and Western Allied military authorities and ask them not to send these ethnic Germans to us. However, our authorities have to be instructed to be vigilant that none of these ethnic Germans enter our country."[36]

4. The intent not to allow any of the evacuated or fugitive Danube Swabians to return into the country is even more explicitly stated in the letter from the *Department for Repatriation of the Ministry for Social Policy* of the Democratic Federative Republic Yugoslavia (DFRY) to the Council of Ministers of Yugoslavia in Belgrade: "Ethnic Germans who formerly were of Yugoslav nationality and fled with the fascist occupation forces are not allowed to return to our country. The national commission for repatriation, concurring with the Presidency of the Council of Ministers of the DFRY and the Foreign Office, also issued a resolution prohibiting the return of such persons."[37]

5. The *"Anti-Fascist Assembly of People's Liberation of Serbia"* on March 29th, 1945, in a declaration confirmed the position of the main People's Liberation Committee of the Vojvodina concerning the rights of the national minorities and declared:

"The Hungarian population, being an old established, native population shall enjoy all rights; punished will be only the criminals and servants of the Horthy occupation regime. The assembly also agrees with the position of the Supreme People's Liberation Committee concerning the ethnic German population which, as a unit served the German fascism and no longer deserves a place in our country. Those ethnic Germans who fought with the partisans and Yugoslav liberation army or in other ways supported the people's liberation battle shall enjoy all civic rights."[38]

6. Slovenian historian Dušan Nečak in a study of the ethnic Germans in Slovenia 1918–1955 states:

"Beginning 1944 the Secretary of the Anti-Fascist Council of the People's Liberation of Yugoslavia (AVNOJ), *Radoljub Colaković,* visited the science institute and the executive council of the liberation body and announced the 'outsettlement' of the ethnic Germans from the entire Yugoslavia."[39] This happened only a few weeks after the 2nd AVNOJ conference of November 1943 at Jajce. Necak adds: "More intensive discussions of the leadership of the Slovenian liberation movement concerning the postwar fate of the ethnic Germans took place from September to November 1944. It reached an almost identical conclusion as two or three years before by the mentioned Ljubljana group: the mass expulsion of the ethnic Germans from Slovenian soil, except the participants of the liberation fight. The last word, however, had the Yugoslav national leadership. It adopted such measures for the entire nation."[40] These measures lead to the conclusion that the two AVNOJ resolutions, the one of Jajce and the other of Belgrade, included not only the expropriation and disfranchise but also the expulsion of the ethnic Germans.

7. *Boris Kidrić*, head of the first Slovenian postwar government, already in June 1945 stated in a speech at Marburg: "The rest of the Germanism in the northern areas has to disappear."[41]

8. Beginning 1946 the Yugoslav government started the first of their *three diplomatic attempts* to obtain permission to collectively expel to Germany the Danube Swabians who had survived up to that date. On January 19th, 1946 it submitted to the American embassy at Belgrade a memorandum regarding the "transfer of the remaining ethnic German minority from Yugoslavia to Germany" and solicited its support at the Allied Authorities (Kontrollrat) in Berlin to issue guidelines concerning the "outsettlement" of the 110,000 ethnic Germans. It repeated the same request May 16th, 1946. However, no response from the Allied Authorities was ever received.[42]

At the end of January 1947, Dr. Mladen Iveković, the Yugoslav delegate to the conference of deputy foreign ministers at London, which dealt with the preparations for a peace treaty with Germany, submitted the third memorandum of his government, which among other issues, requested that the 100,000 ethnic Germans still remaining in Yugoslavia should be taken in by Germany. As far as can be determined, this request too was not considered.[43]

13.5 The Execution of the Elimination

As already verified in the physical state of facts criteria of the Genocide Convention, the continual collective persecution activities against the ethnic German population of Yugoslavia had started from the very first days of the assumption of power by the Communist Tito-regime in 1944 and continued until 1948. The measures taken and the documented statements give an overall picture of the elimination. Its characteristic main features are demonstrated in this publication.

There is no doubt that the highest leadership of the partisan movement had the intent to eliminate the ethnic Germans of Yugoslavia as an ethnic group and demanded that the individual federal states initiate the corresponding measures.

The ethnic Germans in Yugoslavia were submitted for years to all the physical state of facts criteria for genocide; this happened openly and in particularly gruesome manner, executed by a multitude of commanders and helpers throughout the areas settled by the ethnic Germans. Such events could not have happened without the knowledge and approval of the highest leadership of a tightly-controlled dictatorship as existed in the communist Yugoslavia. Therefore, there can be no common sense doubt about their intent of physical destruction. But certainly, the guidelines for execution were only of general nature and the manner and choice was left to the individual states, which is evident by their actions.

13.5.1 The Elimination of the Untersteirer and Gottscheers of the Federative State Slovenia

Initially, as the front lines and the fighting edged closer in April 1945, relatively few persons fled from their homes. When the German army group E retreated towards the end of the war, some partisan groups encouraged this flight in the obvious endeavor to ethnically cleanse Slovenia of the Germans.[44] It was only on May 6th, 1945 that the German authorities ordered the complete evacuation of the Gottscheers and Untersteirer. The first train of Gottscheers reached Austrian territory the same day, however, was sent back towards Marburg/Maribor by the Russians. The second train could only advance up to north of Maribor. The occupants of both trains were completely robbed of their belongings by the partisans and, after two weeks, chased across the Austrian border.[45] When the British occupation authorities in Carinthia and Styria (Steiermark) closed the Austrian border and refused to accept new expulsions, the first Slovenian postwar government, headed by Boris Kidrić, changed its policy and began with the destruction of the group by internment in camps, of which the ones at Sterntal/Strnisce near Pettau/Ptuj[46] and Tüchern/Teharje near Cilli/Celje[47] were the worst. The annihilation of the inmates was achieved by continual execution of the men and the starvation to death of children and women. Additional large work camps and internment camps were Castle Herbertstein, Thesen and Tresternitz, the priest seminary Marburg and the textile factory Tüffer.

After executions, torture and starvation had decimated the number of inmates, the Sterntal camp was closed. A part of the survivors were shipped off by train to Carinthia (Kärnten) and another part to work camps. Camp Tüchern existed up to May/June 1946. On January 6th, 1946 part of the inmates were, during the night, chased across the border to Austria. The same procedure was attempted when the camp was closed down.[48]

It is apparent that the modus operandi of elimination underwent a transformation. First the expulsion, then the physical destruction and finally the clandestine shuffling off the survivors. All these events fulfill the criteria of genocide.

13.5.2 Elimination of the Danube Swabians from the Federative State Croatia

Since up to 90 percent of Syrmia's and Slavonia's Danube Swabians were evacuated to the territory of the then German Reich, with the permission of the German authorities and the order of the German-Croatian Association, the newly formed federal state "People's Republic of Croatia", complying with the order of the AVNOJ decree of November 21st, 1944, had to eliminate only a fraction of its former ethnic German population.

In May 1945 the ethnic Germans of the whole of East Slavonia were taken to the barracks camp at Josipovac, near Essegg/Osijek. From there, on July 8th, 1945 3,000 inmates were dispached by train towards Austria and actually did reach Leibnitz in South Styria (Südsteiermark).[49] A similar attempt with about 1,800 inmates was made on July 22nd, 1945 from camp Valpovo/Walpach, however, the British occupation authorities refused to let them enter Austria. Two further transports were also turned back.[50]

By the summer 1945 the number of "displaced persons" and of ethnic German refugees began to become a critical factor for Austria, particularly due to the "wild expulsions" (not authorized) of the "Sudeten-Germans" by the Czechs. The Austrian government protested to the Allies and insisted that they immediately close the Austrian borders. Vladimir Geiger gives more details on this subject: "This was the reason that the departments for internal affairs of the regional committees and the urban People's Liberation Committees, based on the instructions of the AVNOJ of November 21st, 1944, made a decision regarding the nationalization of the ethnic German properties and their expulsion, with the following statement: 'As long as there are no further possibilities for their shipment out of the country (meaning shipment to Austria) they will have to be held in forced-labor camps'."[51]

Initially the approximately 6,000 ethnic Germans that had remained were concentrated at Velika Pisanica near Bjelovar to be eventually distributed to the concentration camps Kerndia and Valpovo. Due to starvation and epidemics between 1,500 and 2,000 perished.[52] Both camps were dissolved in May 1946. Some inmates were discharged, some were distributed to two smaller work camps and small dispatches reached Austria. In January 1947 old-age and sick inmates were eventually shipped to the concentration camp Rudolfsgnad in the Banat.

In Croatia too, the method of elimination went through some transformations. First came the expulsion, after their failure followed the calculated dying due to starvation and epidemics in two concentration camps and finally shipment to the concentration camp Rudolfsgnad which existed for another year.

13.5.3 Elimination of the Danube Swabians of the Federative State Serbia

There were no direct expulsions from the "Autonomous Province of Vojvodina" (consisting of the Banat, Batschka and Syrmia), which is part of Serbia and was the homeland of the great mojority of ethnic Germans in Yugoslavia. On the contrary, immediately after occupying any village and specially after the capture of Belgrade on October 21st, 1944 the partisans began their bloody terror actions against the ethnic German population, targeting for murder primarily (but not limited to) members of the leadership and intelligence classes. These events, which the Danube Swabians call the *bloody autumn of 1944,* resulted in the death of more than 5,000 ethnic Germans in the Banat and Syrmia as well as 2,000 in the Batschka.[53]

There was an organized system by which these actions were carried out: In occupying the Banat mostly mass executions were carried out in the individual communities, but already in October special regional torture and execution camps were set up. The most notorious ones were at Groß-Kikinda, Groß-Betschkerek and Werschetz.[54] In the Batschka there were also local butcherings, however, most of the casualities were caused by the special execution commandos with their targeted executions carried out mostly at night during November 1944. These methods correspond exactly to the criteria for premeditated, intentional killing of members of a group as described in article II of the UNO Convention.

The executions and murder orgies were followed, at different intervals, with the expulsion from their homes and internment in camps of almost all Danube Swabians. The interment was also carried out systematically according to pre-planned clasifications in local camps, central work camps and concentration camps. Between December 2nd, 1944 and autumn 1945 those unfit to work were shipped to the six concentration camps (Jarek/Jarak, Gakowa/Gakovo, Kruschiwl/Krusevlje, Molidorf/Molin, Rudolfsgnad/Knićanin and Syrmisch-Mitrowitz/Sremska Mitrovica): old-age persons over 60, children up to age 14 and mothers with small children under two years.[55] The complete internment, with a few exceptions in the North Batschka had taken place already by the end of June 1945, that means before the July 17th, 1945 Potsdam Conference of the Allies and, in the Vojvodina, involved about 160,000 ethnic German civilians. Deviating from Hungary, Poland and Czechoslovakia, Yugoslavia did not attempt to have the expulsion of her ethnic Germans sanctioned by the Posdam Agreement.

The establishment of "special camps" for infirm, children and old-age persons, in addition to the work camps, makes it clear that there was a deliberate destruction intent. What other purpose would the separation under "special conditions" have? It was clear even for the politically responsible persons with little far-sightedness that such camps with chronic malnutrition and lack of medicines as well as continual maltreatments quickly had to become stations of mass deaths. The opinion of Dieter Blumenwitz that the camp internment as such would not be sufficient to prove premeditated destruction intent[56] may be applicable to internment in adequately supplied work camps; in the "special camps", as apparent in the reports, however, the death by starvation and epidemics was premeditated and intended. A large part of the almost 50,000 camp victims died during the winter 1945/46 of starvation, epidemic diseases and freezing.

Whoever wants to argue that there was no intent to let people die must allow the question why was nothing done to prevent hunger and starvation? There was plenty of wheat available since, at least as far as the Banat and Batschka are concerned, the entire wheat harvest of 1944 was in storage. Let's assume there were bottlenecks in supplies for the camp inmates, why was there no attempt to obtain international aid? Why was the supply for the camp inmates during the time of December 1944 to May 1946 reduced to a bare, totally insufficient minimum? The strict prohibition of begging or exchange of clothing for food, the barbaric punishment and often even execution for those captured at clandestine procuring of food speaks also a clear language (only from May 1946 onwards food packages were allowed to be sent from outside to the Gakovo death camp).

Why were measures by the Yugoslavian health authorities to reduce the typhoid epidemics in the "special camps" only then taken when the epidemics threatened to spread beyond the camp?[57] Ambulances, operated by non-camp persons were not utilized by the camp administration. The few interned physicians, some of which also died or were murdered, did not receive any medical supplies.[58] Outside physicians and not interned ethnic German physicians were forbidden to treat ethnic Germans with medicines.[59] So it is very obvious that the demise from illness was an instrument of intentional elimination.

The first memorandum requesting the "transfer of the remaining ethnic German minority of Yugoslavia to Germany" was handed to the American embassy on January 19th, 1946. At that time the typhoid epidemics at the liquidation camps reached their peak. The second memorandum with the same transfer request was delivered May 16th, 1946. By then the typhoid epidemic, through the use of DDT, had been conquered. Thus one could have pointed out that there was no danger that the transfer of the ethnic Germans would also import epidemics.

Numerous personal reports demonstrate that the escape from the work and liquidation camps was strictly prohibited and a life-threatening undertaking. Nevertheless, thousands fled from the camps in the Banat to Romania, also thousands from the Batschka to Hungary. It is difficult to state how many lost their life during this so-called "black flight". Chapter 10 of the present book gives an idea of what this flight meant for the desperate people.

The personal experience reports of internees provide good indicators that the more relaxed guarding at some liquidation camps between October 1946 and autumn 1947 was supposed to enable the escape of inmates who were endangered by hunger and epidemics. However, even during this time of the so-called "white flight" the escape was not without problems. As a rule, the commander or the guards had to be bribed. The ones who could not come up with money or valuables still had to risk the dangerous "black" escape. It is estimated that 30,000 to 35,000 inmates escaped from the Vojvodina to Romania and Hungary during such "black" and "white" flights. It is unthinkable that such large-scale escape movement could take place without knowledge of the camp leadership. At the minimum, their passive participation can be considered an indirect form of expulsion.[60]

The method of elimination which was used in the Vojvodina can be considered as the most rigorous. First came the targeted physical destruction with preference of but not limited to the potential leadership class of the Danube Swabians. Then the physical destruction of the unfit to work and the ones that became unable to work any longer by internment in "special camps". Then the forcible transfer of children to other ethnic groups. Finally the attempted direct expulsion ("resettlement") and partial indirect expulsion of the survivors by loosening the camp guard.

Result: The Tito-regime's premeditated elimination in the form of physical killing and expulsion is documentable, both in its general form and from the very inception. The result of this intent to destroy the ethnic Germans of Yugoslavia was: Of the Danube Swabians of Yugoslavia, who had remained at home, roughly one third (60,000 civilians) were physically destroyed, almost one fifth (35,000) escaped from the camps and the survivors, after the camps were closed and their subsequent forced labor employment ended, requested their "outsettlement", mainly during the 1950s.

The then Yugoslav rulers committed a genocide of their ethnic German fellow citizens because they wanted to destroy this group as a social and ethnic dimension in the country. They affirmed their expulsion and the pre-planned methods, namely the destruction of the Danube Swabians native world through expropriation, expulsion from their homes, internment in camps and partial expulsion from the country. The destruction of the settlement structure of their villages which meant the destruction of their bases of ethnic customs, language, social cohesiveness and consciousness are important factors. In addition they affirmed the physical destruction of the German-language ethnicity and carried out premeditated mass executions and willfully created conditions such as starvation and epidemics which led to their demise.

The individual actions against the ethnic Germans of Yugoslavia by the government and her executioners form an overal state of facts and in accord with Dieter

Blumenwitz it can be stated: "The actions in Yugoslavia between 1944 and 1948 against the native ethnic German population group domiciled there for many generations (and long before these territories were incorporated into Yugoslavia), which included, in addition to mass killing, the collective expropriations and disfranchise, internment and expulsion, as well as the forced ethnic re-education of children, fulfill both the physical state of facts and the mental state of facts criteria of genocide as cited in the Genocide Convention of the United Nations, dated December 9th, 1948."[61]

Footnotes to Chapter 13

[1] See official English text of the Convention dated December 9th, 1948 (chapter 16 of this book).

[2] Gilbert Gornig,*Völkerrecht und Völkermord. Definition – Nachweis – Konsequenzen am Beispiel der Sudetendeutschen.* Volume 2 of publication series of Felix-Ermacora-Institute, Viena 2002, p. 26.

[3] Already in 1961 the Israel court alledged this fact and condemned Adolf Eichmann of genocide for crimes committed long before the UNO Convention on the Prevention and Punishment of the Crime of Genocide had been passed. See Gornig, ibid., p. 27.

[4] The Fedarative People's Republic of Yugoslavia signed the Convention on December 11th, 1948, ratified it on August 29th, 1950 and adopted it in article 141 of its penal code. After their separation from Yugoslavia, Slovenia joined the Convention on July 6th, 1992 and Croatia on October 12th, 1992.

[5] According to the International Ruanda Court serious bodily or mental harm is caused by bodily or mental torture, by inhuman or humiliating treatment and persecution. The court adopted this interpretation from the Eichmann trial. See International Criminal Tribunal Rwanda (ICTR), case no. 96–4–T, Tz 502.

[6] Ibid.

[7] See interpretation of the Deutscher Bundesgerichtshof für Strafsachen (BGHSt = Federal Criminal Court of the Federal Republic of Germany), St 45, 6582; also ICTR, case no. 96–4–T, Tz 506.

[8] The International Law Commission (ILC) in 1996 was of the opinion: "The word destruction ... must be taken only in ... its physical or biological sense." ILC Draft Code 1996, p. 90.

[9] Christian Tomuschat, *Die Vertreibung der Sudetendeutschen. Zur Frage des Bestehens von Rechtsansprüchen nach Völkerrecht und deutschem Recht,* in: *Zeitschrift für ausländisches öffentliches Recht,* 1996, p. 13.

[10] See United Nation's Convention on the Non-Applicability of Statutory Limitations to War Crimes and Crimes against Humanity, November 26th, 1968.

[11] According to article 25 of the German Constitution it is mandatory for the German judicature not to recognize other countries' actions which are in conflict with international law. However, German legislation can only protect property within ist own territory of jurisdiction. See Gornig, ibid., p. 68–70 and 85–87.

[12] Negotiations of the German Bundestag, 37th session on July 8th, 1954, print no. 162, p. 1765.

13 Ibid., p. 1766.

14 Ibid.

15 Gornig, ibid., p. 67.

16 Felix Ermacora, *Die sudetendeutschen Fragen,* München (Munich) 1992.

17 Ermacora, ibid., p. 185.

18 Gornig, ibid., p. 64.

19 Ermacora, ibid., p. 187.

20 Völkerstrafrecht (The International Genocide Convention of December 9th, 1948 and the Precept of International Penal Law). ZStW, 1994, p. 193, 213.

21 Gornig, ibid., p. 27.

22 Dieter Blumenwitz, *Rechtsgutachten über die Verbrechen an den Deutschen in Jugoslawien 1944–1948,* published by Donauschwäbische Kulturstiftung, Stiftung des bürgerlichen Rechts (DKS), München 2002, p. 35–46.

23 Interpretation of § 220 a of the German penal code on the occasion of the rehearing procedure in the criminal case Nikola Jorgić. He was accused of systematical destruction and expulsion of the Moslem population of the Doboj area.

24 Bundesverfassungsgericht, 2 BvR 1290/99 of December 12th, 2000.

25 BGHSt 45, 65, 801.

26 Ibid.

27 The predominant interpretation is that a "first grade dolus directus" (legal technical term) has to prevail. See Blumenwitz, ibid., p. 28.

28 The strategy of vindication by declaring a bad secondary effect as not intended but only permitted, is being rejected categorically by the actual moral theology. See for instance Wilhelm Korff, *Ethische Entscheidungskonflikte: Zum Problem der Güterabwägung,* in: Anselm Hertz' *Handbuch der christlichen Ethik,* vol. III, *Wege ethischer Praxis,* Freiburg/Basel/Wien 1982, p. 86.

29 Blumenwitz, ibid., p. 35 and ICTR, case no. 96–4–T, Tz 521.

30 Arbeitskreis Dokumentation, *Verbrechen an den Deutschen in Jugoslawien 1944–1948* (Abbr.: VDJ), issued by DKS, Munich 2000 (3rd edition), p. 321.

31 Milovan Djilas, *Der Krieg der Partisanen. Memoiren 1941–1945,* published by Molden, Viena 1978, p. 540.
Title of Yugoslavian edition: *Revolucionarni Rat.*
Title of US American edition: *Wartime.*

32 Ibid., p. 540.

33 Vladimir Geiger, *Folksdojceri – Pod teretom kolektivne krivnje* (The ethnic Germans under the burdon of collective impeachment), Osijek 2002, p. 32 (translation by Oskar Feldtänzer).

34 Hrvatski drzavni arhiv (Croatian public-record office), Zagreb, legacy Svetozar Ritig, box no. 1, Fasz. 5 *Protjerivanje Nijemaca iz FNRJ.* Zemaljska Komisija za repatriaciju Njemaca pri ministarstvu unutrasnjih poslova Federativne drzave Hrvatske, Broj 1/45, Predmet: Njemaca nasih drzavljana repatrijacija (iselenje Njemaca) – upute –, Zagreb, 7. VII 1945. Geiger, ibid., p. 32 footnote.

35 Geiger, ibid.

36 AJ Beograd, fond 50, fasc 35, spis 73/list 732 (taken from Geiger, ibid., p. 32).

37 AJ Beograd, fond 50, fasc 35, spis 73 (taken from Geiger, ibid., p. 34).

38 Edmund Schweißguth, *Die Entwicklung des Bundesverfassungsrechtes der Föderativen Volksrepublik Jugoslawien* (The Development of the Constitutional Law of the Ferderal People's Republic of Yugoslavia), studies of the Institut für Ostrecht, Munich, vol. 9, 1961, p. 88.

39 Dušan Nečak, *The "Germans" in Slovenia (1918–1955),* issued by Znanstveni Institut Filosofske fakultate, Ljubljana 1948. Summary in German, p. 33.

40 Nečak, ibid., p. 23.

41 Stefan Karner, *Die deutschsprachige Volksgruppe in Slowenien. Aspekte ihrer Entwicklung 1939–1997* (The German speaking ethnic group in Slovenia. Aspects of ist development 1939–1997), Klagenfurt/Ljubljana/Wien, p. 131.

42 *Das Schicksal der Deutschen in Jugoslawien* (the fate of the Germans in Yugoslavia), Volume V of the documentation on the expulsion of the ethnic Germans from East-Central Europe, issued by the German Federal Ministry for Expellees, Refugees and Wronged People, Düsseldorf 1961, p. 99 (abbr.: Dok. V).

43 Dok. V, p. 468.

44 Karner, ibid., p. 130.

45 Karner, ibid., p. 120.

46 VDJ, ibid., p. 229–234.

47 VDJ, ibid., p. 235–241.

48 VDJ, ibid., p. 238, 240; Karner, ibid., p. 141.

49 VDJ, ibid., p. 220.

50 VDJ, ibid., p. 221.

51 Vladimir Geiger, *Radni logor Valpovo 1945–1946.* Dokumenti, Njemacka narodnosna zajednica – Zemaljska udruga Podunavskih Svaba u Hrvatskoj (Work Camp Valpovo 1945–1946. Documents issued by *Volksdeutsche Gemeinschaft – Landsmannschaft der Donauschwaben in Kroatien*), Osijek 1999, p. 10, and Geiger, *Nijemciu Djakovu i Djakovstini,* Hrvatski institut za povijest – Dom i svijet, Zagreb 2001, p. 174.

52 VDJ, ibid., p. 222 and 226.

53 VDJ, ibid., p. 92.

54 Details may be taken from chapter 3 of this book.

55 See chapter 7 of this book.

56 Blumenwitz, ibid., p. 43.

57 See for instance camp Rudolfsgnad.

58 See reports on Syrmisch-Mitrowitz.

59 Anna Niklos-Nyari, *Nachruf auf verlorene Jahre,* Karlsruhe 1991, p. 125, 181–185.

60 Dok. V, ibid., p. 113 E.

61 Blumenwitz, ibid., p. 49.

Chapter 14: Demand for Rehabilitation

14.1 General Attitude of the Expellees

The ethnic Germans of the former Yugoslavia avow to the *Charta der Heimatvertriebenen* (Charter of the Expellees from their Homelands) which was formulated 1950 by the representatives of the expellees living in Germany. As an expression of their basic position it still retains its validity up to this day. It represents the first declaration of renunciation of use of force and the first peace document following World War II.

In the introductory sentence: "We expellees from our homelands renounce revenge and retaliation", the ethnic German expellees disavow thoughts of revenge sanctions against the perpetrating nations. Already at that time they endeavored a European solution. *However, in the Charter, they did not relinguish their elementary rights as anchored in the United Nations Conventions and International Law.*

The currently ruling generation of the perpetrating nations is not guilty of the past; however, based on the natural solidarity of a nation's generations, it has to assume the responsibility and liability for the events of the past and their consequences. The expellees demand that today's generation of politicians of the perpetrating nations feels responsible for the legal consequences of their expulsion and confiscation of property which are considered crimes against humanity and thus do not become statute-barred. The criteria of responsibility for the consequences which the international consciousness of justice has developed during the past decades are also valid for the current governing generation and successors of the perpetrators. They are admonished to reestablish their national honor in the eyes of world history. *The moral and legal rehabilitation of the expellees has become an unavoidable requisite of justice.*

Regrettably, the expellees have to determine that a large percentage of the perpetrating nation's population lack the perception of the factors of guilt. Therefore, when the expellees in their writings, documentations and demonstrations point out these factors of guilt, they do not intend to create a feeling of aversion towards the current generation of their former home countries, but want to induce them to accept their responsibility.

14.2 Legal Viewpoints of the Expellees from Yugoslavia

The expellees from their homeland, the former Yugoslavia, persist in presenting to the successor nations of the dissolved state of Yugoslavia the following legal viewpoints:

1. In view of the fact that it was the partisans leadership intent and determination to eliminate the ethnic German population from its native soil – which it had possessed long before there was a Yugoslavian state – and that this plan was carried out, the ethnic Germans of Yugoslavia hold the legal viewpoint that the crime of genocide, in the sense of customary international law and the UN Genocide Convention of December 9th, 1948, was committed against them. In the process, about 70,000 ethnic German citizens of Yugoslavia lost their life.

2. In view of the fact that during World War II the ethnic Germans living in the devided Yugoslavia were not bound by loyalty pledges to the communist-dominated "people's liberation movement", they consider the collective judgement, passed in an ex-judicial procedure by the "Anti-Fascist Council for the Liberation of Yugoslavia" (acronym: AVNOJ) that branded them indiscriminately as "enemies of the people" and "traitors", as unjust. Therefore, they demand the annulment of the AVNOJ decree of November 21st, 1944 and all laws that are based on this decree.

3. The ethnic Germans of the former Yugoslavia consider the AVNOJ resolution of November 21st, 1944 ordering the total confiscation of their mobile and real properties as unjust and illegal and its execution by expulsion from their homes followed by internment of the entire ethnic group, including infants and old age people, as an act of violence which has to be regarded as part of the comprehensive act of genocide (see chapter 13).

4. Since war crimes, crimes against humanity and genocide do not become statute-barred, based on today's concept of justice and legal practice, the expellees consider it mandatory to prosecute for the crime of genocide those that are the originators of the destruction of the ethnic German population as well as those that participated as murderers, sadists and exploiters.

14.3 Demand for Rehabilitation

The word "rehabilitation" means: to revert back to the prior state of honorable innocence, thus a restitution in a broad sense. The meaning of "rehabilitation", as well as "restitution" and "compensation" includes only a minimum of justice and fairness for the wronged. The loss of home and homeland including destruction of the group identity remains everlasting; injured life remains injured; nobody can revive those tortured to death and starved to death. There are forms of destruction that cannot be remedied.

There is a difference between legal and moral rehabilitation. The legal rehabilitation requires the annulment of the unjust legislation by the current legislators. They are the parliaments of Serbia-Montenegro, Croatia, Bosnia-Herzegovina and Slovenia.

A legal rehabilitation usually includes material rehabilitation: return of or compensation for plundered property. Even a late financial compensation can be one way to partially reestablish the dignity of the wronged.

14.3.1 Material Rehabilitation and Economic Compensation

Losses of real values by the ethnic Germans of Yugoslavia, caused by the AVNOJ decrees and subsequent laws are enormous. The Yugoslavian side itsself registered in detail all agricultural properties that were collectively expropriated from the ethnic Germans without any compensation. For instance, the two experts for agrarian reforms and colonization after 1945, Dr. Nikola L. Gaćeša and Dr. Vladimir Stipetić, published exact figures in the newspaper *Nedjeljna Dalmacija* of May 6th, 1990. Similar figures can also be found in the *Enciklopedija Jugoslavije*, issued 1962 in Zagreb (volume 5, page 19).

The expropriated private German agricultural properties according to Yugoslavian statements consisted of the following:

In the Vojvodina (autonomous Serb Province)	68,036	properties with	389,256 ha
In Serbia	1	property with	193 ha
In Croatia	20,457	properties with	120,977 ha
In Bosnia	3,523	properties with	12,733 ha
In Slovenia	5,474	properties with	114,780 ha
Total			637,939 ha

In addition to these individual private properties of about 638,000 hectare, another 19,000 hectare of German cooperative and church properties were expropriated. The agricultural properties obviously included completely furnished and equipped dwellings and farm-buildings as well as machinery and appliances; there were also great numbers of domestic animals (horses, cattle, sheep, pigs, poultry etc.).

Last but not least, all industries belonging to ethnic Germans were also seized without compensation. The Yugoslav sources admit, that the percentage of the country's industry owned by ethnic Germans was much higher than their share of the population. In the Vojvodina, for instance, the Germans were leaders in brick-works, mills and hemp processing plants; they owned more than 50 percent of these industries.

Beginning with the 1945 values in Dinar of the confiscated German properties and applying the respective exchange rates, for the year 1990 the experts calculated their total value at more than 100 milliards of German Marks (in the USA: 100 billions of German Marks). In 2002 this would correspond to aprox. 50 milliards of Euros or 50 billions of US-Dollars. The ethnic Germans are in agreement with these Yugoslav statistics, there is no difference of opinion on the value of the expropriated assets.

Upon their confiscation all properties passed to the ownership of the Yugoslav State without any indemnification or compensation for the expropriated ethnic German citizens. After the secession of various Federal States and the final total dismemberment of Yugoslavia, the successor nations Serbia-Montenegro, Croatia, Slovenia and Bosnia-Hercegovina became the beneficiaries.

As far as the material rehabilitation is concerned there are varying legal viewpoints among the ethnic Germans of Yugoslavia:

a. A few ethnic Germans of the former Yugoslavia insist on full return of their house and property in their former homeland. They are, however, cognizant of the fact that such "natural restitution" would face obstacles since their demand would entail a forced evacuation of the current owners of their house, land and other properties.

The most significant obstacle would be the international prohibition of use of force. The charter of the United Nations stipulates the prohibition of use of force in its article 2, section 7. In addition, and independently, prevailing opinion is that the prohibition of use of force is also part of the customary international law. It protects people, among other factors, from being forcefully removed from their place of domicile. It is also valid for people who, after the expulsion of the original inhabitants, settled in a certain area. Therefore, the expellees organizations in Germany stressed, rightfully, that the return of the expellees to their original home country must not result in a new expulsion.

b. There are many ethnic Germans of the former Yugoslavia who, in acknowledging the above mentioned factors, demand full financial compensation from the successor nations and they be included in the statutory legislation which the reformed nations of Croatia and Slovenia have initiated. Thus the Donauschwäbische Arbeitsgemeinschaft Österreichs (DAG), the umbrella organization of the Danube Swabian societies in the individual federal states of Austria, take the position that, in addition to the moral rehabilitation, a full material (financial) compensation has to be claimed since the organization does not have the authority to waive the legitimate claims (by virtue of their human rights) of its members.

c. There are also ethnic Germans of the former Yugoslavia who, while not giving up their legitimate demands, are not pressing to achieve them at this time since they realize that the former homelands presently do not have nearly the economic and financial resources to grant full compensation. They are of the opinion that there must be a deliberate discussion of an adequate and fair compensation when the involved countries join the European Union and participate in the European financial adjustment system. A settlement of the restitution question would con-tribute to inter-European peace and would probably be indispensable to the reduction of distrust between the nations and minorities.

d. Many of the ethnic Germans who were still born in their old homeland consider it rather more realistic to demand a symbolic financial rehabilitation because they are afraid they won't see a more extensive one in their lifetime. Hungary, as an example, has granted their expellees and those remaining in their country such a symbolic compensation. This makes sense, in as far as it considers the need for justice and re-establishes a part of the wronged person's honor and dignity.

14.3.2 Moral, Historical and Cultural Rehabilitation

In the eyes of the expellees, a considerable greater importance than the material aspect is given to the moral, historical and cultural rehabilitation.

a. The moral rehabilitation includes the admission of guilt and the plea for for-giveness for the expulsion and genocide by the political leadership of the respec-tive nations. They also expect the show of respect for the dignity of their dead. In the eyes of the ethnic Germans, the possibility of unhindered visitation and care ofthe graves as well as the erection of memorials for the victims of the genocide constitutes an important part of moral rehabilitation.

b. By cultural rehabilitation the ethnic Germans understand the recognition, the factual appreciation of the economic and cultural achievements of the expellees in their former homelands during the course of history as well as acceptance of the expellees as equal partners in the cultural and scientific exchanges of today.

c. The historical rehabilitation includes the demand to retract, in an official de-claration, the incriminating assertion of the communist government of the former Yugoslavia, that the ethnic Germans were "enemies of the people" and "traitors". Such false assertions must be eliminated from the history books and be replaced with the truth, also with regard to how and why the ethnic Germans "disappeared" from their homelands.

Just like all other ethnic groups in the devided Yugoslavia during World War II, the ethnic Germans lived under the governments of Hungary, the Independent State of Croatia, the German-occupied Serbia and Germany. No loyalty obligations existed to the "People's Liberation Movement", dominated by the Josip-Broz-Tito-communists, whose assertion to be representing the "true will of the people" could not be based on a democratic legitimacy of the Yugoslavian people and was considered illegal by the exiled royal government of Yugoslavia as well as by the Serbian nationalistic movements.

14.4 EU Membership and Rehabilitation

All successor nations of Yugoslavia aspire to the membership of the European Union. The ethnic Germans from the former Yugoslavia welcome these efforts for two reasons: firstly because they consider that these nations, their former fellow-citizens and neighbours, belong to Europe as they themselves do; secondly the option for the EU involves the adherence to the European Values, i. e. freedom, democracy, constitutionalism and respecting the human rights. These positive intentions are cause for joy and satisfaction.

Without any doubt, many people in the successor nations of Yugoslavia still need fundamental changes of mentality: They have to comprehend that human rights are indivisible and equally correspond to every human being; they must uncondi-tionally accept parity in the eyes of the law; they must understand, that justice over-rules personal and nationalistic interests; they cannot apply two kinds of measures in their own favour. Since the evident attitude of the successor nations towards the European Values is still rather ambiguous, there are some ethnic Germans and also others including reputed experts on international law, who argue that these people are not yet mature and therefore should not be admitted to the European Union.

However, the problem may also be seen the other way round: Being members of the family, it is easier to guide them out of their deficiencies in a friendly manner; they may be reminded that they obligated themselves to comply with the rules by entering the Community; being admitted even with certain reservations instead of being rejected will surely challenge their national honour to prove that they are not second class members.

As soon as they become conscious of their moral and legal commitment resulting from being a valid member of the European Community of Values, the people in the Yugoslav successor nations will recognize, that they also have to assume the responsibility for their nation's shady past. They will comprehend that a legal, moral, historic and cultural rehabilitation of their former ethnic German fellow-citizens is absolutely indispensable. The amount of a compensation for the ex-propriated properties is less important than the sincere desire to restore the dignity of the innocent victims. Not lip services of agile politicians are required, but the honest sense of duty of the people, the same like the German nation assumed her responsibility towards others. When the people in Serbia-Montenegro, Croatia, Slovenia and Bosnia-Hercegovina will have understood and complied with this high ethic requirement, then and only then will they be members up to the standard of the European Community of Moral and Legal Values!

Chapter 15: Danube Swabian Chronology

Early beginnings up to 1918

1526	Battle at Mohatsch. Turkish victory over Hungary.
1526–1918	The Imperial House of Habsburg also became Hereditary Kings of Hungary and Croatia.
1526–1686	Most of Hungary under Turkish rule.
1683	Imperial and royal Polish forces defeat the Turks at Vienna.
1684–1699	Hungary liberated from Turkish rule. Germans recruited to settle in the territory.
1697	Prince Eugen of Savoy defeats the Turks at Senta.
1699	Peace treaty at Karlowitz: Hungary, Syrmia, Slavonia and the Batschka ceded to the Emperor Leopold I.
1712	The first Swabian settlers arrive at Sathmar.
1716–1718	Prince Eugen defeats the Turks at Peterwardein, Temeschburg and Belgrade.
1717–1779	The liberated Banat becomes imperial crown land with its own administration.
1718	Peace treaty at Passarowitz: the Banat, North Serbia and Belgrade ceded to Austria.
1722–1726	First large-scale Swabian migration trek (Großer Schwabenzug) during Emperor Karl I's rule.
1723	Settlers granted tax exemption and inheritance rights.
1736–1754	Cathedral built at Temeschburg.
1737–1739	War with Turkey and peace treaty at Belgrade result in the loss of North Serbia.
1740–1780	Empress Maria Theresia settles 50,000 Germans in Hungary.
1763–1773	Second large-scale Swabian trek.
1779	The Temescher Banat crown land comes under Hungarian administration.

1780–1790	Emperor Josef II abolishes bondage; decress German as the official language and in school teaching.
1782–1787	Third "Großer Schwabenzug". Protestants included for the first time.
1790	Hungarianizing begins; Hungarian becomes the official language.
1806	End of the "Old Reich", demolished by Napoleon I.
1812	Opening of the German theater at Pest. Ludwig van Beethoven composed the ceremonial music.
1849–1861	The imperial crown land "Serbian Wojwodschaft and Temescher Banat" becomes established.
1867	The double monarchy Austria-Hungary is formed.
1868	The Hungarian parliament passes legislation, guaranteeing equal rights for its ethnic minorities, but they were never honored.
1907	Swabian Society (Schwabenverein) founded at Vienna.
1913	Society of the Germans in Croatia and Slavonia founded.
1914	Crown Prince Franz Ferdinand assassinated by Serbian Nationalists at Sarajevo. Austria-Hungary declares war on Serbia. Start of World War I.
1918	End of World War I. US President Wilson promulgates self-determination rights of nationals. The dual monarchy collapses. 1,500,000 Danube Swabians are split up ($^1/_3$ given to each of the successor nations Hungary, Yugoslavia and Romania).
1919	At the Paris peace negotiations, a peace delegation of the Danube Swabians pleads for keeping the Banat undivided.

The Danube Swabians in the Kingdom of Serbs, Croats and Slovenes (SHS), Renamed Yugoslavia after 1929

1919–1944	In the peace treaties of Paris, Yugoslavia, Romania and Hungary pledged to provide international guarantees for their ethnic minorities which, however, were never adhered to.
1920	Founding of the Swabian-German Cultural Alliance.

1922	Founding of the Germany Economic Organization Agraria.
	Founding of the German Party (Partei der Deutschen).
	The collective term "Donauschwaben" (Danube Swabians) is becoming widely accepted.
1929	Parliament and political parties in Yugoslavia are dissolved and replaced by a "Royal Dictatorship".
1931	German School Foundation and Private Teachers College founded.
1939	Start of World War II.
1941	German forces occupy Yugoslavia. Disintegration of the Yugoslav state. Splitting up of the Danube Swabians: The Batschka and Baranja-Triangle revert to Hungary; the Banat remains with Serbia under German military occupation; Syrmia and Slavonia are attached to Croatia. With the German attack on Russia, Yugoslav partisans begin raids on ethnic German settlements.
1942	Partisan raids lead to evacuation of ethnic Germans from Bosnia and Serbia.
1942–1944	Due to partisan raids all dispersed German settlements in Syrmia and Slavonia are resettled in larger communities.
1943	The Anti-Fascist Council of the People's Liberation of Yugoslavia (acronym AVNOJ), the highest political body of the partisan movement, declares all persons who opposed the People's Liberation Army "enemies of the people and traitors". They lose all civic rights, are disfranchised and face the threat of the death penalty. Without formally mentioning any specific persons, ethnic Germans in Yugoslavia are affected and considered disenfranchised.
1944	As of October 1944 over 1,500 ethnic German civilians are killed by the partisans.

The End of the Danube Swabians in Yugoslavia

1944	By October 4th, 10,600 Danube Swabians from the West Banat and 2,500 from Serbia manage to escape from the partisans and the Red (Russian) army.
	Starting October 3rd: About 100,000 Danube Swabians from Syrmia, Slavonia and Croatia are evacuated, mainly to Austria.

Starting October 8th: About 80,000 Danube Swabians in the Batschka and Baranja heed the evacuation call and flee.

October 20th: Belgrade captured by the Russian Army and partisans.

Supported by the Russian army, the Tito-partisans assume control of Serbia and the Vojvodina. Close to 200,000 Danube Swabians come under the rule of the Tito-regime.

"Bloody autumn" in the Vojvodina. By the end of November about 9,000 Danube Swabian civilians in the Banat, Batschka, Baranja and East Syrmia are murdered.

Beginning November: Camps for civilians and work camps are set up.

November 21st: AVNOJ declares, without judicial process, Danube Swabians collectively as "enemies of the people and traitors" and thus disfranchised. All movable and stationary property is confiscated by the government.

December 2nd: The first liquidation camp for Danube Swabians in the South Batschka is established at Jarek/Bački Jarek.

1944–1945   About 167,000 civilians are disenfranchised and interned between the beginning of December 4th and the end of August 1945.

December 29th, 1944 to January 6th, 1945: 8,000 women and 4,000 men, all Danube Swabians from the Batschka and Banat, are selected for slave labor and shipped to Russia.

March 12th: The liquidation camps Gakowa/Gakovo and Kruschiwl/Krusevlje in the Batschka are set up.

May 8th: German Armed Forces capitulate.

May 15th: 150,000 German and over 200,000 Croatian soldiers lay down their weapons and become prisoners of the partisans.

May 22th: 2,000 Danube Swabian soldiers of the SS Mountain Division Prinz Eugen are butchered by the partisans at Rann/Brezice (Slovenia).

May: The death camp Sterntal/Strnisce and Tüchern/Teharje (Slovenia) established.

May: Liquidation camp Walpach/Valpovo (Slavonia) established.

Liquidation camp Kerndia/Krndija (Slavonia) set up.

August: Liquidation camp "Svilara" (silk factory) established in Syrmian Mitrowitz/Sremska Mitrovica.

September: Liquidation camp Molidorf/Molin (Banat) established.

	October: Liquidation camp Rudolfsgnad/Knićanin (Banat) established.
1945	At the end of the year about 24,000 children, women and elderly starved to death in the liquidation camps.
1945–1946	November to April: Additional 20,000 camp inmates die due to starvation and typhus epidemic. Orphaned children are shipped off to Yugoslav children homes for their "ethnic re-education".
1946	Late autumn: Begin of mass escapes from the camps to Hungary and Romania – sometimes tolerated by the camp administration, sometimes being a mortal risk.
1947	Additional 4,000 civilians die in the liquidation camps.
1947	Autumn: Camp administration stops further escapes.
	Since autumn 1946 about 30,000 to 40,000 Danube Swabians escaped to Hungary and Romania.
1947–1949	Discharge of most slave labor deportees from Russia, mainly to the former East Germany.
1948	March: Closing of the liquidation and work camps in Yugoslavia. The surviving ethnic Germans were forced to enter three-year work contracts.
1948–1959	Search in Yugoslavian children homes for separated children.
1950–1959	Repatriation of children to Austria with the help of the Red Cross.
1952–1960	Emigration of the still remaining Germans by paying Yugoslav government for release from their Yugoslav Nationality.
1960	Only about 10,000 ethnic Germans remain in Yugoslavia.

New Homeland in the West

1946	Aid Society of Danube Swabians in the USA founded by Peter Max Wagner.
1948	About 10,000 Danube Swabians settle in France. (Part of the Danube Swabians are descendants of French settlers.)
1949	Umbrella organization of the Danube Swabian state societies in Austria founded.
	German federal society of the Germans of Yugoslavia founded.
	Southeast German cultural project established in Munich, Germany.

1950	Charter of the Expellees proclaimed at Stuttgart, Germany.
1951	Council of the ethnic Germans of Southeastern European countries founded at Bonn, Germany.
1952	2,000 Danube Swabians resettle from Austria to Brazil. Today this settlement is called Entre Rios.
1954	German state of Baden-Württemberg assumes the sponsorship of the Danube Swabians.
1964	Cultural Center of the Danube Swabians in Austria completed. The German city Sindelfingen assumes the sponsorship of the Danube Swabians of Yugoslavia.
1970	The cultural center of the Danube Swabians opens at Sindelfingen.
1978	The Danube Swabian Institute, a public corporation for the promulgation of Danube Swabian research, documentation and cultural activities founded at Munich, Germany.
1987	Danube Swabian Institute for history and research at the University of Tübingen, Germany founded.
1996	"Haus der Heimat" (Homeland Center), a cultural convention center for the ethnic German societies in Austria opens at Vienna.

Chapter 16:
Appendix: Pertinent United Nations' Documents

CONVENTION ON THE PREVENTION AND PUNISHMENT
OF THE CRIME OF GENOCIDE

Approved and proposed for signature and ratification of accession by General Assembly resolution 260 A (III) of 9 December 1948

ENTRY INTO FORCE: 12 January 1951, in accordance with article XIII

The Contracting Parties,

Having considered the declaration made by the General Assembly of the United Nations in its resolution 96 (1) dated 11 December 1946 that genocide is a crime under international law, contrary to the spirit and aims of the United Nations and condemned by the civilized world,

Recognizing that at all periods of history genocide has inflicted great losses on humanity, and

Being convinced that, in order to liberate mankind from such an odious scourge, international co-operation is required,

Hereby agree as hereinafter provided:

Article I

The Contracting Parties confirm that genocide, whether committed in time of peace or in time of war, is a crime under international law which they undertake to prevent and to punish.

Article II

In the present Convention, genocide means any of the following acts committed with intent to destroy, in whole or in part, a national, ethnical, racial or religious group, as such:

a. Killing members of the group;
b. Causing serious bodily or mental harm to members of the group;
c. Deliberately inflicting on the group conditions of life calculated to bring about its physical destruction in whole or in part;
d. Imposing measures intended to prevent births within the group;
e. Forcibly transferring children of the group to another group.

Article III

The following acts shall be punishable:

a. Genocide;
b. Conspiracy to commit genocide;
c. Direct and public incitement to commit genocide;
d. Attempt to commit genocide;
e. Complicity in genocide.

Article IV

Persons committing genocide or any of the other acts enumerated in article III shall be punished, whether they are constitutionally responsible rulers, public officials or private individuals.

Article V

The Contracting Parties undertake to enact, in accordance with their respective Constitutions, the necessary legislation to give effect to the provisions of the present Convention, and, in particular, to provide effective penalties for persons guilty of genocide or any of the other acts enumerated in article III.

Article VI

Persons charged with genocide or any of the other acts enumerated in article III shall be tried by a competent tribunal of the State in the territory of which the act was committed, or by such international penal tribunals as may have jurisdiction with respect to those Contracting Parties which shall have accepted its jurisdiction.

Article VII

Genocide and other acts enumerated in article III shall not be considered as political crimes for the purpose of extradition.
The Contracting Parties pledge themselves in such cases to grant extradition in accordance with their laws and treaties in force.

Article VIII

Any Contracting Party may call upon the competent organs of the United Nations to take such action under the Charter of the United Nations as they consider appropriate for the prevention and suppression of acts of genocide or any ot the other acts enumerated in article III.

Article IX

Disputes between the Contracting Parties relating to the interpretation, application or fulfillment of the present Convention, including those relating to the responsibility of a State for genocide or for any of the other acts enumerated in article III, shall be submitted to the International Court of Justice at the request of any of the parties to the dispute.

Article X

The present Convention, of which the Chinese, English, French, Russian and Spanish texts are equally authentic, shall bear the date of 9 Debember 1948.

Article XI

The present Convention shall be open until 31 December 1949 for signature on behalf of any Member of the United Nations and of any non-member State to which an invitation to sign has been addressed by the General Assembly.
The present Convention shall be ratified, and the instruments of ratification shall be deposited with the Secretary-General of the United Nations.
Afer 1 January 1950, the present Convention may be acceded to on behalf of any Member of the United Nations and of any non-member State which has received an invitation as aforesaid.
Instruments of accession shall be deposited with the Secretary-General of the United Nations.

Article XII

Any Contracting Party, may at any time, by notification addressed to the Secretary-General of the United Nations, extend the application of the present Convention to all or any of the territories for the conduct of whose foreign relations that Contracting Party is responsible.

Article XIII

On the day when the first twenty instruments of ratification or accession have been deposited, the Secretary-General shall draw up a procès-verbal and transmit a copy thereof to each Member of the United Nations and to each of the non-member States contemplated in article XI.

The present Convention shall come into force on the ninetieth day following the date of deposit of the twentieth instrument of ratification or accession.

Any ratification or accession effected, subsequent to the latter date shall become effective on the ninetieth day following the deposit of the instrument of ratification or accession.

Article XIV

The present Convention shall remain in effect for a period of ten years as from the date of its coming info force.

It shall thereafter remain in force for successive periods of five years for such Contracting Parties as have not denounced it at least six months before the expiration of the current period.

Denunciation shall be effected by a written notification addressed to the Secretary-General of the United Nations.

Article XV

If, as a result of denunciations, the number of Parties to the present Convention should become less than sixteen, the Convention shall cease to be in force as from the date on which the last of these denunciations shall become effective.

Article XVI

A request for the revision of the present Convention may be made at any time by any Contracting Party by means of a notification in writing addressed to the Secretary-General.

The General Assembly shall decide upon the steps, if any, to be taken in respect of such request.

Article XVII

The Secretary-General of the United Nations shall notify all Members of the United Nations and the non-member States contemplated in article XI of the following.

a. Signatures, ratifications and accessions received in accordance with article XI;
b. Notifications received in accordance with article XII;
c. The date upon which the present Convention comes into force in accordance with article XIII;
d. Denunciations received in accordance with article XIV;
e. The abrogation of the Convention in accordance with article XV;
f. Notifications received in accordance with article XVI.

Article XVIII

The original of the present Convention shall be deposited in the archives of the United Nations.
A certified copy of the Convention shall be transmitted to each Member of the United Nations and to each of the non-member States contemplated in article XI.

Article XIX

The present Convention shall be registered by the Secretary-General of the United Nations on the date of its coming into force.

CONVENTION ON THE NON-APPLICABILITY OF STATUTORY LIMITATIONS TO WAR CRIMES AND CRIMES AGAINST HUMANITY

Adopted and opened for signature, ratification and accession by General Assembly Resolution 2391(XXIII) of 26 November 1968

ENTRY INTO FORCE: 11 November 1970, in accordance with article VIII

PREAMBLE

The States Parties to the present Convention,

Recalling resolutions of the General Assembly of the United Nations 3 (1) of 13 February 1946 and 170 (11) of 31 October 1947 on the extradition and punishment of war criminals, resolution 95 (1) of 11 December 1946 affirming the principles of international law recognized by the Charter of the International Military Tribunal, Nürnberg, and the judgement of the Tribunal, and resolutions 2184 (XXI) of 12 December 1966 and 2202 (XXI) of 16 December 1966 which expressly condemned as crimes against humanity the violation of the economic and political rights of the indigenous population on the one hand and the policies of apartheid on the other,

Recalling resolutions of the Economic and Social Council of the United Nations 1074 D (XXXIX) of 28 July 1965 and 1158 (XLI) of 5 August 1966 on the punishment of war criminals and of persons who have committed crimes against humanity.

Noting that none of the solemn declarations, instruments or conventions relating to the prosecution and punishment of war crimes and crimes against humanity made provision for a period of limitation,

Considering that war crimes and crimes against humanity are among the gravest crimes in international law,

Convinced that the effective punishment of war crimes and crimes against humanity is an important element in the prevention of such crimes, the protection of human rights and fundamental freedoms, the encouragement or confidence, the furtherance of co-operation among peoples and the promotion of international peace and security,

Noting that the application to war crimes and crimes against humanity of the rules of municipal law relating to the period of limitation for ordinary crimes is a matter of serious concern to world public opinion, since it prevents the prosecution and punishment of persons responsible for those crimes,

Recognizing that it is necessary and timely to affirm in international law, through this Convention, the principle that there is no period of limitation for war crimes and crimes against humanity, and to secure its universal application,

Have agreed as follows:

Article I

No statutory limitation shall apply to the following crimes, irrespective of the date of their commission:

a. War crimes as they are defined in the Charter of the International Military Tribunal, Nürnberg, of 8 August 1945 and confirmed by resolutions 3 (1) of 13 February 1946 and 95 (1) of 11 December 1946 of the General Assembly of the United Nations, particularly the "grave breaches" enumerated in the Geneva Conventions of 12 August 1949 for the protection of war victims;

b. Crimes against humanity, whether committed in time of war or in time of peace as they are defined in the Charter of the International Military Tribunal, Nürnberg, of 8 August 1945 and confirmed by resolutions 3 (1) of 13 February 1946 and 95 (1) of 11 December 1946 of the General Assembly of the United Nations, eviction by armed attack or occupation and inhuman acts resulting from the policy of apartheid, and the crime of genocide as defined in the 1948 Convention on the Prevention and Punishment of the Crime of Genocide, even if such acts do not constitute a violation of the domestic law of the country in which they were committed.

Article II

If any of the crimes mentioned in article I is committed, the provisions of this Concention shall apply to representatives of the State authority and private individuals who, as principals or accomplices, participate in or who directly incite others to the commission of any of those crimes, or who conspire to commit them, irrespective of the degree of completion, and to representatives of the State authority who tolerate their commission.

Article III

The States Parties to the present Convention undertake to adopt all necessary demestic measures, legislative or otherwise, with a view to making possible the "tradition", in accordance with international law, of the persons referred to in article II of this Convention.

Article IV

The States Parties to the present Convention undertake to adopt, in accordance with their respective constitutional processes, any legislative or other measures necessary to ensure that statutory or other limitations shall not apply to the prosecution and punishment of the crimes referred to in articles I and II of this Convention and that, where they exist, such limitations shall be abolished.

Article V

This Convention shall, until 31 December 1969, be open for signature by any State Member of the United Nations or member of any of its specialized agencies or of the International Atomic Energy Agency, by any State Party to the Statute of the International Court of Justice, and by any other State which has been invited by the General Assembly of the United Nations to become a Party to this Convention.

Article VI

This Convention is subject to ratification. Instruments of ratification shall be deposited with the Secretary-General of the United Nations.

Article VII

This Convention shall be open to accession by any State referred to in article V. Instruments of accession shall be deposited with the Secretary-General of the United Nations.

Article VIII

1. This Convention shall enter into force on the ninetieth day after the date of the deposit with the Secretary-General of the United Nations of the tenth instrument of ratification or accession.

2. For each State ratifying this Convention or acceding to it after the deposit of the tenth instrument of ratification or accession, the Convention shall enter into force on the ninetieth day after the date of the deposit of its own instrument of ratification or accession.

Article IX

1. After the expiry of a period of ten years from the date on which this Convention enters into force, a request for the revision of the Convention may be made at any time by any Contracting Party by means of a notification in writing addressed to the Secretary-General of the United Nations.

2. The General Assembly of the United Nations shall decide upon the steps, if any, to be taken in respect of such a request.

Article X

1. This Convention shall be deposited with the Secretary-General of the United Nations.

2. The Secretary-General of the United Nations shall transmit certified copies of this Convention to all States referred to in article V.

3. The Secretary-General of the United Nations shall inform all States referred to in article V of the following particulars:

(a) Signatures of this Convention, and instruments of ratification and accession deposited under articles V, VI and VII;

(b) The date of entry into force of this Convention in accordance with article VIII;

(c) Communications received under article IX

Article XI

This Convention, of which the Chinese, English, French, Russian and Spanish texts are equally authentic, shall bear the date of 26 November 1968.

IN WITNESS WHEREOF the undersigned, being duly authorized for that purpose, have signed this Convention.

PRINCIPLES OF INTERNATIONAL CO-OPERATION IN THE DETECTION, ARREST, EXTRADITION AND PUNISHMENT OF PERSONS GUILTY OF WAR CRIMES AND CRIMES AGAINST HUMANITY

General Assembly resolution 3071 (XXVIII) of 3 December 1973

The General Assembly,

Recalling its resolutions 2583 (XXIV) of 15 December 1969, 2712 (XXV) of 15 December 1970, 2840 (XXVI) of 18 December 1971 and 3020 (XXVII) of 18 December 1972,

Taking into account the special need for international action in order to ensure the prosecution and punishment of persons guilty of war crimes and crimes against humanity,

Having considered the draft principles of international co-operation in the detection, arrest, extradition and punishment of persons guilty of war crimes and crimes against humanity,

Declares that the United Nations, in pursuance of the principles and purposes set forth in the Charter concerning the promotion of co-operation between peoples and the maintenance of international peace and security, proclaims the following principles of international co-operation in the detection, arrest, extradition and punishment of persons guilty of war crimes and crimes against humanity:

1. War crimes and crimes against humanity, wherever they are committed, shall be subject to investigation and the persons against whom there is evidence that they have committed such crimes shall be subject to tracing, arrest, trial and, if found guilty, to punishment.

2. Every State has the right to try its own nationals for war crimes and crimes against humanity.

3. States shall co-operate with each other on a bilateral and multilateral basis with a view to halting and preventing war crimes and crimes against humanity, and shall take the domestic and international measures necessary for that purpose.

4. States shall assist each other in detecting, arresting and bringing to trial persons suspected of having committed such crimes and, if they are found guilty, in punishing them.

5. Persons against whom there is evidence that they have committed war crimes and crimes against humanity shall be subject to trial and, if found guilty, to punishment, as a general rule in the countries in which they committed those crimes. In that connection, States shall co-operate on questions of extraditing such persons.

6. States shall co-operate with each other in the collection of information and evidence which would help to bring to trial the persons indicated in paragraph 5 above and shall exchange such information.

7. In accordance with article I of the Declaration on Territorial Asylum of 14 December 1967, States shall not grant asylum to any person with respect to whom there are serious reasons for considering that he has committed a crime against peace, a war crime or a crime against humanity.

8. States shall not take any legislative or other measures which may be prejudicial to the international obligations they have assumed in regard to the detection, arrest, extradition and punishment of persons guilty of war crimes and crimes against humanity.

9. In co-operating with a view to the detection, arrest and extradition of persons against whom there is evidence that they have committed war crimes and crimes against humanity and, if found guilty, their punishment, States shall act in conformity with the provisions of the Charter of the United Nations and of the Declaration on Principles of International Law concerning Friendly Relations and Co-operation among States in accordance with the Charter of the United Nations.

Chapter 17: Donauschwäbisches Archiv, München

Management:
Donauschwäbische Kulturstiftung
– Stiftung des bürgerlichen Rechts –
D-81929 München, Germany
Schädlerweg 2
Tel./Fax 0 89/93 77 93

VI Series of Danube Swabian publications have been issued by this institution.

Series III is dedicated to contributions on Danube Swabian ethnic and homeland research, as well as to the history of their educational system. (Identification: ISSN 0172-5165- + volume number)

As of today the series contains 110 volumes, which are listed subsequently (volume numbers in the left column).

Band 1:   Schmied, Stefan: *Heimatbuch der Sathmarer Schwaben* Wangen 1952, 118 S.

Band 2:   Senz, Josef Volkmar: *Geschichte der Donauschwaben* 2. erweiterte Auflage. Mit Karte und 23 Bildern. Freilassing, Pannonia Verlag 1955, 148 S.

Band 3:   Senz, Josef Volkmar: *Bilder aus der Geschichte der Donauschwaben* Mit 1 Karte und 25 Bildern. Freilassing, Pannonia-Verlag 1955, 32 S.

Band 4:   Tafferner, Anton/Schmidt, Josef/Senz, Josef Volkmar: *Die Donauschwaben im pannonischen Becken* Mit Karte, farbigem Wappen und Bildern. Freilassing: Pannonia-Verlag 1957, 3. Auflage 1981, 25 S.

Band 5:   Senz, Josef Volkmar: *Vom heutigen Schulwesen der Donauschwaben hinter dem Eisernen Vorhang* Freilassing: Pannonia-Verlag 1957, 16 S.

Band 6:   Hügel, Kaspar: *Abriß der Geschichte des donauschwäbischen Schulwesens*

Mit den gesetzlichen Bestimmungen der Jahre 1941–1944 und anderen Dokumenten im Anhang. München: Verlag des Südostdeutschen Kulturwerkes 1957, 88 S.

Band 7: *Die Deutschen in den Donauländern*
Bildwandkarte. Herausgegeben von der Bayerischen Landeszentrale für Heimatdienst. München: Schaefer-Verlag 1958. Texte und Zeichnungen von der Arbeitsgemeinschaft Donauschwäbischer Lehrer im Südostdeutschen Kulturwerk (Josef Schmidt).

Band 8: *Donauschwaben – Rumänen – Südslawen*
Herausgegeben im Auftrag der Arbeitsgemeinschaft Donauschwäbischer Lehrer (ADL) von Josef Schmidt. Freilassing: Pannonia Verlag 1960, 44 S.

Band 9: *Deutsche Lehrerbildung im Banat*
Festschrift. Herausgegeben von Josef Schmidt. München 1960, 83 S.

Band 10: *Zehn Jahre Landsmannschaft der Deutschen aus Jugoslawien 1949–1959*
Die Donauschwaben in Bayern.
Hg. von Josef Volkmar Senz. München 1960, 136 S.

Band 11: Weidlein, Johann: *Die Rolle der Assimilanten in der Ausgestaltung des madjarischen Rassennationalismus*
Straubing 1962, 24 S.

Band 12: Schmied, Stefan: *Die Sathmarer Schwaben 1712–1962*
Kurz gefasste Geschichte der Volksgruppe – 250-Jahr-Feier 1712–1962.   Leubas 1962, 24 S.

Band 13: Senz, Josef Volkmar: *Deutsche Schule und Lehrer in Südslawien*
Schulgeschichtliche Beiträge
München 1964, 52 S.

Band 14: Hügel, Kaspar: *Stellungnahme zu den Erinnerungen Dr. Kräuters*
Straubing 1968, 15 S.

Band 15: *Bibliographie der Veröffentlichungen von Anton Peter Petri 1953–1968*
Mit einem Nachwort von Hans Diplich. Mühldorf 1968, 32 S.

Band 16: Leicht, Sebastian: *Ein donauschwäbischer Maler*
28 Abbildungen, davon 12 in Farbe. Mit einer Einführung von Elke Ortrun Senz. Stuttgart/Sindelfingen 1968, 36 S.

Band 17: Hügel, Kaspar: *Das Banater deutsche Schulwesen in Rumänien von 1918 bis 1944*
Das Schulwesen der Donauschwaben 1918–1944. München: Verlag des Südostdeutschen Kulturwerkes 1968, 177 S.

Band 18: Senz, Josef Volkmar: *Das Schulwesen der Donauschwaben im König-reich Jugoslawien*
München: Verlag des Südostdeutschen Kulturwerkes 1969, 303 S.

Band 19: Schmied, Stefan: *Geschichte des sathmardeutschen Schulwesens*
Von den Anfängen bis 1971
Leubas 1972, 40 S.

Band 20: Weifert, Ladislaus Michael: *Banater Spitznamen*
Herausgegeben von der Landsmannschaft der Donauschwaben.
Stuttgart 1973, 30 S.

Band 21: Senz, Josef Volkmar: *Donauschwäbische Siedlungsgebiete*
Straubing 1973, 56 S.

Band 22: Scherer, Anton: *Bibliographie zur Pädagogik und zum Schulwesen*
der Donauschwaben in Deutschland, Österreich, Südosteuropa und
Übersee 1945–1965
Graz 1974, 24 S.

Band 23: Brücker, Christian Ludwig: *Schulische Arbeit der Donauschwaben*
in Übersee aus der Sicht des deutschen Auslandsschulwesens
München 1973, 16 S.

Band 24: Tafferner, Anton: *Donauschwäbische Wissenschaft*
Von den Anfängen bis zur Gegenwart. I. Teil
Herausgegeben von der Arbeitsgemeinschaft Donauschwäbischer
Lehrer e. V., Straubing/München 1974, 154 S.

Band 25: *Deutsch-serbisches schulisches Miteinander*
Die Somborer Präparandie als Ausbildungsstätte deutscher Lehrer
Herausgegeben von Josef Volkmar Senz. München 1979, 120 S.

Band 26: *Bayerische Donauschwaben – donauschwäbische Bayern*
Dreißig Jahre Landsmannschaft der Donauschwaben aus Jugoslawien
1949–1979
Herausgegeben von Josef Volkmar Senz. München 1979, 248 S.

Band 27: Rasimus, Hans: *Die deutsche Schulnot im ehemaligen Königreich*
Jugoslawien
Vom Leben und Wirken des donauschwäbischen Schulmannes
Nikolaus Arnold. Mit einer Auswahl seiner Schriften
München 1979, 198 S., € 10,–

Band 28: *Schneider, Franz: Bibliographie Donauschwäbischer Lehrerblätter 1955–1980 (seit 1979 Donauschwäbische Forschungs- und Lehrerblätter)*
Ein Überblick über die Publikationsarbeit der Arbeitsgemeinschaft Donauschwäbischer Lehrer e. V., München 1983, 48 S., br., € 2,50

Band 29: Binder, Friedrich: *Johannes Wurtz*
Der literarische Künder donauschwäbischer pannonischer Lebensart
Festschrift zum 75. Geburtstag. München 1983, 140 S., br., € 7,50

Band 30: Berauer, Josef: *Geschichte des Volksschulwesens der Erzdiözese Kalotscha-Batsch*
Übersetzt aus dem Ungarischen. Kalotscha 1896. München 1983, 300 S., gb., € 15,–

Band 31: Sonnleitner, Hans: *Karlsdorf im Verlauf donauschwäbischer Geschichte. Erd- und Vorgeschichte, Altertum, Mittelalter und Neuzeit des Donaubeckens*
Ein Denkmal der verlorenen Heimat. München 1985, 107 S., € 16,–

Band 32: Stilling, Katharina: *Aus dem Nest gefallen*
München 1984, 102 br. S., mit Bildern, € 7,50

Band 33: Scheierling, Konrad: *Donauschwäbisches Liederbuch*
Straubing 1985, 220 S. mit Grafiken, Gln., € 11,–

Band 34: *Ein Freundschafts- und Partnerschaftsbeispiel*
Festschrift zum 70. Geburtstag von Friedrich Binder und Friedrich Kühbauch. Beiträge zum donauschwäbischen Nachkriegsschicksal
Redaktion: J. V. Senz. Sindelfingen 1986. 208 S. und 32 Bildtafeln, € 10,–

Band 35: Sonnleitner, Hans: *Aktion Intelligenzija in Karlsdorf*
Gedenkschrift 1944–1948 über die Ermordung von 36 Karlsdorfern
Tatsachen und Hintergründe – Reflexion zur Sinnfrage über Mord und Tod
München: Verlag der Donauschwäbischen Kulturstiftung 1986, 524 S., € 20,–, ISBN 3-926276-00-2

Band 36: Weifert, Mathias: *Die Entwicklung der Banater Hauptstadt Temeschburg*
München: Verlag der Donauschwäbischen Kulturstiftung 1987, 190 S., br., € 11,–, ISBN 3-926276-02-9

Band 37: Senz, Josef Volkmar: *Geschichte der Donauschwaben*
München: Verlag der Donauschwäbischen Kulturstiftung, 7. Aufl. 1990, 277 S., Gln., geb., € 12,50, ISBN 3-926276-03-7

Band 38:   Beer, Josef: *Donauschwäbische Zeitgeschichte aus erster Hand*
Mit fünf Karten. München: Verlag der Donauschwäbischen Kulturstiftung 1987, 270 S., 4. Aufl. 1990, geb., € 12,50, ISBN 3-926276-04-5

Band 39:   Rasimus, Hans: *Als Fremde im Vaterland*
Der Schwäbisch-Deutsche Kulturbund und die ehemalige deutsche
Volksgruppe in Jugoslawien im Spiegel der Presse
München: Verlag der Donauschwäbischen Kulturstiftung 1989,
675 S., geb., € 20,–, ISBN 3-926276-05-3

Band 40:   Oberkersch, Valentin: *Die Deutschen in Syrmien, Slawonien,*
Kroatien und Bosnien
München: Verlag der Donauschwäbischen Kulturstiftung 1989,
614 S., geb., € 31,–, ISBN 3-926276-07-10

Band 41:   *Landsmannschaft Donauschwaben – Patenschafts-Jubiläen*
Christian L. Brücker und Freundeskreis. München/Sindelfingen:
Verlag der Donauschwäbischen Kulturstiftung 1989, 120 S., € 10,–,
ISBN 3-926276-08-08

Band 42:   Sonnleitner, Hans: *Donauschwäbische Todesnot unter dem Tito-Stern*
Verbrechen in den Jahren 1944–1947 mit einer politischen und
moralischen Wertung
München: Verlag der Donauschwäbischen Kulturstiftung 1990,
329 S., € 15,–, ISBN 3-926276-10-X

Band 43:   Brücker, Christian L.: *Donauschwaben in Nordamerika,*
Südamerika und Australien
Sindelfingen: Verlag der Donauschwäbischen Kulturstiftung 1990,
321 S., geb., € 15,–, ISBN 3-926276-11-8

Band 44:   Feldtänzer, Oskar: *Josef II. und die donauschwäbische Ansiedlung*
Dokumentation der Kolonisation im Batscher Land 1784–1787
Herausgegeben von der Donauschwäbischen Kulturstiftung, München
1990. Linz/Donau: Verlag Denkmayr 1990, 504 S., € 29,50,
ISBN 3-901123-02-4

Band 45:   Niklos-Nyari, Anna: *Nachruf auf verlorene Jahre*
Eine Heimatvertriebene erzählt
München: Verlag der Donauschwäbischen Kulturstiftung 1991,
320 S., € 15,–, ISBN 3-926276-12-6

Band 46:   *Leidensweg der Deutschen im kommunistischen Jugoslawien*
Band I: Ortsberichte über Verbrechen an den Deutschen im
kommunistischen Jugoslawien
Verfasst vom Arbeitskreis Dokumentation in der Donauschwäbi-

schen Kulturstiftung, München, und im Bundesverband der Landsmannschaft der Donauschwaben, Sindelfingen. Verlag der Donauschwäbischen Kulturstiftung, München 1991. Bearbeitet von Josef Beer, Georg Wildmann, Valentin Oberkersch, Ingomar Senz, Hans Sonnleitner, Hermann Rakusch. München/Sindelfingen: 958 S., € 15,–, ISBN 3-926276-13-4

Band 47:   Sonnleitner, Hans: *Bibliographie Donauschwäbisches Archiv, München* Darstellung der in der Verlagseinrichtung Donauschwäbisches Archiv erfolgten Veröffentlichungen durch den Arbeitskreis für donauschwäbische Volks- und Heimatforschung. München: Verlag der Donauschwäbischen Kulturstiftung 1991, 40 S., € 3,–, ISBN 3-26276-14-2

Band 48:   Rohr, Robert: *Bayern und seine Donauschwaben* München: Verlag der Donauschwäbischen Kulturstiftung 1991, 190 S., € 5.–, ISBN 3-926276-15-0

Band 49:   Mesli, Paul/Schreiber, Franz/ Wildmann, Georg: *Filipowa – Bild einer donauschwäbischen Gemeinde* 7. Band: Filipowa weltweit. München: Verlag der Donauschwäbischen Kulturstiftung 1992, 304 S., € 47,–, ISBN 3-926276-16-9

Band 50:   *Leidensweg der Deutschen im kommunistischen Jugoslawien Band II: Erlebnisberichte* Hauptredaktion: Josef Beer, zahlreiche Mitarbeiter. Verfasst vom Arbeitskreis Dokumentation in der Donauschwäbischen Kulturstiftung, München, und im Bundesverband der Landsmannschaft der Donauschwaben. München/Sindelfingen: Verlag der Donauschwäbischen Kulturstiftung 1993. 1040 S., € 30,–, ISBN 3-926276-17-7

Band 51:   Milleker, Felix: *Die Familie Weifert und das Brauhaus in Pantschowa 1722/23–1923* Herausgeber der Neuauflage: Mathias Weifert. München: Verlag der Donauschwäbischen Kulturstiftung 1993, 2. Aufl., 40 S., € 6.–, ISBN 3-926276-18-5

Band 52:   Sonnleitner, Hans: *Etymologie des Familiennamens Sonnleitner Dargestellt im Zusammenhang mit der Entstehung der deutschen Familiennamen* München: Verlag der Donauschwäbischen Kulturstiftung 1994, 320 S., € 12,50, ISBN 3-926276-19-3

216

Band 53: Rohr, Robert: *Unser klingendes Erbe*
Aus dem Musikleben der Donauschwaben von 1918 bis zur Gegen-
wart – Band II
München: Verlag der Donauschwäbischen Kulturstiftung 1994,
431 S., € 24,–, ISBN 3-926276-20-7

Band 54: *Leidensweg der Deutschen im kommunistischen Jugoslawien*
Band III: Erschießungen – Vernichtungslager – Kinderschicksale in
der Zeit von 1944 bis 1948
Redaktion: Georg Wildmann. Mitautoren: L. Barwich, E. Lung,
H. Sonnleitner, G. u. K. Tscherny, K. Weber. Arbeitskreis Dokumen-
tation in der Donauschwäbischen Kulturstiftung, München, und im
Bundesverband der Landsmannschaft der Donauschwaben
Sindelfingen/München.
Verlag der Donauschwäbischen Kulturstiftung 1995. 1060 S.,
€ 30.–, ISBN 3-926276-21-5

Band 55: *Leidensweg der Deutschen im kommunistischen Jugoslawien*
Band IV: Menschenverluste – Namen und Zahlen zu Verbrechen an
den Deutschen durch das Tito-Regime in der Zeit von 1944–1948
Bearbeitung und Gestaltung: Karl Weber. Arbeitskreis Dokumen-
tation in der Donauschwäbischen Kulturstiftung, München, und im
Bundesverband der Landsmannschaft der Donauschwaben.
München: Verlag der Donauschwäbischen Kulturstiftung 1993.
1060 S., € 30.–, ISBN 3-926276-22-3

Band 56: Sonnleitner, Hans: *Symbole der Donauschwaben: Wappen, Wappen-*
spruch, Fahne und Hymne
Sonderdruck aus: Entwicklung und Erbe des donauschwäbischen
Volksstammes. München: Donauschwäbisches Archiv 1982, 13 S.,
€ 2,50

Band 57: *300 Jahre im Donauraum*
Schicksal und Leistung der Donauschwaben im europäischen
Südosten
Beiträge von Ingomar Senz, Paul Ginder, Heinrich Lay.
Sonderdruck aus den Heften 49, 50, 51 der Zeitschrift
Der gemeinsame Weg (1988). Herausgegeben vom Ostdeutschen
Kulturrat, Haus des deutschen Ostens, Düsseldorf, 13 S., € 3,50,
ISBN 3-926276-07-X

Band 58: Senz, Ingomar: *Zwischen Bewahrung und Anpassung*
Erbe und Auftrag der Donauschwäbiscben Kulturstiftung
Festschrift zu ihrem zehnjährigen Bestehen

München: Verlag der Donauschwäbischen Kulturstiftung 1988,
32 S., € 3,–, ISBN 3-926276-06-1

Band 59:   *Die Erinnerung bleibt*
Donauschwäbische Literatur nach 1945. Eine Anthologie. Band I:
A–D. Herausgegeben und mit einem Vorwort versehen von Stefan
Teppert. Sersheim: Oswald Hartmann Verlag 1995, 669 S., € 30,–,
ISBN 3-925921-23-0

Band 60:   Senz, Ingomar: *Die Donauschwaben*
Band V der Studienbuchreihe der Stiftung Ostdeutscher Kulturrat
München: Verlag Langen Müller 1994. 240 S., € 14,–,
ISBN 3-7844-2522-4

Band 61:   Kiss, Josef: *Zur Vertreibung und Verschleppung der Ungarn-*
deutschen aus der Schwäbischen Türkei unter besonderer
Berücksichtigung des Ortes Gyönk/Jink
München: Verlag der Donauschwäbischen Kulturstiftung 1995,
84 S., € 8,–

Band 62:   Hauler, Ernst: *Die sathmarschwäbische Gemeinschaft Terebesch*
– ihr Leben mit Rumänen
München: Verlag der Donauschwäbischen Kulturstiftung 1995,
120 S., € 10,–, ISBN 3-926276-25-8

Band 63:   Weiner, Georg: *Heitere Geschichten aus der Heimat der Donau-*
schwaben
München: Verlag der Donauschwäbischen Kulturstiftung 1997,
304 S., € 15,50, ISBN 3-926276-26-6

Band 64:   Senz, Ingomar: *Donauschwäbische Geschichte*
Band II: 1806 bis 1918. Wirtschaftliche Autarkie und politische
Entfremdung
München: Universitas-Verlag 1997, 462 S., € 27,50,
ISBN 3-80841347-7

Band 65:   Hauler, Ernst: *Tausend Jahre deutsche Geschichte in der Region*
Sathmar
München: Verlag der Donauschwäbischen Kulturstiftung 1997,
212 S., € 12,50, ISBN 3-926276-27-4

Band 66:   Senz, J. V.: *Die Deutschen im Batscher Land*
Pioniere und Märtyrer des Abendlandes im europäischen Südosten
Wien: Schutzverein Österreichische Landsmannschaft 1984, 105 S.,
Eckart-Schriften – Band 89, € 3,50

Band 67:   *Verbrechen an den Deutschen in Jugoslawien 1944–1948*
Die Stationen eines Völkermords
Arbeitskreis Dokumentation: Georg Wildmann, Hans Sonnleitner,
Karl Weber. München: Verlag der Donauschwäbischen Kultur-
stiftung 1998, 385 S., € 9,–, ISBN 3-926276-32-0, 2. Aufl. 1998,
3. Aufl. 2000
Englische Ausgabe siehe Bände 91 und 96.

Band 68:   *Märtyrer und Bekenner der Donauschwaben*
Geistliche – Ordensleute – Laien
Georg Wildmann. Anmerkung zur donauschwäbischen Geschichte
von Hans Sonnleitner. Weitere Mitwirkende: Rudolf Fath,
Hans Vastag, Franz Wesinger. Herausgegeben von St. Gerhardswerk,
Stuttgart, und Donauschwäbische Kulturstiftung, München: Verlag
der Donauschwäbischen Kulturstiftung 1999, ISBN 3-926276-34-7
(in Vorbereitung)

Band 69:   Rohr, Robert: *Die Knabenkapellen der Donauschwaben*
München: Verlag der Donauschwäbischen Kulturstiftung 1998,
118 S., € 5,–, ISBN 3-926276-35-5

Band 70:   Senz, Rotraud und Senz, Ingomar: *Ein Leben für die Donauschwaben*
Ein Porträt von Josef Volkmar Senz und seinem Werk
München: Verlag der Donauschwäbischen Kulturstiftung 1999,
212 S., € 15,–, ISBN 3-926276-36-3

Band 71:   Streicher, Therese: *Erinnerungen – Bildband der kreisfreien Stadt*
Pantschowa im Banat
München: Verlag der Donauschwäbischen Kulturstiftung 1999,
200 S., € 30,–, ISBN 3-926276-37-1

Band 72:   Rohr, Robert: *Blasmusik der Donauschwaben in historischen*
Aufnahmen – Begleitbroschüre zu einer MC- bzw. CD-Produktion
München: Verlag der Donauschwäbischen Kulturstiftung 1999, 90 S.,
ISBN 3-926276-38-X – Doppel-CD mit Begleitbroschüre € 18,–,
Doppel-MC mit Begleitbroschüre € 15,–

Band 73:   *Filipowa – Bild einer donauschwäbischen Gemeinde*
Achter Band: Filipowa 1914–1944
Franz Schreiber und Georg Wildmann. Textbearbeitung: Georg
Wildmann.
München: Verlag der Donauschwäbischen Kulturstiftung 1999,
260 S., € 30.–, ISBN 3-926276-39-8

Band 74:   *Ein Volk an der Donau – Das Schicksal der Deutschen in*
             Jugoslawien unter dem kommunistischen Tito-Regime
             Gespräche und Kommentare serbischer und deutscher Zeitzeugen.
             Herausgegeben von Nenad Stefanović. München: Verlag der Donau-
             schwäbischen Kulturstiftung 1999, ISBN 3-926276-41-X. Deutsche
             Ausgabe. Übersetzung: Oskar Feldtänzer. Titel der serbischen
             Originalausgabe, Beograd 1977: Jedan svet na Dunavu – Razgovori i
             komentari. Nenad Stefanović. € 10.–

Band 75:   *Die Erinnerung bleibt*
             Donauschwäbische Literatur seit 1945. Eine Anthologie
             Band 2, E–G 1021 S., € 34.–. Herausgegeben und mit einem Vorwort
             versehen von Stefan Teppert. Sersheim: O. Hartmann Verlag 2000,
             679 S., ISBN 3-925921-24

Band 76:   Scherer, Anton: *Deutschland und Österreich in der öffentlichen*
             Meinung der BR Jugoslawien und Kroatiens von heute
             Graz: Donauschwäbisches Bibliographisches Archiv (A-8044 Graz,
             Waldhofweg 6), 1994, 70 S., € 9,–, ISBN 3-901486-0-1,
             Danubio-Suevia 5

Band 77:   *Kirche und kirchliches Leben der Donauschwaben 1965–1975*
             Bibliographie
             Anton Scherer. Graz: 1995, 44 S., € 8.–, ISBN 3-901486-03-5,
             Danubio-Suevia 9

Band 78:   Scherer, Anton: *Die Donauschwaben in Rumänien, Ungarn und*
             Jugoslawien nach 1945
             Bibliographie 1965–1975
             Graz: 1996, 28 S., € 4,50, ISBN 3-901486-04-6, Danubio-Suevia 10

Band 79:   Scherer, Anton: *Schul- und Bildungsfragen der Donauschwaben in*
             Deutschland, Österreich, Südosteuropa und Übersee
             Anhang: Jugend. Sport. Bibliographie 1965–1975. Graz: 1996, 38 S.,
             € 6,50, ISBN 3-901486-05-4, Danubio-Suevia 8

Band 80:   Scherer, Anton: *Die Donauschwaben und die Deutschen im*
             allgmeinen in den USA, in Canada, Brasilien, Argentinien, Venezuela
             und Australien
             Bibliographie 1965–1975. Graz: 1997, 38 S., € 8.–,
             ISBN 3-901486-06-2, Danubio-Suevia 11

Band 81:   Scherer, Anton: *"Cvaj dojce profesorn – faterland ferlorn"*
             Tendenziöse Darstellungen, unzulässige Verallgemeinerungen,
             unwahre Behauptungen bei deutschen und jugoslawischen
             Historikern
             Graz: 1997, II, 44 S., € 8.–, ISBN 3-901486-07-0, Danubio-Suevia 12

Band 82:   Scherer, Anton: *Irrtümer, Manipulationen und Fälschungen im neuesten Werk über die Donauschwaben in Jugoslawien* Graz: 1997, 28 S., € 6,50, ISBN 3-901486-08, Danubio-Suevia 13

Band 83:   Scherer, Anton: *Deutsche Literatur im Banat (Rumänien) nach dem 23. August 1944* *Künstlerische Normen, politische Tendenzen, typischeVertreter* Graz: 1997, 34 S., € 7,50, ISBN 3-901486-09-7, Danubio-Suevia 14

Band 84:   Scherer, Arbeo Wolfram: *Bibliographie der Veröffentlichungen von Prof. Dr. Anton Scherer* Graz: 1998, 96 S., € 12,50, ISBN 3-901486-11-9, Danubio-Suevia 15

Band 85:   Scherer, Anton: *Donauschwäbische Bibliographie 1965–1975* *Schöngeistiges Schrifttum* Graz: 1998, 36 S., € 7,50, ISBN 3-901486-12-7, Danubio-Suevia 16

Band 86:   Schramm, Josef: *Prof. Dr. Anton Scherer* *Persönlichkeit und Werk. Zu seinem 75. Geburtstag* Das Donauschwäbische Bibliographische Archive, Graz. Graz: 1999, 60 S., € 10.–, ISBN 3-901486-10-0

Band 87:   Scherer, Anton: *Donauschwäbische Bibliographie 1965–1975* *Deutschland* Anhang: Frankreich. Vorwort: Hans Sonnleitner. Graz: 2001, 56 S., € 9,–, ISBN 3-901486-13-1, Danubio-Suevia 18 (in Vorbereitung)

Band 88:   Scherer, Anton: *Donauschwäbische Bibliographie 1965–1975.* *I. Landeskunde, Bevölkerung, Geschichte des mittleren Donauraums unter besonderer Berücksichtigung des Nationalitätenproblems, Geschichte der Donauschwaben* Graz 1999, 200 S., € 22,50, ISBN 3-901486-14-0, Danubio-Suevia 19

Band 89:   Scherer, Anton: *Vereinswesen, Wirtschaft, Soziale Fragen und Bewegungen, Recht, Gesundheitswesen* Bibliographie 1965–1975. Graz: 2001, 28 S., € 6,50, ISBN 3-901486-16-X, Danubio-Suevia 20

Band 90:   Scherer, Anton: *Donauschwäbische Bibliographie 1965–1975* *II. Volkskunde, Bildende Kunst, Musik, Theater, Forscher und Forschungsstellen, Literaturgeschichte und Literaturkunde, Sprachforschung und Sprachpflege, Presse-, Verlagswesen, Buchdruck und Büchereien* Graz: 2000, 240 S., € 25,–, ISBN 3-901486-15-1, Danubio-Suevia 21

Band 91:   *Genocide of the Ethnic Germans in Yugoslavia 1944–1948* Englische USA-Ausgabe des Bandes 67 (Verbrechen an den

Deutschen in Jugoslawien 1944–1948). Danube Swabian Association of the USA 2001. INC. 12626 Vista Panorama Santa Anna, California 92705, U.S.A. 133 S. USA-Ausgabe. ISBN 0-9710341-0-9. LCCN 2001126379. Dollar 20,–

Band 92: Rohr, Robert: *Unser klingendes Erbe – Band III Zur Musikkultur der Donauschwaben (Nachträge und Ergänzungen zu Band I und II)* München: Verlag der Donauschwäbischen Kulturstiftung 2001, ISBN 3-926276-44-4, 350 S., € 25,–

Band 93: Hauler, Ernst: *Lesebuch zur Geschichte der Deutschen in Sathmar* München: Verlag der Donauschwäbischen Kulturstiftung 2001 ISBN 3-926276-43-6, 120 S., € 6,–

Band 94: Sonnleitner, Hans: *Gefordert in bewegter Zeit* *Biographische Notizen, bibliographische, chronologische Daten mit Perspektiven eines geforderten Lebens zwischen 1931 und XY* München: Verlag der Donauschwäbischen Kulturstiftung, München 2004, ISBN 3-926276-45-2, 340 S., € 12,50 (in Vorbereitung)

Band 95: Metz, Franz (Herausgeber): *Beiträge zur südosteuropäischen Musikgeschichte* *Musikleben der Deutschen im Kontext südosteuropäischer Musikkultur. Positionen und Traditionen* Gesellschaft für Deutsche Musikkultur im südöstlichen Europa. Verlag der Donauschwäbischen Kulturstiftung, München 2001, ISBN 5-926276-46-0, 161 S., € 12,50

Band 96: Arbeitskreis Dokumentation: Herbert Prokle, Georg Wildmann, Karl Weber, Hans Sonnleitner: *Genocide of the Ethnic Germans in Yugoslavia 1944–1948* European English-Language Edition/Europäische Englischausgabe, ISSN 0172-5165-96 Verlag der Donauschwäbischen Kulturstiftung, München 2003, ISBN 3-926276-47-9, 224 S., € 10,–

Band 97: Lay, Heinrich: *Das Banat 1849–1867* *Die Wojwodschaft Serbien und das Temescher Banat 1849–1860* *Die liberale Ära und der Österreichisch-Ungarische Ausgleich 1860–1867* Historische Dokumentation, ISBN 3-00-008295-6, Töging am Inn 2001, 347 S., € 17,50

Band 98: Prof. Dr. Blumenwitz, Dieter: *Rechtsgutachten über die Verbrechen an den Deutschen in Jugoslawien 1944–1948* Sonderausgabe: Juristische Studien

Herausgeber: Vorstand der Donauschwäbischen Kulturstiftung, München, 65 S., € 5,–, ISSN 0172-5165-98
Verlag der Donauschwäbischen Kulturstiftung, München 2002, ISBN 3-926276-48-7

Band 99: Donauschwäbische Kulturstiftung, München (Herausgeber):
Auf langem Wege
Dem donauschwäbischen Musikforscher Robert Rohr zum
80. Geburtstag
Verlag der Donauschwäbischen Kulturstiftung, München 2002, ISBN 3-926276-44-4, 96 S., € 7,50, ISSN 0172-5165-99

Band 100: Hauler, Ernst: *Deutsches für Sathmarer Kinder*
Sathmarbezogene kindergerechte Geschichte der Deutschen in Sathmar
Donauschwäbisches Archiv, München 2002, ISSN 0172-5165-100, 130 S., € 7,–

Band 101: Scherer, Anton: *Die Geschichte der donauschwäbischen Literatur*
von 1848–2000
Mit einer Einführung von Hans Sonnleitner
Verlag der Donauschwäbischen Kulturstiftung, München 2003, ISBN 3-926276-51-7, ISSN 0172-5165-101, 156 S., € 15,–, Donau-schwäbisches Bibliographisches Archiv, A-8044 Graz, Waldhofweg 6, ISBN 3-901486-17-8

Band 102: Rohr, Robert: *Spätlese – Gedichte und Geschichten*
Verlag der Donauschwäbischen Kulturstiftung, München 2002, ISBN 3-926276-50-9, ISSN 0172-5165-102, 104 S., € 8,–

Band 103: Redaktion: Karl Weber: *300 Jahre Donauschwaben*
Herausgeber: Donaudeutsche Landsmannschaft in Rheinland-Pfalz e.V., D-67346 Speyer, Friedrich-Ebert-Straße 106
Verlag der Donauschwäbischen Kulturstiftung, München 2003, ISBN 3-926276-52-5, ISSN 0172-5165-103, 150 S., € 12,–

Band 104: Kopp-Krumes, Magdalena: *Druckgraphikkunst in unserer Zeit*
Die Themen sind vielseitig – einige donauschwäbisch
Verlag Freisinger Künstlerpresse W. Bode, Freising 2003, 76 S., davon 53 S. in Farbe, € 25,–, ISSN 0172-5165-104, ISBN 3-927067-26-1

Band 105: Scherer, Anton: *Wortkundliche Studien. Etymologien und*
deutschsüdosteuropäische sprachliche Interferenzen
Graz 2002, Donauschwäbisches Bibliographisches Archiv, A-8044 Graz, Waldhofweg 6, ISBN 3-901486-17-8, 116 S., € 14,–

Band 106: Metz, Franz (Herausgeber): *Die Kirchenmusik in Südosteuropa Historische und typologische Studien zur Musikgeschichte südosteuropäischer Regionen*
Kongressberichte Temeswar/Timisoara 1998 mit überwiegend musikwissenschaftlichen Referaten aus der Musikgeschichte der Donauschwaben, ISSN 017-5165-106
Verlegt bei Hans Schneider, Tutzing 2003, ISBN 3-7952-1117-4, 346 S., € 50,–

Band 107: *Weißbuch der Deutschen aus Jugoslawien – Ortsberichte 1944–1948*
Inhaltsgleiche Lizenzausgabe von *Leidensweg der Deutschen im kommunistischen Jugoslawien*. Band 46 des Donauschwäbischen Archivs, München. Universitas Verlag in F. A. Herbig, Verlagsbuchhandlung GmbH, München 1991, ISBN 3-8004-1270-5, € 15,–

Band 108: *Weißbuch der Deutschen aus Jugoslawien – Erlebnisberichte 1944–1948*
Inhaltsgleiche Lizenzausgabe von *Leidensweg der Deutschen im kommunistischen Jugoslawien*. Band 50 des Donauschwäbischen Archivs, München. Universitas Verlag in F. A. Herbig, Verlagsbuchhandlung GmbH, München 1993, ISBN 3-8004-1298-5, € 15,–

Band 109: *Weißbuch der Deutschen aus Jugoslawien – Erschießungen – Internierungslager – Kinderschicksale 1944–1948*
Inhaltsgleiche Lizenzausgabe von *Leidensweg der Deutschen im kommunistischen Jugoslawien*. Band 54 des Donauschwäbischen Archivs, München. Universitas Verlag in F. A. Herbig, Verlagsbuchhandlung GmbH 1995, ISBN 3-8004-1325-6, € 15,–

Band 110: Sonnleitner, Hans: *Die Donauschwaben – Leistung und Schicksal im südöstlichen Mitteleuropa*
Sonderausgabe Historische Brennpunkte
ISSN 0172-5165-110, Verlag der Donauschwäbischen Kulturstiftung, München 2004, ISBN 3-926276-53-3, € 12,50 (in Vorbereitung)

Band 111: *Donauschwäbische Siedlungsgebiete*
Historische Farb-Wandkarte 59,4 × 84,1 cm – oder gefaltet –
Herausgeber: Hans Sonnleitner
Donauschwäbisches Archiv, München, ISSN 0172-5165-111
Kartographie: Magdalena Kopp-Krumes MA
Verlag der Donauschwäbischen Kulturstiftung, München 2003
ISBN 3-926276-54-1, € 12,—